THE POI

'Roger Hardy distils the imperial past of the Middle East down to its essentials. Through memorable vignettes and powerful insights, he has produced a sharply-focused and brilliant history of the modern Middle East.' —Eugene Rogan, author of *The Fall of the Ottomans: The Great War in the Middle East, 1914–1920*

'Why is the Middle East plagued by perpetual conflict, violence, and misrule? The reasons are rooted in imperial history, and Roger Hardy unearths them skilfully in this concise, clearly-written, and accurate analysis.' — Thomas W. Lippman, Middle East Institute, Washington, DC; former Middle East bureau chief of the Washington Post, and author of *Saudi Arabia on the Edge*

'A short and popularly accessible history of the late colonial period in the Middle East, combining general comment and analysis with country by country studies. The author's personal authority and sensibly quiet and judicious tone adds greatly to its general impression and effect.' — Roger Owen, Emeritus Professor of Middle East History, Harvard University

'*The Poisoned Well* offers a thought-provoking and insightful study of the colonial legacy in the Middle East. Clear, concise and beautifully written, the book is a pleasure to read.' — Nigel Ashton, Professor of International History, London School of Economics

'[Hardy] navigates the rocks and eddies of the region's history with a sure touch and brilliant eye for detail. In *The Poisoned Well* he provides a superb overview of events from the early 19th century ... Hardy skilfully zooms in on individual narratives, showing how major events were witnessed and influenced by observers at the time. His book is peopled with a variety of characters, great and humble, deftly sketched and brought to life.' — *The Financial Times*

'Despite the familiarity of the subject matter, Mr Hardy provides us with a gripping and illuminating addition to this literature. He is even-handed throughout, passionate without being sentimental and has a great turn of phrase ... He also has a particular talent ... for simplifying complex situations on the ground for the benefit of his reader.' — *The Economist*

'Roger Hardy's lively new account of British and French imperialism in the region is bursting with memorable anecdotes, intriguing detail and splashes of colour that illuminate a canvas of power, greed and double standards—and other legacies left standing amidst the wreckage of the Palestine Mandate or Algerie Française.' — Ian Black, *LSE Review of Books*

'This historical drama is narrated through the memoirs of political leaders, diplomats and journalists who witnessed those times, making this book highly readable and rich in Governance, law and ethics.' — *International Affairs*

ROGER HARDY

The Poisoned Well

Empire and its Legacy in the Middle East

HURST & COMPANY, LONDON

This revised and updated paperback edition published 2018.

First published in the United Kingdom in 2016 by
C. Hurst & Co. (Publishers) Ltd.,
41 Great Russell Street, London, WC1B 3PL
© Roger Hardy, 2018
All rights reserved.
Printed in Great Britain by Bell & Bain Ltd, Glasgow

The right of Roger Hardy to be identified as the author of
this publication is asserted by him in accordance with the
Copyright, Designs and Patents Act, 1988.

A Cataloguing-in-Publication data record for this book
is available from the British Library.

ISBN: 9781849049542

This book is printed using paper from registered sustainable
and managed sources.

www.hurstpublishers.com

For Jola, a freedom fighter,
& for Peter and Ania, the post-colonial generation

CONTENTS

INTRODUCTION

REMEMBERING COLONIALISM

The crises and conflicts of today's Middle East are rooted in the colonial past. The Israeli-Palestinian dispute, radical Islamism, Iran's hostility towards the West, the fraught relationship between Turkey and Europe, and between France and Algeria—all these, and a host of other issues, have their origins in the era of European colonial rule. To begin to understand the contemporary Middle East, we need to grasp how it emerged, in essentially its present form, in the half-century between 1917 and 1967.

The modern Middle East—as a string of recent anniversaries has reminded us—was the product of the First World War. After 1918 the victors in that war, Britain and France, divided between them the Arab portions of the Ottoman empire. To their chagrin, the Turks themselves refused to accept defeat and, under Mustafa Kemal, rescued the Anatolian part of the empire and turned it into the modern-day republic of Turkey. But elsewhere in the Middle East European colonial rule was the order of the day. In the post-war carve-up, Britain was allotted Palestine, Transjordan (now Jordan), and Iraq, while France got Syria and Lebanon—each power receiving a mandate to prepare these territories, in theory at least, for eventual independence. Persia (as Iran was then called) and the Arabian peninsula were not formally colonised, but they were heavily influenced, directly or indirectly, by the *pax Britannica*.

1

Whatever their motives—the defence of the route to India, the acquisition of oil and military bases, a desire to keep out rivals or protect Christian holy places—the European powers believed they were there to stay. They failed to reckon with the spirit of nationalism—stronger in some places, weaker in others—which was already in the air. Once Turkey had achieved statehood in 1923 and Saudi Arabia in 1932, others in the region were determined to follow suit. The Second World War was the turning-point. After six years of conflict, Europe's grip on empire was enfeebled. International opinion—reflected at the new-born United Nations and shared by an up-and-coming United States—was increasingly hostile to imperialism. In the post-war years, state after state broke free from European rule. By the late 1960s, after the French had withdrawn from Algeria and the British from Aden, the process was more or less complete.

But if the European powers have gone, the memory and folk-memory of their rule remains. In the Middle East, events of a century ago such as the Sykes-Picot agreement and the Balfour Declaration are remembered as if they happened yesterday, and in the blackest terms. In the West, meanwhile, as the number of those directly involved in the European empires dwindles, our opinion of imperialism has changed. We are less inclined to accept the claims made on its behalf, and more inclined to the view that it is wrong for one people to impose foreign rule and foreign occupation on another.

Historians of the period have approached the subject in different ways. Elizabeth Monroe, in *Britain's Moment in the Middle East*, wrote an incisive account of the rise and fall of British power in the region from 1914 to the Suez crisis of 1956. Others have focused on individual countries, producing studies of, say, the Palestine mandate or Algeria's war of independence, or on particular aspects of the drama of decolonisation. In a novel twist, soldiers and counter-insurgency experts now look back to Palestine in the 1930s and Algeria in the 1950s for lessons in fighting the new wars of the twenty-first century.

This book focuses on the struggle for independence in ten countries stretching from north Africa to south Arabia. It follows an overall chronology, from the emergence of modern Turkey in the 1920s, to that of Saudi Arabia in the 1930s, of Syria, Israel, and Jordan in the 1940s, Egypt and Iraq in the 1950s, and finally Algeria and the People's Democratic

Republic of Yemen in the 1960s. In each case the key date is that of actual, rather than formal, independence. Purists may object that Algeria is not a Middle Eastern country, and that the Iranian chapter (on the rise and fall of Muhammad Mossadeq) describes a failed, rather than a successful, attempt to break free from foreign tutelage. But both were important episodes in the struggle between nationalism and imperialism in the region, and hence intrinsic parts of the overall story.

The advantage of a country-by-country approach is that it captures the specificity of each—in geography, history, and culture—while highlighting how differently the struggle played out in different settings. Egypt was more homogeneous than Iraq; central Arabia far less developed than the Fertile Crescent. Statehood might be achieved through contraction (Turkey) or through expansion (Saudi Arabia). It might involve great violence (Algeria) or be largely peaceful (Jordan). It might be a straight fight between an indigenous people and a colonial power (as in Egypt)—or involve a third party with demands of its own (the *colons* in Algeria, the Zionist settlers in Palestine).

The Poisoned Well draws as far as possible on eye-witness testimony. It casts a wide net, taking in rulers and ruled, men and women, the famous and the unknown. The *dramatis personae* (listed at the end of the book) include nationalists and colonial administrators, soldiers and spies, consuls and courtesans, oilmen and missionaries, journalists and schoolteachers. Some played a role in the struggle for independence; others simply observed it. I have made use of memoirs, diaries, and letters—published and unpublished—and where possible have interviewed survivors from the period, or their children. I have listened to their stories and looked at their photographs and letters and other mementoes. Human memory is fallible, and it is not always possible to check the accuracy of such testimony. But if there are risks there are also abundant rewards: at its best, oral history tells us not just what happened, but what it felt like to be there.

The origins of this book go back to the early 1990s when, as a journalist with the BBC World Service, I made a radio series called 'The Making of the Middle East'. There were eventually ten programmes. In Ankara, I was lucky enough to meet people who had known Atatürk; and in Cairo, two of the surviving Free Officers who had overthrown the British-backed monarchy in 1952. I came across one retired soldier and diplomat, Sir Gawain Bell, who could have taken part in virtually all of the programmes: he had been a colonial administrator in Sudan, joined Glubb's Arab Legion in Jordan, helped put down the Arab revolt in Palestine in the 1930s, fought alongside the Free French in Syria in the Second World War, served as British Resident in Kuwait during the Suez crisis, and in the 1960s had taken part in a mission to draw up a new constitution for south Arabia. What's more, his memory was remarkably intact. Many of those I met then are no longer alive, but their voices live on in the unedited tapes of their interviews.

What was the colonial legacy in the Middle East? I return to this question in the epilogue. First and foremost, the Europeans drew borders—lines in the sand—which, however arbitrary or unwanted, have proved remarkably durable. Some boundaries have been contested, either successfully or unsuccessfully. In Palestine, the Jewish state emerged by conquest during the first Arab-Israeli war. More than four decades later, the Iraqi leader Saddam Hussein laid claim to Kuwait—which Iraqi nationalists had long seen as their country's natural outlet to the sea—and was driven back only by a large international army. As I write, jihadists are doing their utmost to eliminate the borders of Syria and Iraq. But by and large rulers have chosen to live within the frontiers they inherited from colonial rule, rather than challenge them.

At the same time, the Europeans set the peoples living within these borders on a particular (Western) path of nation-building and modernisation. The building of roads and schools and hospitals, which had begun haltingly in Ottoman times, gathered pace under colonial rule. The results were patchy. When Britain left Iraq and Egypt, illiteracy, disease, and poverty were rife. But the foundations of a modern infrastructure had been laid. At the same time, a cultural shift with far-reaching consequences was under way: schoolchildren were taught English or French, Shakespeare or Molière, and began to imbibe a secular culture often at odds with that of their parents. In the process, Middle Easterners acquired a range of attitudes to the West. New élites spoke Western languages and embraced a Western lifestyle. This cut them off from those of their compatriots who were suspicious of the West and clung to a traditional culture and identity—and who, as the nationalist project faltered, became foot-soldiers in the Islamic revival of the 1970s. A third attitude—perhaps more prevalent than either of the others—was a deep ambivalence towards the West. Many admired its scientific and material progress but at the same time nursed an abiding resentment of Western power and domination, grounded in the memory and folk-memory of the colonial period. All three attitudes persist today.

Western imperialism is not responsible for all of the ills of the modern Middle East. But the Western world has played a significant role in shaping the region and its destiny. This book tells the story of how it did so, and how the Middle East emerged from the shadow of empire.

To set the scene, the story begins with the Ottoman inheritance.

1

OUT OF THE ASHES

On 30 May 1919 a young woman, draped in black, stepped forward to address a packed throng in the square in front of the Sultan Ahmed mosque in Istanbul. The mood was one of national mourning. The Turks had been defeated in the First World War, their country occupied by British, French, Italian—and now, in a final insult, Greek—troops. They faced not merely the loss of their far-flung empire, which was by now irrevocable, but the dismemberment of their country.

The woman in black, Halidé Edib, was a 35-year-old writer and feminist who had been swept up in the national struggle. It was scarcely usual in a Muslim society for a woman to address a public rally. 'I could hardly stand on my feet,' she recalled, 'so fast and loud was my heart thumping: it was only when I entered the huge square that this violent thumping was stopped by the mere surprise of the spectacle. The minarets of Sultan Ahmed mosque rose into the brilliant white flutes of magic design. From their tiny balconies high in the air the black draperies waved softly, flying like long, black detached ribbons in the sky.'

The square and the surrounding streets were packed with a huge crowd of some 200,000 people. Allied planes flew overhead in an effort, the young woman suspected, to intimidate the crowd. She advanced nervously to the podium.

'Brethren, Sons, and Countrymen!' she declared. 'From the tops of the minarets nigh against the heavens, seven hundred years of glory are watching this new tragedy of Ottoman history...

7

'The European powers ... have found a pretext ... to break to pieces the last empire ruled by the crescent ...

'You have two friends: the Muslims and those civilised peoples who will sooner or later raise their voices for your rights.

'Governments are our enemies, peoples are our friends.

'The day is not far off when all nations will get their rights.'[1]

Modern Turkey, like the modern Middle East, emerged out of the ashes of the Ottoman empire. That empire, ruled from Istanbul by the Turkish sultan, had in its heyday been a Muslim superpower. It stretched across three continents, from north Africa to the Crimea. Among its kaleidoscope of twenty-two races and fifteen creeds were Turks, Arabs, Kurds, Greeks, Armenians, Jews, Bulgarians, Serbs, and Romanians.

The empire's heartland was Anatolia. It was here that Turks from Central Asia had settled and that Osman, the first Ottoman sultan, had established his dynasty sometime around 1300. But the empire's dramatic early expansion was not in Asia or the Middle East, but in Europe. Indeed for several centuries the sultan probably had more Christian subjects than Muslims. Having conquered the Balkans, his armies advanced into the heart of Europe. In 1529, after taking Hungary, they laid siege to Vienna but failed to capture it. They failed again in 1683, which proved to be the high-water mark of their expansion.

From the early sixteenth century, the Ottomans had extended their rule into the Arab Middle East, absorbing not only Egypt and Syria but also the western coast of the Arabian peninsula. Here they became custodians of Mecca and Medina, the holiest places of Islam, with all the prestige this entailed. With the conquest of Iraq, they acquired control of the revered Shi'a shrines of Najaf and Karbala.

But when expansion stalled and Europe's military and naval power grew stronger, the empire entered a long decline. By 1800 the symptoms were unmistakable. Ottoman rule had become weak and corrupt. The Janissaries, once the sultan's élite praetorian guard, had degenerated into a lawless clique. The empire's debts and much of its trade were in the hands of Europeans. Under the hated Capitulations, foreigners and their local protégés enjoyed immunity from the law and from taxation. Meanwhile two powerful new ideas—nationalism and the liberating message of the French revolution—had sown the seeds of revolt among the empire's subject peoples.[2]

Throughout the nineteenth century, European chancelleries were preoccupied with what was known as the Eastern Question, a euphemism for 'What to do about Ottoman decline?' If the empire collapsed, everyone wanted a piece of it. But in the meantime the European powers kept it on a kind of life-support, each fearful that its abrupt demise would benefit a rival.

The break-up began in earnest in Europe, with revolts by the Serbs and the Greeks. In 1830 Serbia achieved local autonomy, and in 1832 the European powers forced the Turks to accept Greek independence. Meanwhile a troublesome soldier called Muhammad Ali, an Albanian of Macedonian ancestry, wrested Egypt from Ottoman control. Worse still, in 1831 his son Ibrahim captured Syria and threatened Istanbul itself. The sultan was obliged to call for help from the Russian Tsar, who sent 30,000 men to fend off the Egyptian threat. By the time Muhammad Ali died in 1849, Egypt had been cut down to size. But the episode showed how desperately weak the empire had become.

The fate of the Turks depended not only on the role of outsiders (which was considerable) but on the quality of their rulers. This varied wildly. Some of the early sultans—most famously, Suleiman the Magnificent in the sixteenth century—were able and intelligent. But many of their successors were, in the words of one historian, 'incompetents, degenerates, and misfits'.[3]

In the nineteenth century, however, two reforming sultans initiated a process of modernisation which, if sustained, might have halted or slowed the empire's decline. This was the period of the *Tanzimat*—the Reorganisation—or, as the British ambassador in Istanbul playfully dubbed it, the 'great game of improvement'. The *Tanzimat* began under Sultan Mahmud, who came to the throne in 1808 at the age of twenty-three. Visible changes were soon apparent at court. The young sultan scandalised the religious by acquiring a taste for champagne. He preferred sitting on a chair rather than a divan. And he broke with custom by attending the imperial council, where the grand vizier (the Ottoman prime minister) normally held sway.

As a prelude to wide-ranging reforms, Sultan Mahmud crushed the powerful Janissaries, who had become an obstacle to progress. Then he set about modernising the empire's ramshackle bureaucracy and limiting the power of the *ulema* (scholars of Islam), denying them a role in administering education and justice. He decreed new forms of civilian dress, introducing the fez to replace the turban, and even insisted, controversially, that his cavalry adopt a European-style saddle. The process Mahmud had begun was continued by his son Abdul-Mejid, who succeeded him in 1839. On 3 November 1839, Abdul-Mejid issued the Gülhane edict (named after the rose garden in the Topkapı palace). The edict set out four main aims: to guarantee the life, honour, and property of the sultan's subjects; to establish an orderly (rather than predatory) system of taxation; to introduce conscription for the army; and to uphold the equality of all under the law, regardless of religion. This last was a significant break with tradition, since it implied that Islam would lose its pre-eminence.

The edict was addressed not only to the sultan's subjects but also to the European powers, in a bid to assure them that the Ottoman state was seriously committed to reform and modernisation. The object of the *Tanzimat*—which lasted for about four decades—was the transformation of Ottoman society, and in some areas it succeeded. 'If we compare the empire of 1870 with what it had been in 1820,' observes the historian Albert Hourani, 'there is no doubt that standards of administration and justice had risen; the non-Muslims were freer ... the provincial administration had been reformed ... a certain idea of Ottoman "nationhood" was spreading.'[4] Above all, reforms to education began to create a new and more modern-minded élite, both civil and military, that was committed to European ideas of progress.

But if the successes were real, the obstacles and setbacks were considerable. Implementation of reform was uneven. Sultans were reluctant to accept constraints on their power. The *ulema* were hostile to anything that might undermine the rule of Islamic law and the dominant position of Muslims in the empire. One intellectual loudly complained: 'The Muslim community is the ruling community, but it has been deprived of its sacred rights.'[5]

In practice, the idea of equality made little headway. 'Despite all statutes to the contrary,' wrote the British diplomat Sir Charles Eliot, 'religious equality does not prevail, nor is Turkey constitutionally governed.'[6]

By now, the main external threat came from Russia. Tsar Nicholas wanted to bring about the partition of the Ottoman empire—which he famously described as the 'sick man of Europe'—using as a pretext his claim to be the protector of its Orthodox Christians. When, in response, the sultan declared war on Russia, Britain and France came to his aid. This precipitated the Crimean war of 1853–56, which succeeded in forestalling the Tsarist threat.

But nothing could halt the empire's decay. Every attempt at serious reform aroused fierce opposition from political and religious conservatives. After Abdul-Mejid's death, the reactionaries took over—including the most powerful of them, Sultan Abdul-Hamid, whose reign of more than three decades, from 1876 to 1909, proved to be the turning-point in the story of Ottoman decline.

It was during the rule of Abdul-Hamid that Halidé Edib grew up. She was born in 1884 in Istanbul, where her father was a secretary at the royal court. As a girl she watched, dazzled, as the sultan's men marched past:

> Abdul-Hamid's Albanian bodyguard in bright red, his Tripolitan black guards in green and red, his numberless aides-de-camp in gilt uniforms … the royal sergeants (chosen for their good looks) in blue jackets with long hanging sleeves lined with red, the incredibly beautiful horses pawing the ground impatiently, or stepping in time to the lively 'March of his Majesty'.

Following the procession in his carriage, on his way to Friday prayers, came the sultan himself. 'I did not realise then,' wrote Halidé in her memoirs, 'that the man with the imposing nose and shifty eyes was the last Turkish emperor at his highest ascendancy.'[7]

At first Abdul-Hamid paid lip-service to reform. In 1876, thanks to the reforming zeal of his grand vizier, Midhat Pasha, the first Ottoman constitution was introduced, leading to the opening of the first Ottoman parliament. It was, on the face of it, a great victory for the reformers. But within weeks Abdul-Hamid had sent Midhat Pasha, whom he mistrusted, into exile (where he subsequently had him strangled), and in 1878 he dismissed the parliament and suspended the constitution. The sultan's behaviour became increasingly autocratic and paranoid. Fearful he would be deposed, he shut himself away in his palace, seldom emerging into public view. He imposed strict control of books and newspapers and, relying on an extensive network of spies, stamped out any sign of opposition.

The whole city [wrote Sir Charles Eliot] groans under the tyranny of the Minister of Police ... The highest functionaries may be summoned in the middle of the night, and interrogated by persons much their inferior in rank on utterly frivolous charges ... A man is spied on by his colleagues, his subordinates, and his servants, who all write reports of his daily doings.[8]

But despite the pervasive climate of fear, dissent grew among students, intellectuals, and army officers. In 1889 a group of medical students in Istanbul set up a secret society which soon became known as the Committee of Union and Progress—and its members, more popularly, as the Young Turks. Among its most prominent figures was a dashing and ambitious soldier called Enver Pasha, and among its junior members a young army officer, as yet unknown, called Mustafa Kemal. The self-appointed mission of the Young Turks was to free the empire from dictatorship and decline.

On 23 July 1908, in the face of an ultimatum from the CUP, Abdul-Hamid announced the restoration of the constitution he had suspended three decades earlier. There was wild rejoicing in the capital. Muslims, Christians, and Jews embraced in the street. The city, wrote a British observer, 'was glowing like a rose'.[9] 'We are all brothers,' declared Enver to an ecstatic crowd in Salonica, one of the main centres of revolutionary fervour. 'There are no longer Bulgarians, Greeks, Serbs, Romanians, Jews, Muslims—under the same blue sky we are all equal, we are all proud to be Ottomans.'[10]

The new Ottoman parliament—made up of 142 Turks, sixty Arabs, twenty-five Albanians, twenty-three Greeks, twelve Armenians, five Jews, four Bulgarians, three Serbs, and a Romanian—met for the first time in Istanbul in December 1908.[11] For the Young Turks, however, the heart of their revolution was not the capital—where their following was limited, and opposition to them remained strong—but Salonica, which they revered as 'the Mecca of freedom'. The main Ottoman port on the Aegean, it was the key to control of the Balkans. From its waters steamships sailed to Europe, returning with 'Manchester cottons and Rouen silks, beer from Austria, watches and jewellery from Switzerland'. Although Turks had run the city since the Ottomans captured it in 1430, much of its commerce was in the hands of Greeks and Jews, the two largest communities. Salonica's four main languages were Greek, French,

Turkish, and Spanish (the language of the Sephardi Jews who had settled there after being driven out of Spain and Portugal).[12]

It was in this vibrantly cosmopolitan world—brilliantly evoked by Mark Mazower in *Salonica: City of Ghosts*—that Mustafa Kemal, the founder of the modern Turkish republic, had been born in 1881. His father Ali Rıza, a junior civil servant and unsuccessful merchant, died when he was only seven, and he was brought up by his mother Zübeyde, a barely literate and deeply religious woman of peasant origin. Like her, he had fair hair and blue eyes, and may well have had Balkan ancestors.[13]

Zübeyde did not want him to become a soldier. But he persuaded her to let him enter a military preparatory school at Manastir, near Macedonia's border with Greece. Hard-working but proud and aloof, Mustafa Kemal developed a love of mathematics, learned French— considered the language of freedom—and admired the political ideas of Rousseau and Voltaire. He hated wearing traditional Turkish clothes and longed for the uniform of an officer.

He got his wish in 1899, when he entered the War College in Istanbul. This was the factory that produced the band of nationalists who created modern Turkey. The cadets found discipline harshly enforced. In Abdul-Hamid's police state, the works of the French political philosophers were banned as subversive, and Mustafa Kemal had to read them secretly at night. By the time he graduated and entered the Staff College, he and his friends were committed opponents of the sultan's autocratic rule. But their activities—which included the production of a hand-written newspaper—had been observed, and they were arrested and interrogated. The young cadets got off lightly: after several weeks in prison, they were posted to Damascus. Here, in 1906, they founded a secret revolutionary society that before long they merged with the CUP, whose aims they shared.

The slogans of the Young Turks, who were imbued with the ideals of the French revolution, were freedom, brotherhood, and union. But they were political novices, divided and conspiratorial, who lacked a strategy around which to unite. Their politics, remarked Halidé Edib, who was by no means unsympathetic to their aims, were 'raw, impetuous, and tactless'.[14] Some were Ottomanists, seeing their future in a revived and reformed Ottoman empire. Others, like Mustafa Kemal, were moving towards a more specifically Turkish nationalism—a belief that Turks had to find their future in a Turkish, rather than an Ottoman, state.

The CUP had powerful enemies. In April 1909 there was a counter-revolution calling for the defence of Islam and the restoration of Islamic law. The Young Turks were forced to flee from Istanbul; but they regrouped and fought back. Enver and Mustafa Kemal were among a force of Young Turk loyalists in Salonica who marched on the capital and deposed Abdul-Hamid.

Politically, the CUP was in the ascendant and the old guard on the defensive. But neither group could prevent the continuing disintegration of the empire. Piece by piece, Ottoman lands in Europe were lost, as local nationalism gained momentum. A bitter personal blow to Mustafa Kemal was the loss of Salonica, which was captured by the Greeks in 1912. He was indignant that the city had surrendered without a shot being fired. His mother, sister, and cousin were forced to flee to Istanbul, where he found them in a refugee camp and managed to resettle them.

His disenchantment with the Young Turks grew. After being briefly ousted from power in 1912, they carried out a coup in January 1913. The empire was now ruled by a triumvirate. At its head was Enver, 'flamboyant, reckless, and self-indulgent', dreaming of being a Turkish Napoleon. The older and shrewder Jemal was a skilful organiser and a man of 'cold, fanatical ruthlessness'. Talat, dubbed the 'Danton of the revolution', had started life as a postal clerk in Thrace and was the most senior civilian member of the CUP. The three men ran a military dictatorship which was to last until 1918.[15]

Halidé Edib, too, was caught up in the fervour of the times, becoming active as a writer and social reformer. She too had grown up in a cosmopolitan world, taking for granted the fact that many of her friends and neighbours were Greeks and Armenians. She was educated at home, learning English, French, and Arabic, and then studied at the American College for Girls, a school founded in Istanbul by American missionaries. She read Western literature avidly, acquiring a passion for Shakespeare. (In later life, as professor of English at Istanbul University, she translated *Hamlet* into Turkish.) After graduating in 1901 at the age of seventeen, she married a much older man, the scholar Salih Zeki, and settled down to a life as writer, wife, and mother of two sons. In 1908, the year of revolution, she helped found the Society for the Elevation of Women, which had links with the British suffragettes. The following year, following the counter-revolution, when reformers were being attacked and killed, she found her name on a blacklist. At the urging of friends, she escaped with her two boys to Egypt.

On her return, she suffered the first great crisis of her family life. It became clear that Salih Zeki intended to take a second wife, a decision which Islam sanctioned but which Halidé strongly opposed:

> There was a long and painful struggle between us, but at last he consented to a divorce, and I left what had been for nine years my home. It was a cold April night when I drove with the boys to Fatih [a district of Istanbul], to the big old-fashioned house of Nakié Hanum [a woman teacher and life-long friend], where I stayed till I found a suitable house. What now seems an almost ordinary incident in a woman's life was then of supreme importance and the cause of great suffering to me.

In her new life, she shared a house with her 80-year-old grandmother. The relationship between the two women was close. For all her commitment to social change, Halidé could understand her grandmother's distress at the bewildering changes going on around her.

> She was much shocked by the new women. Their talk, their walk, their dress, and their general aspect hurt her. She felt lonely, like a stranger in a world where she felt she had stayed too long … She suffered because they shook their arms as they walked, looked into men's eyes, had loud voices, and smoked in public; above all they did not iron their clothes as she did every morning.[16]

When the First World War broke out in 1914, Enver—his army heavily dependent on German advisers—took Turkey into the war on Germany's side. It was a fateful decision that Mustafa Kemal, by now a lieutenant-colonel, opposed. Nevertheless, when Allied forces menaced the Dardanelles, the straits that guarded Istanbul, he was one of the commanders entrusted with its defence.

In the Gallipoli campaign of 1915–16, the Turks succeeded in holding back the advance of British and Anzac (Australian and New Zealand Army Corps) forces. Though Mustafa Kemal was not quite the saviour of Istanbul he later claimed to be, there is no doubting his dogged determination and his ability to inspire the loyalty of his men—for the most part poorly-armed, ill-fed Anatolian peasants. 'I do not order you to attack,' he famously told them, 'I order you to die.' And they did. The eight-month campaign cost at least 86,000 Turkish lives.[17] In the end the Allied forces were obliged to make a humiliating withdrawal. Word soon spread of the young colonel's exploits, despite Enver's efforts to play them down.

Mustafa Kemal was thirty-eight. Elevated to the rank of General Mustafa Kemal Pasha, he was sent to fight the Russians, who had advanced into eastern Anatolia, and then to Syria, which was soon to fall as British forces swept through the Ottomans' Arab domains. Militarily he was useful to the Young Turk government, but politically he was a thorn in their side. In September 1917 he sent Enver and Talat an outspoken report on the condition of the empire:

> There are no bonds left [he declared] between the present Turkish Government and the people ... Public life is full of anarchy. Each new step taken by the Government increases the general hatred against it ... All officials take bribes ... The police forces do not function ... If the war lasts much longer the whole structure of the Government and the [Ottoman] dynasty, decrepit in all its parts, may suddenly fall to pieces.[18]

When the report was ignored, he resigned in disgust.

The story of the death throes of the Ottoman empire has countless victims and few heroes. In the inter-communal fighting that accompanied its demise, over three million people—Turks, Greeks, Armenians, Bulgarians, and others—were killed, and countless others forced from their homes.[19] As violence bred violence, victims became perpetrators and vice versa. The destruction or dispersal of whole communities left a legacy of bitterness and changed irrevocably the demographic composition of former Ottoman lands.

This process was under way well before the First World War, even if the war hastened it to its grim conclusion. Massacres and the flight of refugees had accompanied the Balkan uprisings. But by far the most significant and most contentious case of what we now call ethnic cleansing was that of the Armenians between the 1890s and 1917. Underlying the Turkish attitude towards the empire's Christian minorities was a deep-rooted sense of paranoia, a fear that the enemy within was in league with the enemy without—the foreign (Christian) powers who had long schemed to carve up Ottoman territory. This feeling was articulated by Sultan Abdul-Hamid:

> By taking Greece and Romania, [the Great Powers] cut off the feet of the Turkish state. By taking Bulgaria, Serbia, and Egypt they cut off our hands. Now by stirring up trouble among the Armenians they are getting close to our vital organs and want to cut out our intestines. This is the beginning of mass destruction. We must defend ourselves at all costs.[20]

Large-scale massacres of Armenians, at first local in character, began in 1894. The following year they spread to a much wider area. The British diplomat Sir Charles Eliot estimated that 50,000 Armenians perished. The killings, he wrote, were carried out 'with military precision'. 'The authorities did not interfere, and in some cases encouraged the mob.' In the harsh winter that followed, many of the survivors, mostly widows and orphans, died of hunger or cold. The massacres provoked a wave of indignation in Europe.[21]

By the time of the First World War, the sense of Turkish paranoia had grown more intense. As the empire fought for its life, Enver, Talat, and their colleagues saw the Armenians as a fifth column in league with Tsarist Russia. Armenian nationalists believed that, in the event of a Russian victory, they would be able to establish an Armenian state in eastern Anatolia. In April 1915 the government decided, at the suggestion of Talat, the minister of the interior, to relocate the entire Armenian population of the war zone to the Syrian desert. In fact the deportations were not limited to the war zone, and were accompanied by acts of appalling brutality.

> Men were separated from their women and children and massacred. Rivers clogged up with bodies. Kurdish tribesmen looted the columns of survivors and carried off marriageable girls slung over their saddles. Of columns of up to 20,000 refugees, sometimes only one or two hundred survived. Even grandmothers were stripped of their clothes and left to stumble on naked.[22]

How many Armenians died, either in massacres or during the forced march into exile, has been fiercely debated. The historian Eric Zürcher thinks the likely figure is between 600,000 and 800,000—by his estimate, about half the pre-war Armenian population of Anatolia. Other historians believe the true figure is 1.5 million. As to the vexed issue of culpability, Zürcher writes: 'There are indications that ... an inner circle within the [CUP] under the direction of Talat wanted to "solve" the Eastern Question by the extermination of the Armenians and that it used the relocation as a cloak for this policy.'[23]

In 1917 the Turks lost Mecca, Baghdad, and Jerusalem—heavy blows to both their morale and their prestige in the Islamic world. In October 1918, their empire destroyed, they were forced to accept an armistice. It was a moment of national humiliation. Enver, Talat, and Jemal fled to the Crimea in a German warship, and from there to Berlin. A French general entered Istanbul on a white horse, to the cheers of local Greeks, Armenians, and Europeans. A fleet of over fifty Allied warships steamed into the Bosphorus. Nationalists regarded the current sultan, Mehmed VI, the last surviving son of Abdul-Mejid, as a stooge in the hands of the victorious Allies.

The idea of creating a movement of national resistance originated not in the palace or among the established politicians, but among patriotic army officers—including Mustafa Kemal—with the active or passive support of members of the general staff. In April 1919 the nationalists had a stroke of luck when Mustafa Kemal was appointed inspector-general of eastern Anatolia and the Black Sea coast. His brief was to bring law and order to areas of unrest, but he had a very different object in mind: to mobilise resistance to Allied plans for the country's partition.

The following month a 20,000-strong Greek force landed at Smyrna (modern-day Izmir), on the western coast of Anatolia. The Greeks laid claim not only to the port itself but also to a slice of western Anatolia. The invasion had been approved by Britain, France, and the United States, and took place under the protection of Allied warships. Its most enthusiastic supporter was the British prime minister, David Lloyd George, who wanted to reward the Greeks (a war-time ally) and punish the Turks (a war-time enemy). The Turkish surrender of the city, with three to four hundred Turkish casualties, prompted the national mourning which found expression at the mass meeting addressed by Halidé Edib in Istanbul. At the same time, the electric shock of the Greek invasion gave a powerful stimulus to the nationalist cause.

Mustafa Kemal based himself first at Samsun, on the Black Sea, then moved further inland, building up his forces and ignoring orders from

Istanbul for his arrest as 'a mutineer and a traitor'. In July 1919 he summoned nationalists to a congress at Erzurum, in eastern Anatolia, which elected him as its president and issued a rallying-call to the country in the form of a National Pact. He was quick to grasp the importance of publicity, making good use of the telegraph system which Abdul-Hamid had created to strengthen his control and assist his spies.

Mustafa Kemal had thrown down the gauntlet to the sultan—and to the British, who were deeply unhappy at the challenge he posed but reluctant to confront him militarily. He now moved to Angora (modern-day Ankara), then a small, dusty provincial town in central Anatolia, which became the centre of the national movement and the seat of a rival government.

The history of the struggle for independence has tended to be dominated by the personality of Mustafa Kemal. He was undoubtedly the driving force of the national movement. But four of his close colleagues played an indispensable role: Hussein Rauf, Ali Fuat, Ibrahim Refet, and Kazım Karabekir. All were his contemporaries, or near contemporaries; all were military men, products of the War College in Istanbul; all were to fall out with him once independence had been won.[24]

A new parliament with a nationalist majority met in Istanbul in January 1920 and endorsed the National Pact. But the British were not ready to acquiesce in a nationalist victory. In March they seized full control of the capital and arrested 150 leading nationalists, including Mustafa Kemal's colleague Rauf, who was deported to Malta. Among those who went into hiding were Halidé Edib and her second husband, Adnan Adıvar, a respected doctor and writer. On 18 March 1920—with Dr Adnan disguised in the black robe and white turban of a *hodja* (a Muslim cleric) and Halidé in the dowdy dress of a *hodja*'s wife—they boarded the ferry to cross to the Asian side of the Bosphorus. They were in constant fear of discovery.

> The Bosphorus [Halidé recalled] was brilliantly illuminated by the lights of the [British] warships, the guns glistened, and the sailors walked the decks; the waters were harsh and white with foam and the cold was penetrating.[25]

Once they landed, they hastened through the dark streets to a *tekké*—a Sufi lodge—which the nationalists were using as a safe house.

Here they met four members of parliament, also on the run from the British. There were posters all over the city, in English and Turkish, threatening anyone who harboured a nationalist with death. They heard a rumour that the British were offering £500 to anyone who could reveal their whereabouts.[26]

Leaving her two sons in the care of friends, Halidé embarked with Dr Adnan on a difficult and dangerous two-week journey through bandit-infested country to Angora. In remote villages, supporters of the cause gave them shelter and fed them eggs and yoghurt and black bread. The experience opened the eyes of a woman who had enjoyed a comfortable middle-class existence to the life of the people. The last part of their journey was by train, and on the evening of 2 April 1920 they finally reached Angora, to be greeted by Mustafa Kemal. In the months that followed, Halidé was to become his translator, secretary, and public-relations officer, and the only woman in his inner circle.

A war of words now ensued between the two rival governments. The sultan, backed by a *fatwa* (religious decree), declared war on the nationalists—to which Mustafa Kemal retorted with a counter-*fatwa* issued by the religious leaders of Angora. On 23 April 1920 a nationalist parliament, the Grand National Assembly, met in Angora and elected Mustafa Kemal as its president. For the time being he kept secret his true goal—the creation of a republic—in the interests of maintaining unity. To call for the destruction of the sultanate was too bold a step, even for some of his close associates; instead he claimed his object was to rescue the sultan from the clutches of the European imperialists.

But despite the nationalists' efforts, the final break-up of the empire seemed a foregone conclusion. Under the post-war settlement, set out in the Treaty of Sèvres of May 1920, the Greeks were to obtain Thrace (depriving the Turks of their last European foothold), and the prospect of some sort of statehood was held out to the Armenians and the Kurds—while the Turks were to be left with a rump state, with Istanbul (under Allied control) as its capital. It was to foil this Western plan that Mustafa Kemal now devoted his energies.

The immediate task was to drive back the Greek invaders. The nationalists' first success came in January 1921, when Mustafa Kemal's trusted colleague Ismet defeated the Greeks at the battle of Inönü.

Then, in March, Ismet held off another Greek offensive. But final victory was far from assured. The Greeks advanced eastwards, forcing Mustafa Kemal to pull back his forces and make a stand only fifty miles from Angora. The National Assembly, in alarm, granted him exceptional powers for three months. In the next few crucial weeks, he requisitioned supplies and vehicles and mobilised all able-bodied citizens for the coming struggle. At the battle of Sakarya, which lasted twenty-two days, the Greeks were thrown back. Angora was saved.

The nationalists' position was by now stronger diplomatically as well as on the battlefield. They were receiving support and weapons from Russia, France, and Italy, leaving Britain isolated in its opposition to them. Mustafa Kemal nevertheless faced vocal dissent in the National Assembly, and within his inner circle, from those who suspected that, for all his fine words about the sovereignty of the people, he was at heart an autocrat. Halidé Edib admired his strength and commitment, but considered him amoral in the pursuit of his aims.

> He was by turns cynical, unscrupulous, and satanically shrewd. He bullied, he indulged in cheap street-corner heroics. Possessing considerable though quite undistinguished histrionic ability, one moment he could pass as the perfect demagogue—a second George Washington—and the next moment fall into some Napoleonic attitude.[27]

Moreover, as a feminist, she could not fail to observe that, while championing female emancipation, he frequently treated women abominably.

The final battle against the Greeks came the following year, in August 1922. After fifteen days of fighting, half the Greek army was killed or captured and the other half in headlong flight. The dénouement was brutal. The retreating Greeks adopted a scorched-earth policy, destroying villages as they went, until they reached Smyrna, the port where they'd arrived three years earlier. Turkish forces entered the city, proclaiming their desire to re-establish law and order. But a few days later a fire broke out in the Armenian quarter, quickly spreading through the city as far as the waterfront. Tens of thousands of Greek refugees sought to escape the flames. A British journalist, G. Ward Price, of the *Daily Mail*, witnessed what ensued.

21

As darkness fell the scene became a terrible one … The long waterfront was packed with Greeks of all ages penned up between fire and sea … Mothers were holding up their babies; old women came staggering down to the front, bent double under bundles of their possessions. Blind men were being led along. The sick and aged from the hospitals were carried down on improvised stretchers … The fire was now a conflagration two miles long. The surface of the sea shone like burnished copper.[28]

The fire, which destroyed three-quarters of the city, was almost certainly an act of revenge by Turkish soldiers against the city's Greeks and Armenians, whom they regarded as traitors.

As Mustafa Kemal watched the smouldering embers of Smyrna, he remarked to a colleague: 'They think that this is the end, that I have reached my goal. But it is only now that our real work is beginning.'[29] He had challenged the Western powers and won, but in London and Paris it took time for the implications to sink in. The way was now open for the nationalists to advance on Istanbul, still under Allied occupation, where Sultan Mehmed was proving reluctant to step aside. Mustafa Kemal was not willing to compromise with him. He persuaded the National Assembly—after a long and difficult debate—to take the momentous step of abolishing the sultanate.

It was by force [he declared] that the sons of Osman seized the sovereignty and Sultanate of the Turkish nation … Now the Turkish nation … has effectively taken sovereignty and Sultanate into its own hands.[30]

He did not go as far as to abolish the caliphate: the sultan's religious role as caliph was preserved, but shorn of political power.

In the early morning of 11 November 1922, the last Ottoman sultan escaped from his palace, amid elaborate secrecy, to a British warship that took him to exile in Malta.

Six centuries of Ottoman rule had come to an inglorious end.

On the ground, Mustafa Kemal had demonstrated his supremacy. What remained was to secure the formal reversal of the Treaty of Sèvres, now a dead letter. In January 1923 he sent a reluctant Ismet as his representative to peace talks in Lausanne. It was hard going. Pressed by his interlocutors, Ismet would frustrate them with the refrain: 'Sovereignty, sovereignty, sovereignty'. When Lord Curzon, the British Foreign Secretary, demanded his immediate signature to an agreement, Ismet refused and the talks broke up. It was not until July that the parties returned and, after further negotiation, the treaty was signed.

The Western powers had been forced to accept the reality of a new Turkey, in essentially the borders it has retained to this day. Once again, a heavy price was to be paid in human suffering. The contentious decision was taken at Lausanne for a compulsory exchange of populations between Greece and Turkey, which led to the uprooting of more than one and a half million people. The new Turkey, largely shorn of non-Muslims, was predominantly Turkish in ethnicity (with a large Kurdish minority) and 98 per cent Muslim.[31]

The Allies withdrew their ships and their soldiers from Istanbul. In a calculated break with the past, the National Assembly declared Angora (renamed Ankara) to be the new Turkish capital. The birth of the republic of Turkey was proclaimed on 29 October 1923, with Mustafa Kemal as its first president.

What was the Ottoman legacy? For Turkey itself, it was one that for decades was denied. The aim of Mustafa Kemal's one-man revolution, between 1923 and his death in 1938, was to achieve a complete break with the past. Islam was deprived of its officially enshrined status as the religion of state. The new republic was a secular state modelled on European lines. In schools and universities, modern science was accorded pride of place. Women were given the vote and discouraged from wearing the veil. Men were told to exchange the fez for the European-style hat (which provoked riots). The Turkish language was modernised to accommodate new terms and remove Arabic and Persian accretions. History was re-written to discount Ottoman achievements. The republic became the embodiment of progress and enlightenment, while the imperial past was consigned to oblivion.

At the same time, the war of independence left long-lasting scars. The Turks had not been formally colonised, but European powers had acted in concert to prevent, or at the very least circumscribe, their rebirth as a nation-state. Turkish nationalism had, from the first, an embattled character, and this was to colour Turkey's future relations with the West, which were sensitive to the point of paranoia.

Mustafa Kemal took the name Atatürk (father of the Turks). Politically, his legacy was populist rather than truly democratic. Although he championed the sovereignty of the people, he could not brook opposition. Some of his closest associates in the war of independence fell out with him and were either imprisoned or forced into exile. Among the latter were Halidé Edib and her husband Dr Adnan, who fled the country after an opposition group they had helped to found was shut down. They did not return until after Mustafa Kemal's death in 1938.

To the naked eye, his legacy and the personality cult that still surrounds him are alive and well. But closer inspection suggests that, while the shell of his achievement has survived, its core has been hollowed out. In the decades after his death, Turks became more open in expressing their Muslim identity. Multi-party politics replaced one-party rule. The military asserted its role as guardian of stability and secularism in three coups between 1960 and 1980. Only recently have civilian politicians begun to curb the political influence of the generals. At the same time, the Ottoman centuries have begun to be viewed in a fresh light. While some Turks remain loyal to the Kemalist conception of the past, for many others there is a greater readiness to recognise Ottoman achievements, not least in art and culture, and to feel a certain pride in the fact that for six centuries Turks were at the helm of a Muslim superpower which affected the destiny of Europe and the Middle East.

In the Middle East itself, there has similarly been a process of rejection followed by reassessment. For decades, Arab historians regarded the centuries of Ottoman rule as a dark page, one that was best ignored or passed over as briefly as possible. But this view could not be sustained indefinitely. As Albert Hourani remarked:

> Anyone who has travelled in the lands which the Turks once ruled ... must have noticed how deep the Ottoman impress went and how lasting is the unity it has imposed on many different countries and peoples: the buildings, from the domes and graceful slender minarets of mosques in the Ottoman style, to the solid barracks and government houses of a later period; the formal and elaborate manners of the old families of Istanbul and the provincial capitals ... a certain style of government and politics, difficult to describe but which continued almost until our time, not only among Turkish politicians but in the palaces in Baghdad, Amman, Cairo and Tunis, among the older statesmen of Egypt before the revolution, and the older nationalist leaders of Syria [and] Iraq ...[32]

This legacy, both visible and invisible, will be apparent in the chapters that follow. The modern Middle East shook off the Ottoman yoke but remained profoundly influenced by Ottoman culture and politics. The men who played a part in shaping the new order—King Faisal of Iraq and his loyal minister, Nuri al-Said; Emir Abdullah of Transjordan; the Syrian nationalist leader Shukri al-Quwatli and his Lebanese counterpart Riad al-Solh—these and countless others were, for good or ill, products of the Ottoman age.

2

SWORD OF ARABIA

The tall, one-eyed, battle-scarred king loved nothing better than telling stories of his exploits as a desert warrior. Once, when recalling to a young British diplomat the moment he'd charged on camelback towards an enemy, he got up and seized one of the swords displayed on the wall. 'I drew nearer and nearer, and raised my sword'—and here, to the Englishman's consternation, he waved it aloft—'and chopped off his head, and sent it rolling away in the sand.'[1]

In the course of thirty years and more than fifty battles, Abdul-Aziz ibn Abdul-Rahman al-Saud—better known in the West as Ibn Saud—created the country we know today as Saudi Arabia. Of all the feats of nation-building in the modern Middle East, this was one of the most extraordinary. The Saudi kingdom occupies three-quarters of the Arabian peninsula. Only one per cent of its land is cultivated. Its biggest and cruellest desert, the Rub al-Khali, or Empty Quarter, is larger than France. It was this vast, sparsely populated territory, riven by tribal rivalries, that Ibn Saud united by the sword in the first three decades of the twentieth century.

Muhammad Almana arrived in Jeddah, on Arabia's Red Sea coast, in May 1926 to take up a post as Ibn Saud's translator. He had been born in Zubair, in southern Iraq, to a family whose roots (like those of the king) were in Nejd, the heartland of central Arabia. At the age of ten he was taken by his father to India and spent the next twelve years in Bombay, where he studied at an English school. But the young Almana was eager to return to Arabia and pulled strings to get a job at the royal court. He was fluent in English, Urdu, and Arabic, at a time when Ibn Saud badly needed linguists to help him understand and communicate with the outside world.

The job was hard; he worked an average fourteen hours a day, translating documents and interpreting for the king and his officials. Conditions in Riyadh, the Saudi capital, were a far cry from British-ruled Bombay. As Almana recalled in a memoir, Riyadh in the 1920s was a small town surrounded by a mud wall some twenty feet high, with 'a maze of twisting streets, some so narrow that it was difficult for two men to walk abreast down them'. He stayed at court, at Ibn Saud's side, for the next nine years, an eye-witness to the birth of the Saudi kingdom.[2]

The founding father of Saudi Arabia had been born in Riyadh, probably in 1876. His family, the house of Saud, believed it had a mission to dominate central Arabia. Twice it had tried—in the eighteenth century and again in the nineteenth—and twice it had been pushed back by rival clans. By the beginning of the twentieth century, the young Ibn Saud and his father, Abdul-Rahman, whom he revered, were languishing in poverty and self-imposed exile in neighbouring Kuwait—while Riyadh and Nejd were in the hands of their great rivals, the Rashids.

For two centuries these two powerful dynasties had been engaged in a struggle for hegemony in central Arabia. Now their rivalry was to enter a decisive phase. At the end of 1901 the 26-year-old Ibn Saud set out with a few dozen men to capture Riyadh and revive his family's fortunes. No one believed they could succeed. But in January 1902 they scaled the walls of the town in a daring night-time raid. They hid in a house near that of the Rashidi governor, Ajlan, and at dawn attacked him as he stepped out of his fortress. Ajlan managed to escape back inside but, in fierce fighting, was struck down near the mosque. The garrison surrendered, and Ibn Saud publicly proclaimed the return of the house of Saud to its ancestral capital. The capture of Riyadh has become the founding myth of the Saudi state.[3]

But dramatic though it was, this was only the beginning of a long struggle. At first the Rashids underestimated their enemy. 'The rabbit is in the hole,' scoffed their leader, Ibn Rashid, when told of Ibn Saud's coup.[4] He was slow to act against the Saudi upstart, and this enabled Ibn Saud to consolidate his hold on Riyadh, strengthen its fortifications, and extend his rule over surrounding areas. But the Rashids were far from finished, and for several years there was an uneasy stalemate, with Nejd effectively partitioned between the two warring clans.

Ibn Saud had hitherto relied on Nejdi townsmen ready to fight for his cause. Now he mobilised the tribesmen of the region under the banner of jihad, or holy war. He began to recruit a force known as the Ikhwan, or Brotherhood. These were tough bedouin fighters motivated by the lure of booty and a burning zeal to spread the message of Wahhabism—the austere, literalist form of Sunni Islam which the Sauds had espoused in the middle of the eighteenth century. The essence of Wahhabism was a strict monotheism and a fierce iconoclasm: it abhorred the worship of trees, stones, or saints.

To harness the Ikhwan, Ibn Saud encouraged them to live in new settlements and take up farming. He gave them land and sent Wahhabi preachers to instruct them. 'He wanted the wandering bedouins to settle on fertile plots near wells,' wrote the Dutch diplomat and traveller Daniel van der Meulen. 'From being herdsmen they would become agriculturalists, from free lords of the desert, poor and often lazy but proud of their independence, they would become tillers of the soil, a people living in mud huts instead of the *buyut-ash-sha'r*—houses of goats' hair.'[5] The first Ikhwan settlement was founded in Artawiya, north of Riyadh, around 1912. By 1918 there were over 200 settlements throughout Nejd, able to muster some 60,000 fighting men.[6]

Having spent much of his life abroad, Muhammad Almana was unaccustomed to the rigours of Wahhabi Islam. The Ikhwan's puritanism was so intense, he records, that they regarded a wristwatch as the work of the devil. 'The same applied to cars, telephones, wireless sets and almost every other modern tool which the King needed in order to bring progress to his kingdom.' These things were regarded as *bida*, illegitimate innovation. In this spirit, the Ikhwan frowned on music and smoking; they shunned silk, gold, and jewellery; they even banned children's games.[7]

The Ikhwan were Ibn Saud's shock troops and the necessary instrument of his conquests. But their zeal and independent-mindedness

29

made them hard to handle, and the forceful imposition of their austere faith bred resentment among those they conquered. The Arabian peninsula was far from being uniformly Wahhabi; there were different forms of Sunni Islam, and sizeable Shi'a and Sufi minorities. For many Arabians, Wahhabism was both alien and threatening.

Such was the case in Hasa, the region on the east coast which Ibn Saud conquered in 1913. This brought under his control an area— known today as the Eastern Province—which was later found to contain Arabia's richest oilfields, and whose population was (and is) mainly Shi'a. In the eyes of the Ikhwan, the Shi'a were 'rejectionists': they denied the true faith and hence were little better than infidels. Wahhabi religious leaders told Ibn Saud he must either convert the Shi'a to Wahhabism or deport them. He was reluctant to take such drastic measures; but Wahhabi proselytisation nevertheless got under way in Hasa, and Ikhwan settlements were established there to dilute the Shi'a population.[8] The region's forcible incorporation into Ibn Saud's domains fostered a deep-rooted sense of grievance which persists to this day.

Arabia had hitherto been of little interest to outside powers. For centuries it had been nominally part of the Ottoman empire. As a Muslim power, the Ottoman Turks took an interest in Mecca and Medina, the holy cities of western Arabia which were the focus of the Hajj, the annual Muslim pilgrimage. But they cared little about the rest of the peninsula, which was largely left to fend for itself. When, however, the Turks entered the First World War on the side of Germany, Arabia ceased to be a backwater and the rivalries of its tribal leaders took on a new significance. The Rashids remained loyal to the Ottoman empire, while Ibn Saud allied himself with the British, who signed a treaty with him in 1915 and began supplying him with guns and £5,000 a month in gold. His first meetings with British officials, in 1915 and 1916, gave him a set of novel experiences: he took his first ride in a car and a train, had his first glimpse of a plane and his first encounter with a Western woman, the writer, traveller, and colonial official Gertrude Bell, whose shrill voice and imperious manner he found disconcerting.[9]

His relationship with the British was ambivalent. He needed their support and could not afford to antagonise the strongest power in the

Gulf; but he was conscious that they were infidels with imperial designs. The British, for their part, saw him as a potential ally but also a potential nuisance. For one thing, he was at odds with their main wartime ally in Arabia, the Sherif Hussein of Mecca, whose family, the Hashemites, was leading the war-time revolt against the Turks. For another, they had no desire to see him extend his domain into the sheikhdoms along the coast of the Gulf—Kuwait, Qatar, and the Trucial States (today, the United Arab Emirates)—with which they had signed treaties of protection. 'I have no doubt that Bin Saud could eat up Qatar in a week,' warned a British official after the conquest of Hasa in 1913, 'and I am rather afraid that he may do so.'[10]

The defeat of Germany in 1918 marked, as we have seen, the demise of the Ottoman empire. The Arabs of the Middle East believed they had received a British pledge to grant them independence in return for their role in defeating the Turks. Instead Britain and France divided the region between them. The Arabian peninsula was never formally colonised but was unmistakably part of Britain's sphere of influence. At a conference in Cairo in 1921, Britain's Colonial Secretary, Winston Churchill, put the finishing touches to his plans for the post-war Middle East. To Ibn Saud's consternation, he gave pride of place to the Hashemites, setting one of the Sherif's sons, Faisal, on the throne of Iraq and another, Abdullah, on that of Transjordan (the desert kingdom which became modern Jordan). 'They have surrounded me with enemies,' the Saudi prince remarked bitterly to his biographer, the Lebanese-American Amin Rihani.[11]

At home he turned his attention to his unfinished business with the Rashids. The long and bitter rivalry between the two dynasties came to a head in 1921, when Ibn Saud and his Ikhwan captured their stronghold of Hail—in the Jebel Shammar region of northern Arabia—and their leader Muhammad ibn Talal. In a show of magnanimity, he invited Ibn Talal to Riyadh as a guest in his palace. But once they arrived he was imprisoned for two years and, when released, put under house arrest with a fifty-man guard. His property in Hail was confiscated and he was deprived of income and left dependent on Ibn Saud for food and provisions. He remained politically marginalised until his death in 1952. Some of the Rashids made their peace with the house of Saud, but the fate of others was imprisonment, humiliation, or exile.[12]

By now, Ibn Saud had conquered much of the centre, the east, and the south of the peninsula. What remained was the important prize of the Hijaz, in the west.

The Hijazis, like the Shi'a of the east, were not Wahhabis. Their society, with its Red Sea port of Jeddah, was more open and cosmopolitan than the closed world of central Arabia. What's more, as the site of Islam's two holiest cities, Mecca and Medina, the Hijaz occupied a position of special importance in the Islamic world. Its ruler, the Sherif Hussein, was counting on the British to support him in his rivalry with Ibn Saud. But while they had valued his war-time role in fighting the Turks, they were alarmed by his growing obstinacy and megalomania. His autocratic behaviour and his ruthless fleecing of pilgrims had damaged his reputation both at home and abroad. The final straw was when he declared himself caliph of all Islam, which many Muslims saw as an unpardonable act of hubris. As to his military strength, British officials tended to believe that, if it came to a showdown, Ibn Saud would get the better of him.

The battle for the Hijaz began inauspiciously. When the Ikhwan captured the mountain resort of Taif in September 1924, they massacred some 300 of its inhabitants. Hijazis were filled with alarm. Seizing their chance to get rid of the hated Sherif, they persuaded him to abdicate. He did so the following month, departing by ship with £800,000 in gold, stored in kerosene cans.[13]

Ibn Saud knew he had to reassure the Hijazi merchants—and the rest of the Muslim world—that he was a fit custodian of the holy places. He gave strict orders that there should be no more massacres. Mecca fell without a fight. To show his peaceful intentions, the Saudi leader entered the city in the garb of a pilgrim. In a further gesture, he set up a *majlis al-shura*, or consultative council, made up of local leaders, to help him run the city.

But Jeddah's 20,000 inhabitants held out, enduring months of siege and privation. Many merchants, fearful of the Ikhwan, either fled or sent their families out of the city. Finally, a group of notables emerged to negotiate its surrender. Ibn Saud entered the city on 23 December 1924. His conquest of the Hijaz was complete. This boosted his prestige in Arabia and beyond, and brought him, in the era before oil, much-needed revenue from the pilgrimage. In 1926 he was proclaimed

King of Hijaz and Sultan of Nejd, and this enhanced status was acknowledged in a new treaty with Britain the following year.[14]

What was he like, this desert warrior? Every account, Arab and Western, concurs in depicting a man of stature and authority. He was a giant of six foot three, barely literate, bearing the scars of battle across his face and body, and blind in one eye as a result of an old infection. His features were volatile: he had considerable charm, aided by a winning smile, and was capable of great gentleness; but he also possessed an explosive temper. He was religious but not fanatical. When there were no Ikhwan present, he would tolerate singing and smoking. But on one occasion, when he felt the need to appease them, he publicly destroyed a gramophone he had brought with him from Kuwait. His experience of life outside Arabia was distinctly limited: on only two or three occasions did he leave the land of his birth, and then only to visit neighbouring countries. Yet he was shrewd enough to learn as he went along how to deal with an alien world for which his life had done nothing to prepare him.

Daniel van der Meulen arrived in Jeddah on a 'decrepit mail steamer' in February 1926. The son of a country schoolteacher, he had begun his diplomatic career in the Dutch East Indies (present-day Indonesia). Then, after studying Islam and Arabic for three years under the 'severe rule' of one of the foremost Dutch Orientalists, Snouck Hurgronje, he took up the post of Dutch consul in Jeddah, at the very moment when Ibn Saud was consolidating his control of the Hijaz. He found much of Jeddah in ruins:

> Bombardment had wrecked parts of the city. The inhabitants themselves, when fuel became scarce, had destroyed other sections. Famine and disease had killed thousands and everyone was desperately short of water. Thus the people were more relieved that their ordeal was over than concerned that the enemy had won.[15]

The people of Jeddah, wrote the consul, had no sympathy for Wahhabi puritanism. 'To them it seemed a most dangerous creed for a country whose sole source of income was the annual pilgrimage. What they wanted was a tolerant, liberal régime that would welcome pilgrims of every type who brought money into the country.'[16] Nevertheless the impact of Wahhabi doctrine soon began to be felt. When the *muezzin* called the faithful to prayer, 'the streets and shops emptied as if an air raid siren had sounded'. The Wahhabi religious police enforced a ban on smoking and music. They 'would commonly strike the cigarette from a smoker's lips without a word of warning'. Men were forbidden to shave their beards. (Wahhabis believed that, in this, they were emulating the Prophet.) Consuls were allowed to play their gramophones only if the sound did not carry into the streets. A devout Christian, van der Meulen developed a deep knowledge of Arabia, a considerable empathy for Islam, and an abiding antipathy to the Ikhwan.[17]

The consuls residing in Jeddah in the 1920s were a colourful and resilient bunch. In the age before air-conditioning, the intensely humid city offered few comforts. Water had to be brought on donkey-drawn carts, there was no electricity (other than from backyard generators), and no entertainment other than at the social gatherings organised by the consuls and their families (if any). Asked by officials in London what foreign institutions existed in the city, Reader Bullard replied that there were two—'a bank, which is closed, and a cemetery, which is open'. Bullard's letters to his family in Britain provide vivid glimpses of the sheltered world of the few Westerners living in early twentieth-century Arabia.[18]

Bullard was far from the conventional British diplomat. Born in 1885, the son of a London dockworker, he had mastered a string of languages in order to sit the exam for what was then called the Levant Consular Service. His first posting was to Istanbul, where he stayed for six years as a dragoman (literally, interpreter; the intermediary between a foreign consul and the Ottoman court) and witnessed the Young Turk revolution of 1908. After six years in Iraq, he was sent to Jeddah as consul in 1923. He had, as his vice-consul, a man of very different temperament, Laurence Grafftey-Smith, an *homme moyen et sensuel* who found Bullard's work ethic and ascetic tastes (he allowed seven minutes for lunch) a little hard to take. Grafftey-Smith's elegant, witty (and politically incorrect) memoir, *Bright Levant*, has become a classic of its kind.[19]

Then there was Philby, the *enfant terrible* of the Western community. Harry St John Philby, whose son Kim was to become a notorious spy for the Soviet Union, was a gifted but cantankerous writer and traveller who converted to Islam and was for thirty years a friend and adviser to Ibn Saud. Bullard and other British officials found him impossible, but he was a fixed and unpredictable feature of the Jeddah scene.[20]

Following the conquest of the Hijaz, Ibn Saud left in place the officials who had been running it under the Hashemites. As his domain expanded he needed men with experience of administration and of dealing with the outside world. Since Arabia lacked such people, he brought them in from other Arab countries. There was Hafiz Wahba, a former Egyptian school-teacher who joined the court in 1923, becoming the king's adviser on foreign affairs and later his ambassador in London. Yusuf Yassin, a Syrian from Latakia, became his director of publicity (and procurer of concu-bines). Fuad Hamza, a Lebanese who had trained as a lawyer, rose to become deputy foreign minister under Ibn Saud's son Faisal (who was to become king in the 1960s). These were the officials—together with the court's chief translator, Muhammad Almana—whom the foreign diplo-mats dealt with when they needed something done. The experience was often frustrating. A senior British diplomat, Sir Gilbert Clayton, accused Wahba and Yassin of 'low cunning' and 'consistent obstruction', and nick-named them 'the vultures'.[21]

One man, however, had a special importance for the king, and this was Abdullah Sulaiman, a Saudi from Nejd who was finance minister throughout his reign. He had received no formal education but as a young man had gone to Bombay (as Almana had done), where he learned about commerce from a leading Nejdi merchant. An uncle found him a job at Ibn Saud's court, and eventually he made himself indispensable to a king who was well known for his largesse, and as a result always short of money. Almana describes him as 'the ultimate éminence grise, always self-effacing and keeping himself in the wings'.[22] Unwilling or unable to delegate, he worked eighteen or nineteen hours a day. When the king needed cash, Sulaiman would somehow supply it, even if he had to milk the wealthy merchants, who accordingly did their best to avoid him. But he did much more than manage the king's money, and was his prime minister in all but name. Sulaiman had his faults. 'He was the only Finance Minister I ever met,' wrote Grafftey-Smith laconically, 'who drank methylated spirits.'[23] His heavy drinking and acerbic manner gave ammunition to his detractors. (He had many

Saudi critics, and both British and American officials tried at different times to get rid of him.) But the king always stood by the man he dubbed 'my support'.

Ibn Saud had conquered most of the Arabian peninsula. But he faced one more challenge that might yet deprive him of final victory. In 1927 the Ikhwan rose up in revolt against him. Fiercely proud, they resented the way in which, under British pressure, he had curbed their raiding expeditions into neighbouring Iraq and Transjordan, depriving them of conquest and booty. They believed he was not zealous enough in enforcing a strict interpretation of Wahhabi doctrine and in fighting the infidels (who included the Shi'a of southern Iraq, as well as the Christian imperialists). And, in Faisal al-Dawish, one of the most out-standing Ikhwan commanders, they had a leader who was to prove a stubborn thorn in Ibn Saud's side.

In November 1928, in an attempt to isolate the dissidents, the king summoned tribal and religious leaders to a large gathering in Riyadh. Then, in what Almana, who witnessed the event, calls 'a masterly piece of bluff', he offered to abdicate and be replaced by anyone the assembly cared to choose. This provoked, as he must have expected, loud uproar followed by strong affirmations of loyalty to his leadership. The dele-gates returned home—laden, Almana recalls, with 'generous gifts of swords, incense, money, [and] food'—and the king, now apparently secure, set off on his annual journey to perform the Hajj in Mecca.[24]

But the Ikhwan persisted in their defiance, until Ibn Saud felt he had no choice but to crush them. The two sides confronted one another in March 1929 at Sibillah, near Artawiya, where the first Ikhwan settle-ment had been established. Faisal al-Dawish believed the king had become old and soft; and it was true he had not fought a battle for over a decade. But Dawish's forces were heavily outnumbered, and the king's men had the added advantage of a dozen machine-guns. Their use, to devastating effect, took the Ikhwan rebels by surprise. After a battle that lasted only half an hour, they were in headlong flight.

Dawish escaped, seriously wounded, but eventually surrendered. Remarkably, Ibn Saud pardoned him and let him go. He may have thought the rebel leader was close to death. But Dawish recovered and returned to the fray. The rebellion was re-kindled with even greater ferocity. Only in January 1930, after further defeats, did Dawish finally surrender to the British authorities in Kuwait, who handed him over to Ibn Saud on condition that he should be spared. The Ikhwan rebellion was over. Their demise represented the victory of town-dwellers over bedouin, and of men with cars and machine-guns over fighters on camels.

In September 1932 the birth of the kingdom of Saudi Arabia was proclaimed, with the 56-year-old Ibn Saud as its king. It was the consummation of his thirty-year campaign of conquest and unification.

But if the life of the desert kingdom had undergone one extraordinary transformation, it was about to experience another. On 3 March 1938 a group of American oilmen—despondent after the failure of four years of back-breaking toil—struck oil in substantial quantities at Well No. 7 in Dammam, on the kingdom's east coast. The following year Ibn Saud arrived to watch the first tanker pick up the first cargo of Saudi oil. The king himself turned the valve through which the first thread of oil began to flow.

With the creation of the state, the king's long and difficult struggle to unify and pacify most of Arabia was over. But he was broke. When in 1933 a Californian oil company offered him £50,000 in gold for the right to prospect for oil—and a further £50,000 if oil was found in commercial quantities—he told Abdullah Sulaiman, 'Put your trust in God, and sign.'[25] The award of the concession marked the beginning of the kingdom's transition from poverty to wealth—and from dependence on Britain to dependence on the United States.

Why Britain, which had such close ties to Ibn Saud, lost out in the quest for oil remains something of a puzzle. One reason may have been that the king preferred the United States as it had no colonial baggage. Another was that British officials were far from convinced that significant oil deposits existed. They were also unaware that Philby, a staunch anti-imperialist, was working for the American company (Standard Oil of California) that won the concession. In any event, the king had received no better offer and jumped at the chance to get the money he so badly needed.

The first American oilmen arrived. Their first settlement, known as American Camp, was founded in Dammam in 1934. As the chronicler of US-Saudi relations, Thomas Lippman, records, their life in this wholly unfamiliar environment was arduous. Everything had to be imported, 'from drinking water to trucks to pre-fabricated dwellings'. They ate mostly tinned food and had to cope with sand, malaria, and boredom. Their comforts were few: the company had a special dispensation to bring in alcohol for its non-Muslim workers; and the first wives arrived in 1937. Most of the local Arabs had never seen a Western woman before.[26]

Reader Bullard returned to Jeddah in 1936, and stayed until 1939, observing how much had changed since his earlier stint as consul in the 1920s. There was now visibly greater law and order. But oil money was proving to be a mixed blessing. Bullard reported that on one occasion Ibn Saud made the journey from Mecca (near the coast) to Riyadh (in the interior) with a caravan 'of 558 motor vehicles'. 'To find a comparison,' he observed, 'one has to think of Louis XIV.'

Bullard was fifty-three; Ibn Saud, sixty. The British diplomat admired him—as most Western visitors did—but was conscious of his foibles. The king had difficulty with European names: Mussolini came out as 'Miss O'Looney'. Bullard also remarked on the king's pleasure in women. He was thought to have had over 200 marriages (though, as a pious Muslim, never more than four wives at a time). 'There is no doubt,' wrote Bullard, 'that failing sexual vigour is a cause of worry to the king.' He noted the extent of royal waste—this in the mid-1930s, when oil wealth was only a trickle compared with the flood that was to follow.[27]

Philby had converted to Islam in 1930. He did so less from conviction than from calculation: as a Muslim he could get closer to the king and the court, and so further his business interests. (He had set up a company to import Ford cars into the kingdom.) A delighted Ibn Saud gave him a Muslim name, Sheikh Abdullah. He could now accompany the king, and some 200,000 other pilgrims, on the Hajj. In a talk broadcast by the BBC, Philby recorded his impressions of 'the great pilgrimage which was instituted by the Prophet Muhammad over thirteen-hundred years ago'.

> It is the proud boast of His Majesty the King of Saudi Arabia, the Guardian of the Holy Places of Arabia, that the ceremonial of the pilgrimage is still carried out today in exactly the same way as it was in Muhammad's day ... It is difficult to imagine a more impressive ceremonial, especially on the

return journey after dark when the thousands of white figures, bobbing up and down to the gait of their camels, suggest a cavalcade of ghosts making its way along the valley winding among the Meccan mountains.[28]

The outbreak of the Second World War had a severe impact on the country. It delayed the exploitation of Saudi oil; cut the king's revenue by reducing the number of pilgrims performing the Hajj; and coincided with a severe drought which caused food shortages, even starvation, in parts of the kingdom. The war was also the turning-point in the transition from British to American influence, as Britain entered its long decline and the United States began to assert itself as a Middle East power.

The new and increasingly special relationship between the United States and Saudi Arabia was sealed at a war-time meeting, in February 1945, between Ibn Saud and the American president, Franklin D. Roosevelt. The man who worked tirelessly to set up the encounter, and who served as translator for the two leaders, was Colonel William Eddy. Bill Eddy did more than any other individual to lay the foundations of the new relationship—in oil, in defence, in diplomacy, in economic co-operation—between the two countries. He had been born in Lebanon in 1896, the son of American Protestant missionaries. After distinguished service as a marine in the First World War, he had joined the OSS (forerunner of the CIA), before being sent to Jeddah as head of the US diplomatic mission in 1944.[29]

Before the Second World War Saudi Arabia was of more interest to the oil companies, which had personnel in the kingdom, than the State Department, which did not. (Until 1942 Saudi affairs were handled from Cairo.) But in the 1940s several factors combined to arouse Roosevelt's interest in the kingdom. One was the prospect that, when the war was over, Saudi Arabia would become a major oil producer. The United States' need for oil was growing but its domestic production had peaked. Another factor was that American officials were looking for bases in the Gulf that would serve as transit points for the war in Asia—and that were not under British control. (The British were unwilling to share their base in Bahrain.)

Slowly, the relationship blossomed. The first US diplomatic mission was opened in Jeddah in April 1942, headed by the first chargé d'affaires, James Moose. The following year, conscious of the kingdom's economic difficulties, Roosevelt declared it eligible for aid under the Lend-Lease programme (a scheme to provide war-time assistance to allies). In 1944, because of the distance between the diplomats in Jeddah and the oilmen on the eastern coast—over 800 miles—an American consulate was opened in Dhahran. The king took some persuading that this expansion of the infidel presence was justified.

In the same year, after the Saudis complained that Moose lacked enthusiasm, he was recalled and replaced by Bill Eddy. Eddy's brief was to build up a personal rapport with Ibn Saud as the only effective means of nurturing relations between the two countries. This was not easy. Eddy, like all foreign diplomats, was in Jeddah, while the old king was over 500 miles away in Riyadh, which foreigners could enter only by royal invitation and wearing Arab dress. Communications were difficult. There were no roads, no airports (other than a few landing strips), and few telephone lines. But Eddy had two advantages—his fluent Arabic, and the fact that the king liked him. What's more, Ibn Saud was not averse to loosening his ties with the British, whom he had needed but (so he told the Americans) had never loved.

So, in the final months of the Second World War, Ibn Saud and Roosevelt met on a US naval destroyer in Great Bitter Lake, in the Suez Canal. For Eddy, setting up the meeting—in haste, in secrecy, and in war-time conditions—was a logistical nightmare. One US naval vessel, the *Murphy*, was to bring the old king from Jeddah to Egypt, while another, the *Quincy*, would bring the American president to meet him. The Saudis initially proposed a royal retinue of 200. Eddy whittled this down to twenty. But on the appointed day, forty-eight showed up— together with 100 sheep, to provide fresh lamb for the voyage. After tricky negotiations between Eddy, the Saudis, and the ship's commander, the latter reluctantly agreed to bring seven sheep on board.

Thomas Lippman has captured the extraordinary moment when the *Murphy* came into sight.

As the *Murphy* approached, everyone in President Roosevelt's party was mesmerised by the spectacle, at once majestic and bizarre. On a deck covered with colourful carpets and shaded by an enormous tent of brown canvas, a large black-bearded man in Arab robes, his head-dress bound with golden cords, was seated on a gilded throne. Around him stood an entourage of fierce-looking, dark-skinned barefoot men in similar attire, each with a sword or dagger bound to his waist by a gold-encrusted belt. On the *Murphy*'s fantail, sheep grazed in a makeshift corral.[30]

In the event, the two rulers hit it off. Both wanted the meeting to succeed; both used their personal charm to make sure it did. Roosevelt gave the Saudi ruler a DC-3 passenger aircraft, which was to become the nucleus of the kingdom's national fleet. The king gave the president a diamond-encrusted sword. On the vexed issue of Palestine, however, there was no meeting of minds. The king, like most Arabs, opposed large-scale Jewish immigration to a predominantly Arab land. When the president asked him to show sympathy for the Jews because of the Nazi holocaust, the king replied: 'Amends should be made by the criminal, not by the innocent bystander.'[31]

When the American president pledged to take no action hostile to the Arabs, and to consult with the Arabs on the future of Palestine, the king took this to be a cast-iron commitment by the United States. But within weeks Roosevelt was dead, and the Saudi king regarded the pro-Zionist policies of his successor, Harry Truman, as a personal betrayal.

Churchill was furious about the meeting in Egypt and insisted on seeing Ibn Saud himself shortly afterwards. But the king did not warm to a British leader who drank alcohol in his presence and puffed cigar smoke in his face. Tensions over Saudi Arabia were a constant feature of Anglo-American relations in the post-war years.

British fears grew when Bill Eddy pulled off one of his biggest coups: an agreement to build an American air base at Dhahran. Sensitive to opposition from religious conservatives and to anything that might seem to diminish Saudi sovereignty, the king and his principal negotiator, Yusuf Yassin, drove a hard bargain. Ibn Saud was aware that the British strenuously opposed the plan, seeing it as an encroachment on their traditional preserve, and he was reluctant to take so significant a step without their acquiescence. British officials were particularly shocked to discover that, after the war, a US commercial airline, TWA, would have exclusive landing and transit rights at the base. Dispatches from Jeddah to London became incendiary, one official accusing the Americans of 'diplomatic gangsterism in the service of an unscrupulous economic imperialism'.[32]

The negotiations were tough. The Saudis insisted that their flag be flown around the perimeter of the base (which would be referred to by the less sensitive term 'airfield'). They wanted assurances that the Americans stationed there would behave themselves. (They were quietly assured that no prostitutes would be allowed onto the site.) They secured agreement that TWA would train Saudi pilots and help the kingdom build up a national airline of its own. For his part, Eddy insisted that American government employees at the base should not be subject to Saudi law—a modern form of the much-hated Capitulations dating from Ottoman times. In the end Eddy got most of what he wanted, and the British bowed to the inevitable and reluctantly allowed the deal to go ahead. It was signed in August 1945.[33]

The aftermath of the war witnessed a surge in the growth of the oil company, now renamed Aramco (the Arabian American Oil Company, a consortium of Standard Oil, Texaco, Exxon, and Mobil). It opened the first oil refinery, at Ras Tanura, and began work on a giant pipeline linking Dhahran to the Mediterranean, thus bypassing the Suez Canal. (Both these big projects were carried out by the American construction giant Bechtel.) At Saudi insistence, the company also began a programme of building roads, schools, and hospitals in the Eastern Province.

Aramco was becoming a state within a state. Even in the 1930s it had been, in Lippman's words, 'the *de facto* government of Saudi Arabia's Eastern Province'.[34] Now its tentacles were spreading ever wider. The company had a bigger workforce and a much bigger area of operations. Its network of contractors and sub-contractors was mushrooming. Apart from technical specialists, it had its own body of experts on Arab affairs, who often thought they knew better than the diplomats. It had its own departments involved in politics, public relations, and intelligence-gathering. It lent the king money, dug wells for him, and helped him build a railway from Riyadh to Dhahran. It worked to enhance the kingdom's image (not least in a sceptical American Congress), wrote its own history of the opening-up of modern Arabia, and compiled and updated lists of government officials.

The State Department began to fret that the company was a law unto itself, and looked for ways to rein it in. One of their concerns was the company's treatment of its Arab workforce—made up mostly of

Saudis, together with Egyptians, Palestinians, and others—which in the post-war years grew to some 14,000. It was undeniable that many of the Arabs who worked for Aramco received a unique apprenticeship in a host of new skills. A few went on to become successful businessmen or high-ranking government officials. But the majority suffered from the racist behaviour of some of their American colleagues and from the company's blatant discrimination in jobs and housing. While American workers and their families lived in segregated compounds, with swimming pools and a cinema and excellent food and medical facilities, Arab workers lived in poor housing, ate inferior food, and received a much lower standard of healthcare.

In 1945 these grievances found expression in a series of strikes, the first in the company's history. In June, there were riots by Arab workers at the Ras Tanura refinery over their food rations and their treatment by company guards. In July, Arab drillers in Dhahran (part of the skilled workforce) went on strike over their pay and conditions. Hundreds of other workers joined them. At the orders of the local emir, a demonstration on 16 July was broken up and several workers were beaten. The strike grew, and was soon backed by 2,000 workers. The situation briefly calmed down when the emir urged the company to take the workers' demands seriously. But the strike resumed in August, this time involving all 9,000 Arab workers at Dhahran and Ras Tanura. On 9 August, the king told Eddy, in unusually blunt language, that the company had let him down. A negotiating committee was set up to investigate the workers' grievances.

Aramco's initial response had been to put the blame for the strikes on nationalist or communist agitators. But gradually the company was forced to abandon what many regarded as the 'caste system' in the camps and to spend more on the health and education of its Arab workers. [35]

The strike, and others that followed in the 1950s, were among the birth pangs of the modern Saudi state. With oil came the ideas as well as the machines of the twentieth century. Arab nationalism was slow to arrive in Saudi Arabia, but the country was not immune to the political turbulence that swept through the region. Workers from Egypt, Palestine, and elsewhere brought nationalist and anti-imperialist ideas into the kingdom. Political change could be resisted, but not indefinitely.

Untold oil wealth was also accompanied by corruption and excess on a far bigger scale than that witnessed by Bullard in the 1930s. In his old age, Ibn Saud, sick, blind, and crippled by arthritis, grew despondent about the floodgates of change his actions had unwittingly opened. Rivalries were emerging among his sons. He repeatedly urged the eldest of them, Saud and Faisal, to work together for the good of the family and the state (which were, after all, one and the same). Ibn Saud's nation-building project had been remarkable, but he understood better than anyone the constraints and vulnerabilities of the house he had built, and was apprehensive that divisions within the family could bring the whole edifice crumbling to the ground.

The old king, exhausted in body and spirit, died at the age of seventy-seven on 9 November 1953.

3

THE STRUGGLE FOR THE LEVANT

On 1 June 1945 the Syrian president, Shukri al-Quwatli, made an impassioned plea to Winston Churchill:

> Every part of Syria is being destroyed. French bombs pitilessly pour on to peaceful defenceless towns. Homs, Hama, and Aleppo are subjected to unprecedented bombardment. For three days Damascus ... has undergone savage bombardment by aircraft, artillery, and tanks. Fires resulting from the bombardments are breaking out everywhere. Whole streets and districts [have been] ravaged by fire bombs and destruction ... All this slaughter is only justified by our having refused to grant France special privileges incompatible with our sovereignty and independence.[1]

The bombing of Damascus, an act of defiance by a dying colonial power, marked the brutal climax of a quarter of a century of French rule in Syria and Lebanon.

Syria was the birthplace of Arab nationalism. In nationalist eyes, *bilad al-sham*—the land of Syria—stretched from the Sinai desert to the Taurus mountains, embracing Syria, Lebanon, Palestine, Transjordan, and part of southern Turkey. For nationalists, the great crime of Britain and France in the aftermath of the First World War was to dismember this Greater Syria, limb from limb.

What were the origins of Arab nationalism in Greater Syria? For four centuries, from 1516 until 1918, Syria and Lebanon had been under the rule of the Ottoman Turks. But outside the main towns the Ottoman writ had not run far, and feudal landowners exercised a good deal of local autonomy. A process of modernisation got under way in the 1830s, with the beginnings of centralised government and the establishment of both local and foreign schools. As the empire began to decline, European powers increasingly interfered in its affairs. France in particular felt it had a special responsibility to protect Lebanon's Christians, dominant among whom were the Maronite Catholics. In the 1840s tensions built up between the Maronites and the Druze (a heterodox Muslim sect) which in 1860 exploded into violence. Following the massacre of some 10,000 Christians, France sent in troops, and the European powers forced the Turks to create an autonomous province of Lebanon, with a Christian majority and a Christian governor.

In the decades leading up to the First World War, as the Ottoman empire crumbled, Arabs increasingly began to see themselves as Arabs rather than as Ottoman subjects. Many resented the autocratic rule of Sultan Abdul-Hamid, and initially welcomed the Young Turk revolution of 1908. But they soon discovered that the Young Turks were no more sympathetic to their aspirations than the sultan had been. Arab secret societies sprang up which at first favoured Arab autonomy under Turkish rule, but soon began to champion Arab independence.

One of the factories of nationalist awakening was Beirut, which became a vibrant centre of Arab culture and commerce:

> Ships from all over the world dropped anchor in its harbour ... The population soared from 19,000 in 1846 to 115,000 in 1893 ... By 1859, Beirut was linked by telegraph to the rest of the world ... The first bank in the Arab world opened its doors in Beirut, and the first newspaper was published there in 1858.[2]

With its schools, printing presses, and rich intellectual life, the city's influence spread throughout the region. In 1866 American missionaries established the Syrian Protestant College (which in 1920 became the American University of Beirut, one of the most prestigious universities in the Arab world). French Jesuits followed suit, establishing the college of Saint-Joseph in 1875. Among the graduates of these colleges were some of the pioneers (both Christian and Muslim) of the nationalist movement.

It was into this late-Ottoman world that Wadad Makdisi was born in 1909. She grew up in Beirut with a love of the sea. Her childhood memories were of the sights and sounds of the cobblers, potters, and braziers who sang to advertise their wares as they walked down her street. Her father, a Christian Arab, was a professor of Arabic at the Syrian Protestant College. She lived with her parents, three brothers, and two sisters in a beautiful old house in the Ras Beirut area of the city.

The idyll of her childhood was shattered by the First World War, which the Turks entered on the side of Germany. 'Half-naked people, hopeless and hungry, walked the streets of Beirut begging for scraps of bread, searching through garbage. Babies cried incessantly. The Turks and Germans needed every provision for their armies, so there was little left for the people.' Even when Wadad was in bed, she was kept awake by 'the sound of wailing that came to us at night'.[3]

As many as 300,000 people may have died of starvation or malnutrition in war-time Syria and Lebanon.[4] The Turks press-ganged tens of thousands of Arabs to join the Ottoman army, many of whom later deserted. They also resorted to fierce repression in a desperate bid to hold on to the Arab provinces of the empire. In 1915 and 1916, on the orders of the ruthless Jemal—the Ottoman governor of Syria (and member of the Young Turk triumvirate) who earned the nickname Al-Saffah (the Butcher)—dozens of Arab nationalists were hanged in the public squares of Beirut and Damascus. Others were imprisoned or deported to remote corners of the empire.

The Makdisi family left Beirut in July 1917 for the safety of the mountains above the city. They returned in the autumn of 1918, in time to see Germans and Turks 'streaming out of the city as the British army marched in from the Sidon road'.[5] For the Makdisis and many other families, the war generated a prolonged and intense debate about the Arabs' future. Struggling to respond to the new order taking shape around them, they began to acquire a new political consciousness which drew on their common history, culture, and language. But it was as yet an embryonic nationalism, capable of developing in markedly different ways. Should the Arabs seek autonomy under Turkish rule or try to shake off the Turkish yoke altogether? Should their loyalty be local, focused on a single country, or pan-Arab, founded on the belief in a single nation stretching across all the Arabic-speaking lands? Should

Arab nationalism be secular or Islamic? And, crucially, should they co-operate with the European powers in the hope of securing independence once the war was over?

During the war, the British made no less than four sets of promises concerning the future of the Middle East. In the McMahon-Hussein letters of October–November 1915, they promised the Sherif Hussein of Mecca, of the Hashemite family of Arabia, that if he joined the war and helped defeat the Turks, he would become the leader of an independent Arab state. In the secret Sykes-Picot agreement of May 1916, Britain and France agreed to divide up the Middle East between them. In the Balfour Declaration of November 1917, Britain promised the infant Zionist movement a Jewish 'national home' in Palestine. Finally, in November 1918, Britain and France issued a declaration promising 'the complete and final liberation of those peoples who have been for so long oppressed by the Turks'.

How, if at all, could these contradictory and ill-defined promises be honoured? The Sherif and his son Faisal launched the Arab Revolt against the Turks in 1916. After two years of hard fighting, the Arabs expected their reward. Things began promisingly when, following the defeat of the Turks in 1918, Faisal entered Damascus amid scenes of jubilation. But as the Paris peace talks dragged on and the fate of the Middle East remained undecided, Arab nationalists grew impatient. Overruling the cautious Faisal, a nationalist congress in Damascus proclaimed him king of Syria (including Lebanon and Palestine). This infuriated the French, who saw the emergence of the new state as an Anglo-Arab conspiracy to destroy their influence in the Middle East. In fact, the British regarded the congress's action as reckless, and withdrew their support from Faisal. The new kingdom lasted only twenty-two months. At the battle of Maysaloun, in July 1920, the French crushed a small, badly-equipped Arab army, ejected Faisal, and assumed control of Syria and Lebanon.[6]

The French believed they had a historic mission to rule the Levant and protect its Christians. When the victorious French general, Henri Gouraud, a bearded giant who had lost an arm at Gallipoli, reached Damascus, he went straight to the tomb of Saladin—the renowned warrior who had led the Muslims during the Crusades—and declared, 'Saladin, we're back.'

In the post-war settlement, the British received mandates from the League of Nations to govern Iraq, Palestine, and Transjordan, and the French a mandate for Syria and Lebanon. The mandatory power was supposed to groom the people it ruled for eventual independence. But nationalists saw the mandates as a cover for colonial rule, and felt betrayed. 'The ghost of the Peace Settlement,' wrote the historian Albert Hourani, 'has haunted Arab politics ever since.'[7]

Syria and Lebanon presented a complex tapestry of ethnic and religious groups, but there were important differences between the two. Syria had a large Sunni Arab majority, with Christian, Druze, and Alawi minorities. (The Druze and the Alawis are offshoots of Shi'a Islam.) In contrast, Lebanon had a slender Christian majority. Politically dominant were the Maronites (in alliance with France and in communion with Rome), who coexisted, not always easily, with a bewildering variety of other Christian and Muslim sects.

The French divided and ruled. One of their first acts, in 1920, was to carve out a separate Lebanese state, or Greater Lebanon, doubling the size of the autonomous province the Turks had established, by adding the coastal towns of Beirut, Sidon, and Tripoli, and, in the east, the fertile Beqaa valley. Their aim was to create a predominantly Christian state under French protection. But the effect was to fuel a sense of abiding grievance among Lebanese Muslims, who resented the way the French had redrawn the borders to suit their Christian protégés, and who regarded Lebanon as an integral part of Greater Syria.

Employing the same logic, the French divided Syria into mini-states: the two 'states' of Damascus and Aleppo (the country's main cities, together with their hinterland), a Druze state in the south, and an Alawite state in the west. The object was to cut off communities from one another and forestall any effort to unite them under the banner of a common nationalism.

A High Commissioner was appointed to govern the two countries from his headquarters, the Serail, in Beirut. The first two High Commissioners, Henri Gouraud and Maxime Weygand, were military men and devout Catholics. Throughout the mandate, lobbies representing business and clerical interests in France exerted powerful pressure on policy-making in the Levant. High Commissioners who toyed with making political concessions to the nationalists were invariably slapped down by these lobbies in France and by the military chiefs in the Levant.

Syria had a mostly rural population of about one and a half million, only a third of which lived in the four main cities—Damascus in the south, Homs and Hama in the centre, and Aleppo in the north. These towns became the main centres of nationalist opposition to colonial rule. In the early years of the mandate there were revolts in several parts of the country. But, to the great surprise of the French, the first significant challenge came from the Jebel Druze, a mountainous region of black rock some seventy-five miles south of Damascus. From there it spread to the rest of the country. Lasting from 1925 to 1927, the rebellion became known as the Great Syrian Revolt.

The Jebel was home to a Druze population of 50,000, many of whom had migrated to the area from Lebanon following the massacres of 1860. They had also settled in the neighbouring Hauran, a fertile plain where much of Syria's wheat was grown. The French had always found the Druze troublesome and regarded them, with justice, as allies of the British—but were nevertheless caught unawares when the revolt flared up in July 1925. Its leader was Sultan al-Atrash, an eagle-nosed, hawk-eyed warrior with a huge moustache, piercing blue eyes, and a fierce pride in his Druze heritage. In 1910 he had been conscripted into the Ottoman army and served in the Balkans, where he learned to read and write. But after the Turks hanged his father for leading an earlier revolt, he became bitterly anti-Ottoman and aligned himself with the British and their Hashemite allies. Sultan al-Atrash was a Druze patriot and an Arab nationalist. While the revolt had local origins, its avowed goal was the liberation of the whole of Greater Syria.

The Druze deeply resented French rule, and in particular the arrogant governor who had been imposed on them, General Gabriel Carbillet. Believing he had a mission to transform the backward society of the Jebel, Carbillet introduced a programme of public works using the much-resented *corvée* (forced labour).[8] Druze leaders lobbied without success to have him removed. Despite warnings from some of his colleagues that trouble was brewing, the French High Commissioner, General Maurice Sarrail, badly misread the situation. The early military successes of Sultan al-Atrash brought thousands more Druze to join his army, which soon numbered over 8,000 men. In July, his forces entered the provincial capital, Suwaida, and besieged its French defenders in the citadel. For Sarrail, worse was to come. At the end of July, a force of some 3,500 men under General Roger Michaud set out to restore order in the south, only to be routed by Sultan al-Atrash and his men and forced into humiliating flight.

By the time the young Bennett Doty arrived in the Jebel that sweltering summer, the region was aflame. The memoirs of this young American recruit to the French Foreign Legion provide a vivid account of the brutality of the fighting and the tough, rumbustious life of a legionnaire. His first encounter with the conflict came on the journey south from Damascus in an armoured train.

> The tracks were now closely guarded ... Now and then we stopped at some post to revictual it. They were virtually in a state of siege, surrounded with barbed wire and trenches, all the walls loopholed. On the flat roof above always a sentinel stood, anxiously scanning with his binoculars the hills from which the Druses descended. Their razzias [raids] of late had been frequent, several posts had been surprised at night and annihilated.[9]

Doty was a southerner, born in Alabama in 1900. Lying about his age (he was only sixteen), he'd enlisted to fight in the First World War and had seen action in France. After returning home at the end of the war, he enrolled as a university student, then dropped out and went to sea. In June 1925, on an impulse, he travelled to France to join the Foreign Legion, using the name 'Gilbert Clare'. Twenty-four years old, speaking little French, he was sent for training to Algeria where he discovered the Legion's stern discipline, its camaraderie, and its legendary addiction to alcohol. He joined a company of 120 men—'a remarkable assortment of villainous gentlemen'—who included French, Germans, Russians, Poles, Italians, Arabs, and Spaniards. After four days at sea, they arrived in Beirut and from there were sent into Syria.[10]

Stung by the defeat of General Michaud's force, the French tried desperately to regain the initiative. The disgraced Michaud was replaced by General Maurice Gamelin. As Gamelin prepared a large force to recapture Suwaida, an advance group of infantrymen and legionnaires reached the nearby village of Musaifra. The French classified villages as *soumis* (submissive) or *insoumis* (in revolt). Musaifra had been *soumis* but had been found to harbour rebels; it had to be taught a lesson. The advance group, under Colonel Charles Andréa, occupied the village, but soon found itself under fierce attack from the Druze.

It was Doty's first big battle as a legionnaire. In the early dawn he watched the extraordinary spectacle of a large force of Druze, on horseback and on foot, 'pouring down upon us as if it were the very earth itself moving in landslide'.[11] After hours of tough fighting, seven or eight French aircraft arrived to bomb the rebels. Then, with the legionnaires' ammunition running dangerously low, there came from a distance the 'tiny brassy sound' of bugles, marking the arrival of a relief column. The Druze were forced to flee, leaving their dead behind them.

The battle took a heavy toll. 'We looked like scarecrows,' wrote Doty. 'Our eyes were bloodshot and half shut; we were caked with dirt and blood, our uniforms were in rags.' Colonel Andréa ordered that the corpses of the Druze fighters should be laid out in a line, as an example to the villagers—and that prisoners should be executed by firing squad. Some of Doty's comrades grew rich from looting.[12]

On 23 August 1925 a leaflet circulated in Damascus, signed by 'Sultan al-Atrash, Commander of the Syrian Revolutionary Armies'. It was a call to arms.

> At last the day has come when we can reap the harvest of our struggle for liberty and independence …
>
> The imperialists have stolen what is yours … They have divided your indivisible homeland. They have separated the nation into religious sects and states. They have strangled freedom of religion, thought, conscience, speech, and action…
>
> To arms, sons of the nation! …
>
> Let us free our country from bondage.[13]

It was an appeal, first and foremost, to the people of Damascus. But the city's leading families were ambivalent. They had much to lose if they took an active part in the revolt; yet to stand aloof would damage their nationalist credentials. Foremost among the nationalist figures who pledged their support for the uprising was Abdul-Rahman al-Shahbandar, leader of the newly-created People's Party. Shahbandar, a popular orator, had been born in Damascus in 1880, the son of a merchant, and had studied medicine at the Syrian Protestant College in Beirut, where he became a student activist. He had supported the Arab Revolt of 1916 and afterwards took part in Faisal's short-lived government in Damascus, serving briefly as his foreign minister. As leader of the People's Party, he advocated a secular, left-wing nationalism, and drew support mainly from the educated urban élite.[14]

Shahbandar urged Atrash to bring the fight to Damascus. An initial attempt to do so failed, when French forces pushed back the rebels only a few miles from the capital. The French authorities proceeded to crush the infant People's Party, arresting and jailing many of its supporters. But Shahbandar managed to escape to the safety of the Jebel, where he and Atrash proclaimed the establishment of a nationalist government.

The revolt soon spread. In early October, in the city of Hama—famous, then as now, for its Islamic conservatism—a cavalry commander in a French-backed force, the Syrian Legion, mutinied with his men and took possession of the city. The commander was a Lebanese soldier of fortune, Fawzi al-Qawuqji, who after fighting the French in Syria would go on to fight the British in Palestine and Iraq. The French had been caught napping, but the following morning they responded with aerial bombardment which destroyed much of the city and killed more than a hundred people, mostly civilians. In panic, a group of notables persuaded Qawuqji and his men to leave, which they did the following day.[15]

Unrest in the Ghuta, the extensive orchards around Damascus, was met with equal brutality. After a number of rebel attacks, French troops entered a village near the capital and executed scores of villagers. They brought back the mutilated bodies of sixteen of them and displayed them in the city's main square. The scene was witnessed by a French woman, the writer and painter Alice Poulleau.

> All around the square were soldiers, guns in hand. In the middle were gendarmes, their hands in their pockets, the chief of police in his cravat, and civilian and military officials. On the ground were long trails of blood. It was a Dantesque horror: the corpses' shoes were scattered all about; they had tragic faces, their arms outstretched. One, so very young, still had his mouth open, as if he were crying something out. Bloody brains, guts spilling from opened stomachs—it was a scene of human carnage.[16]

The spread of the rebellion to Damascus meant its significance could no longer be hidden or denied. On 18 October a group of rebels entered the city in an attempt to capture the High Commissioner, General Sarrail. He wasn't there; but the rebels nevertheless took over large parts of the city, and the French were made to look impotent. They responded by bombing every quarter where an insurgent presence had been reported. The two-day bombardment destroyed whole quarters and left 1,400 people dead, provoking an international outcry.

Sarrail was recalled to Paris in disgrace, and died not long afterwards. His replacement, Henry de Jouvenel, the first civilian High Commissioner, arrived in December 1925. A liberal and a former journalist, he offered the nationalists peace talks, proposed an amnesty, and set up a new government. But the military chiefs, and their hardline allies in Paris, believed the rebellion had to be crushed by force, not through concessions.

In the event, it took a full year to end the revolt. In early 1926 Colonel Andréa surrounded the Old City of Damascus with a security cordon to prevent the rebels penetrating it. In May General Gamelin used aerial bombardment to break the resistance of the Maydan, the Damascus quarter that had become a rebel stronghold and refuge, turning a district of 30,000 people into 'a virtually deserted ruin'.[17] With equal ferocity, the orchards of the Ghuta were cleared; and finally the Jebel Druze itself was subdued. By the middle of 1927 it was all over.

The French sentenced Sultan al-Atrash to death, but he escaped with other rebels into neighbouring Transjordan. He spent a decade in exile, but was eventually pardoned and returned to Syria in 1937. He lived to a ripe old age, a revered warrior and nationalist, dying of a heart attack in 1982.

The revolt's signal achievement was to have shown the French, and the world, the breadth and depth of Syrian opposition to colonial rule. It proved, contrary to French claims, that there was an authentic— albeit embryonic—nationalism in Syria which united a large part of the society in a common hostility towards the mandate. French efforts to divide and rule had largely failed. It was true that certain communities (notably the Alawis and the Christians) had played little part in the revolt; but it had nevertheless brought together urban and rural, young and old, rich and poor, in an entirely new way. For the rebels, the price had been high: 6,000 Syrian dead and over 100,000 made homeless. On the French side, 2,000 soldiers were reported killed or missing.[18]

Bennett Doty had meanwhile deserted from the Foreign Legion, along with a Welshman and two Germans. He had relished the fighting and been awarded the Croix de Guerre for bravery; but he hated the intervals in between, when he and his comrades were made to shift heavy stones and build walls in broiling heat. The four men's attempt to escape by night to British-controlled Transjordan turned into a comedy of errors. They got lost, were captured, and Doty was sentenced to eight years in prison—first in Damascus and then in France. But thanks to the efforts of his father in Mississippi and the American consul in Paris, he served only eight months and eventually returned home. Mystery surrounds the remainder of his unusual life.[19]

The Damascus notables were glad to see the end of the revolt, not just because it had damaged their livelihoods but because they were now able to resume control of the nationalist movement. The vehicle through which they did so was the National Bloc, a loose alliance of landowners, merchants, and middle-class professionals, most of them Sunni Muslims with a sprinkling of Christians. These men were nationalists, but they believed that after the crushing of the Great Revolt it was necessary to reach some kind of compromise with the colonial power. The attempt to secure such a compromise lasted for the remainder of the mandate.[20]

In the latter stages of the revolt, his efforts to negotiate with the nationalists having failed, Jouvenel had resigned after only eight months as High Commissioner. His successor, Henri Ponsot, allowed some of the prominent nationalists to return from exile, in the hope of finding Syrians and Lebanese with whom he could reach an accommodation.[21]

In October 1927 the first congress of the National Bloc was held in Beirut, attended by Syrian and Lebanese nationalists. While affirming the demand for independence, the congress gave its backing to the idea of 'honourable co-operation' with the French. Among the Bloc's supporters was the young Riad al-Solh, the rising star among Lebanon's Arab nationalists. Solh had been born in the port city of Sidon in 1894. His father and grandfather had been loyal servants of the Ottoman empire: breaking with the Turks had been no easy decision. But once they had done so, Solh and his father had worked with Faisal's short-lived Arab kingdom, and following its demise had, like many other nationalists, gone into exile. Solh's growing renown alarmed the French and their Christian protégés, who had long sought to exclude

Arab nationalists from the political arena. He now divided his time between Beirut and European capitals, where he lobbied for support for the nationalist cause.[22]

The Bloc soon came to command the loyalty of a large part of the Syrian population. But there were rifts and rivalries among its leaders. No love was lost between the popular nationalist Jamil Mardam (an ally of the Hashemites) and his younger rival Shukri al-Quwatli (an ally of Ibn Saud, who was hostile to the Hashemites). More radical than either was Shahbandar, leader of the People's Party, who became the Bloc's most powerful critic. The nationalists of Aleppo, Syria's commercial capital, resented the dominance of the Damascenes. The French were not slow to exploit these divisions whenever the opportunity arose.

The canniest of the nationalist leaders proved to be Quwatli, who used the wealth from his family's orchards in the Ghuta—he was known as 'the apricot king'—to build up an impressive network of support in the quarters of Damascus's Old City. This was to pay dividends in the crucial years leading up to independence.[23]

Education became an important battleground in the nationalist struggle. In 1927 Wadad Makdisi entered the American University of Beirut, where her father had taught, one of only a dozen women to do so. The AUB president was an enlightened American, Bayard Dodge, who was a scholar of Arabic and sympathetic to Arab aspirations. The United States, lacking colonial baggage, was seen as a counterweight to the French and a potential ally in the struggle for independence. 'We never felt we were in an American institution,' recalled Wadad, 'but rather a great centre of liberal ideas.'[24]

After graduating from AUB and a spell of teaching in British-ruled Iraq, in 1935 Wadad became the principal of her alma mater in Beirut, the Ahliah National School for Girls, a post she held for the rest of her professional life. She was only twenty-six. Her students were Lebanese, Syrian, and Palestinian. The French disliked the school because of its pronounced Arab ethos, and at one point tried to close it down. They imposed a curriculum which gave pride of place to French language and literature. Students were punished if they spoke Arabic on the school grounds. 'I could see,' Wadad wrote later, 'that bit by bit Lebanon was being detached from its Arab roots.'[25]

Students were caught up in the nationalist struggle, and played a leading role in the strikes and demonstrations that occurred throughout the 1930s. The leaders of the National Bloc welcomed their zeal, but often found them hard to control.[26]

These were years of political radicalisation and economic hardship. Under the impact of the world recession, shops and businesses lost money and were forced to close down. There was large-scale unemployment. The value of Syria's main exports (wool, raw silk, and textiles) fell sharply. The National Bloc decided to target French economic interests—the much-resented *Interêts Communs*. In 1935 they launched a boycott of the Damascus Tramway and Electricity Company. Shopkeepers in Damascus, Aleppo, and Beirut refused to use electricity and instead used oil lamps. Young demonstrators overturned trams, sometimes setting them alight, and tore down electricity cables.[27]

In January 1936 the French struck back. They shut down the National Bloc's headquarters in Damascus, provoking demonstrations and clashes with the police. There were violent protests in Aleppo in which French property was destroyed and two Syrians were killed. Twenty thousand people attended their funerals the following day. On 27 January the Bloc called for a general strike. In response the French declared martial law, outlawed public gatherings, shut down schools and newspapers, and imposed an 8pm curfew. The protests spread to the Lebanese cities of Beirut, Sidon, and Tripoli.[28]

The scale of the unrest created a political opening for the nationalists. Comte Henri de Martel, who had succeeded Ponsot as High Commissioner, entered talks with them, and in March an agreement was reached in which the French for the first time recognised the National Bloc leaders as the legitimate representatives of the Syrian people.[29] The strike was called off after thirty-six days, and a National Bloc delegation set off for Paris to negotiate a treaty which they hoped would pave the way to independence. The advent to power of a Popular Front government in France, under Léon Blum, gave the Syrian nationalists encouragement, since the French socialists were regarded as sympathetic to their aims.

Almost six months later, on 9 September 1936, a Franco-Syrian treaty was signed stipulating that at the end of the mandate Syria would become a sovereign and independent state. Although conditions were attached—French interests would be protected, including the use of two air bases, and the Alawis and the Druze would retain a degree of autonomy—the treaty was nevertheless an unprecedented achievement. The delegation received a heroes' welcome on its return to Damascus. In November the National Bloc won a big majority in elections. Jamil Mardam became prime minister, with Shukri al-Quwatli as minister of finance and defence. The following month the Syrian parliament approved the treaty.

Meanwhile the French secured a Lebanese treaty with far less difficulty, after negotiations in which not a single Arab nationalist took part. The Lebanese Christians were delighted; the Muslims launched protests that turned violent.[30] But the Syrian treaty had not yet been ratified in Paris—and the colonial and clerical lobbies worked hard to ensure it would not be. Despite repeated efforts by Mardam to rescue the treaty—he returned to Paris in 1937 and again in 1938 and was repeatedly forced to make concessions—the collapse of the Popular Front government effectively killed it off. This was a huge blow to the credibility of the National Bloc.

The French provoked further nationalist anger in July 1938 when they ceded part of northern Syria—the *sanjaq*, or district, of Alexandretta—to Turkey. Mardam resigned, and the High Commissioner, Gabriel Puaux, dissolved parliament and ruled by decree. 'The clock,' writes the historian of Syria, Patrick Seale, 'had been turned back to 1920.'[31]

The Second World War marked the turning-point in the struggle of Syria and Lebanon for independence. With the fall of France in 1940 and the entry of Mussolini's Italy into the war, the Mediterranean became an important theatre of conflict. Protecting Egypt and the Suez Canal was of vital importance to Britain, and this required pushing back the Germans and the Italians and countering their efforts to woo the Arabs.

The French were now divided, with the Vichy régime loyal to Germany, and the Free French, under General Charles de Gaulle, allying themselves with Britain. Syria and Lebanon fell under Vichy control. At first, to de Gaulle's intense frustration, the British, with their hands full elsewhere, preferred to placate the Vichy forces in the Levant rather than supplant them. They blockaded French-held territory, by land and sea, with the result that prices in Beirut and Damascus soared and food and fuel became scarce. But British generals argued that they had no troops to spare for an invasion of Syria and Lebanon.

German successes forced them to change their minds; and when in April 1941 a pro-German coup took place in Iraq (described more fully in Chapter 8), the British were forced to respond. They sent in troops to crush the coup, but were alarmed to discover that German aircraft were using Syrian airfields to refuel on their way to Iraq. The fear was that if the Germans, with Vichy connivance, turned Syria and Lebanon into a base, this would threaten Britain's position in the Middle East. An invasion plan—codenamed Operation Exporter—was put together in great haste, with the aim of expelling the Vichy from the Levant. In June 1941 an Allied force—comprising British, Indian, Australian, and Free French forces—invaded Lebanon and Syria. At the same time General Georges Catroux, de Gaulle's representative in the Middle East, issued a proclamation declaring the end of the mandate and promising independence to the Syrians and the Lebanese. This pledge was supported with a British guarantee.

One of the British soldiers who took part in the operation was the future travel writer Wilfred Thesiger, who crossed from Transjordan into Syria with a group of Druze horsemen. 'As we rode across the lava fields [of the Jebel Druze] towards the distant mountain, my men roared out the songs their fathers had sung twenty years earlier as they rallied to Sultan Pasha al-Atrash, when the war-fires blazed on the village roofs, summoning the Druzes to war …'[32]

The British had been careful to forewarn the Druze and secure their co-operation. The messenger chosen for this task was a beautiful and headstrong Druze princess, Amal al-Atrash. Amal had grown up in the Jebel; Sultan al-Atrash was her great-uncle. But in the early 1920s, to escape French bombardment, her mother had taken her to Cairo.[33] Here, not yet twenty, she became a singer under the stage name Esmahan, and before long rivalled the great Umm Kulthum. The Atrash family disapproved of her new life and did their utmost to get her back. In 1933 she married a Druze emir, Hasan al-Atrash, and for a while settled down with him in a villa in the Jebel. But she grew bored and returned to Cairo, where her increasingly scandalous lifestyle led Hasan to divorce her.

At the outbreak of the war, Amal became an ardent supporter of the Free French and would be seen wearing their symbol, 'a large gold Cross of Lorraine which nestled in the cleavage of her ample bosom'.[34] When contacted by the British, she readily agreed to act as a messenger to her ex-husband, the emir. According to one British account,

> She was smuggled across the frontier to Suwaida clutching a goatskin bag full of sovereigns with which to help the discussion. She succeeded dramatically. The Emir stayed staunchly pro-British and remarried her into the bargain. Amal hung onto most of the gold.[35]

But the Vichy forces put up a tough fight, and it took five weeks to defeat them. The British and the Free French lost 4,500 men, and the Vichy about 6,000.[36] An armistice was signed on 14 July, with Catroux representing the Free French. A week later, a furious de Gaulle turned up in Cairo, complaining that Catroux had given too much away. The terms were renegotiated, and this led to an uneasy Anglo-French condominium in the Levant. The Free French, insisting that despite Catroux's declaration the mandate remained in force, were in administrative control of the two territories. But the British remained militarily dominant, and determined that the French should do nothing to complicate their task of winning the war.

The powerful figure of Sir Edward Louis Spears now entered the Levantine stage. He was an old friend of Winston Churchill and had seemed an obvious choice to handle relations between the British and de Gaulle. He had flown with him to London after the fall of France in 1940 and worked with him to establish the Free French movement. But Spears was a complex man, haunted by the feeling of being an outsider. He was neither French (although he had been born in Paris and spoke French fluently) nor fully English (his father was of German Jewish origin, his mother Anglo-Irish). While capable of charm and sensitivity, he could also be abrasive and cruel. He was a soldier rather than a diplomat, and his role in the Levant was to prove both significant and controversial.[37]

Spears was captivated by the remarkable Amal al-Atrash, who, he observed, 'bowled over British officers with the accuracy and speed of a machine gun'.[38] In July 1941, at the end of the fighting, she had remarried Hasan, an event which both Spears and Catroux attended. (The Druze elders were prevailed upon to allow this irregular proceeding.) Hasan was appointed defence minister in the new government. But Amal, like other Druze, felt betrayed by the British, believing Syria had merely exchanged one set of French masters for another. When in the summer of 1942 Spears received intelligence reports that she was on a train heading for the Turkish frontier—'to tell, or rather sell, to the Turks all she knew'—he ordered that she be detained and brought back to Beirut. Here he confronted her, 'terrifying in her rage'.[39] She was put under house arrest in Beirut, then left for Jerusalem, where stories were soon rife of her wild parties at the King David Hotel. Conservative opinion in the Jebel was by now thoroughly scandalised by her behaviour, and Hasan again divorced her. She returned to Cairo and her musical career, made two films (still popular with Arab audiences), and had a brief and turbulent marriage to an Egyptian film director. In July 1944, on a journey from Cairo to Alexandria with a female companion, her car drove into a canal and the two women were drowned. It was discovered that the doors of the car were locked and the driver had disappeared. The mystery of her death, at the age of only thirty-two, was never solved.[40]

Spears returned to Beirut in March 1942 as British Minister to the Levant States. Having been an ardent supporter of de Gaulle, he was now one of his strongest critics. Whereas de Gaulle was determined to keep the French empire intact, Spears believed it was vital to the war effort for Britain to remain committed to Syrian and Lebanese independence. He made it his business to cultivate the Arab nationalists, particularly Riad al-Solh.

The nationalists wanted the restoration of constitutional life and the holding of elections. In March 1943, under pressure from Spears, Catroux announced that elections would be held in both Lebanon and Syria. In Syria the elections duly went ahead and Shukri al-Quwatli was elected president. He was only fifty-one, and his rise to power through the shrewd cultivation of popular support, and skilful outmanoeuvring of rivals, was little short of spectacular.

In Lebanon the picture was very different. The French set about rigging the vote in favour of their Christian allies—only to be thwarted by Spears, who was determined to end the practice of excluding Arab nationalists from the political game. The elections of August 1943, although marred by widespread bribery and intimidation, were a resounding success for Riad al-Solh. He became prime minister and began a fruitful partnership with the new Christian president, Bishara al-Khoury. The two men were the authors of the National Pact, an unwritten formula for Muslim-Christian entente. In essence, the Muslims gave up their desire to be part of Greater Syria, and the Christians, aware that the French would not always be around to protect them, accepted that Lebanon was an Arab country.[41]

Hence the elections succeeded in bringing to power the father of Syrian independence (Quwatli) and the father of Lebanese independence (Solh)—two nationalists who were close friends; who had grown up as children of the Ottoman empire, as fluent in Turkish as in Arabic; who had made the all-important shift of allegiance from Ottomanism to Arabism; who had won their political spurs in Faisal's Arab Revolt of 1916; and who had founded their careers on opposition to French colonial rule.

While Spears was delighted at the outcome of the elections, de Gaulle was livid. In his eyes, the nationalists, aided and abetted by the British, were out to destroy French influence in the eastern Mediterranean. The actions of the new Lebanese parliament did nothing to reassure him: the nationalists announced their intention to terminate the mandate, end France's economic domination, and make Arabic the only official language—an infuriating snub to French cultural pretensions.[42]

The General Delegate (as the High Commissioner was now called) was the unimpressive Jean Helleu. Spears reported that, when the going got tough, Helleu withdrew to a shed at the bottom of the garden, armed with a bottle of whisky. But now, faced with nationalist pressure and apparently acting on de Gaulle's instructions, Helleu responded with unexpected force to nationalist pressure. During the night of 11 November 1943, soldiers arrested and imprisoned Bishara al-Khoury, Riad al-Solh, and other ministers, and the next day Helleu suspended parliament and named a pro-French lawyer, Emile Eddé, as head of state. This provoked uproar. The coup was so brazen and unexpected that it thrust Christians and Muslims together in a new-found solidarity. A general strike was declared. Demonstrations turned violent. Two hundred Lebanese women, both Muslim and Christian, marched to the British and American legations to urge them to intervene. French troops—including the much-resented colonial Senegalese—fired indiscriminately on unarmed civilians. After several days of unrest, Catroux was sent in to retrieve the situation. The British gave him an ultimatum—release the Lebanese leaders, or British troops would intervene and impose martial law. On 22 November the president and the prime minister were freed and returned to Beirut amid scenes of jubilation.[43]

Spears may have felt his assertive approach had been vindicated; but in fact his position was becoming untenable. His enemies in London believed he had gone too far in humiliating the French, who, however disgraceful their behaviour, were still war-time allies. The Foreign Secretary, Anthony Eden, decided he had to go. In the end, even his old friend Churchill was unwilling to rescue him. To save face, he was allowed to resign, which he did in December 1944, after four turbulent years in Beirut.

The French clung on to the bitter end, resisting demands to withdraw their forces from the Levant—the one action that would give substance to Syrian and Lebanese sovereignty. In May 1945 there were violent demonstrations in Beirut and Damascus, leading to a breakdown of law and order. On 29 May the French resorted to the methods they had employed in the 1920s and launched a ferocious bombardment of Damascus. They shelled the citadel and even the parliament building. The assault went on for three days, leaving at least 480 dead and 1,500 wounded.[44]

But French power was waning. After urgent appeals from Quwatli to Churchill, Eden demanded a ceasefire, and a British armoured column entered Damascus to restore order. By the end of 1946, the last French soldier had left Beirut, and Syria and Lebanon were free.

4

LOVERS OF ZION

There were no trumpets or drums, no ringing of bells or flying of flags. When General Edmund Allenby entered Jerusalem on 11 December 1917—the first Christian to capture the holy city since the Crusades— he did so on foot, in a show of humility designed to assure its people that he came as a liberator rather than a conqueror. It was a carefully choreographed moment, recorded in film and photography and later in painting, which became one of the iconic images of the imperial age. Coming amidst the darkest days of the First World War, Allenby's triumph was what the British prime minister, David Lloyd George, had so badly wanted: a much-needed Christmas present for the British people.

The city's assembled dignitaries could scarcely have imagined what was to come, as they stood in line to watch Allenby's arrival and hear him guarantee freedom of religion and the sanctity of the city's holy places, and announce the imposition of martial law. Little more than three decades later, the British departed, Palestine ceased to exist, the state of Israel was born, and a problem was bequeathed to the world which haunts it still.

Palestine was smaller than Belgium. At the start of British rule, it was a backwater of the Ottoman empire with a population of fewer than 700,000. At the end of the First World War Britain was awarded the mandate for Palestine by the League of Nations. What made the

Palestine mandate special was that a fateful British pledge, the Balfour Declaration of 2 November 1917, was formally incorporated into its terms. The declaration, signed by the British Foreign Secretary, Arthur Balfour, committed Britain to support the creation in Palestine of a 'national home' for the Jewish people. What this meant was purposefully vague, but the proviso was attached that nothing should be done to prejudice the rights of 'the existing non-Jewish communities'; in other words Palestine's Arab majority. Britain was caught in a tangle of war-time promises. While pledging a national home to the Jews, it had also, as we have seen, promised independence to the Arabs in return for their help in defeating the Turks.

British rule in Palestine began in a mood of remarkable optimism. The conquering power confidently expected that wise imperial administration would satisfy Arab and Jewish aspirations and safeguard British interests in the Middle East. The country was initially governed by a military administration under Allenby. It was in a wretched state. Edward Keith-Roach, a British official described by a contemporary as 'big and bluff and hearty with an exterior like a prize fighter', arrived at the end of 1919 and travelled around Palestine in a Model T Ford. He found a neglected, under-developed country devastated by war. 'The Jerusalem streets were a series of pitted ruts,' he wrote. 'Tel Aviv was little more than a cluster of cottages on a sand hill; Jaffa was an entirely undrained town and Haifa a picturesque village.' There was not a single town with a public water supply. Much of the arable land was left untilled. Malaria was rampant. The people were forlorn and hungry.[1]

Fadwa Tuqan was born in Nablus, in the West Bank, in the year of the Balfour Declaration. The Tuqans were a wealthy family, prominent in the social and political life of a city which, because of its nationalist sentiment, was known as the 'mountain of fire'. Fadwa grew up in a strictly conservative Muslim household, one of ten children. Like the other women in her family, she was largely confined to the home. Malaria, she recalled, was the 'constant companion of my childhood'; other children made fun of her sallow complexion. One of her earliest memories was of the British arresting her father for his political activities and deporting him to Egypt.[2]

As the 1920s unfolded, more and more Jews arrived to settle in Palestine, prompting growing Arab suspicion of their intentions. In the past religious Jews had come to the country and coexisted relatively peacefully with their neighbours. But the new settlers were inspired by Zionism, the movement of Jewish nationalism which had developed in the nineteenth century in response to anti-Semitism, and was to gain an altogether new momentum as a result of the Balfour Declaration.

These new settlers began to build up the infrastructure of a state under the leadership of two remarkable and contrasting men. The Russian-born Chaim Weizmann was Zionism's consummate diplomat. He was the head of the Zionist Commission, based in Tel Aviv, which was soon carrying out some of the functions of a government. It ran Jewish schools, collected taxes from Jewish settlements, and won the right to determine which Jews qualified for immigration to Palestine. The commission wanted fit and preferably unmarried young men who could work the land. Weizmann was adept at pulling strings to influence British policy.[3]

The other key figure was David Ben-Gurion, who ran the Zionist labour movement, the Histadrut. Born David Gruen (Green) in Tsarist-ruled Poland, Ben-Gurion had arrived in Palestine in 1906. The Histadrut, set up in 1920, was much more than a trade-union federation. It undertook 'activities in land settlement, work contracts, the improvement of working conditions and productivity, vocational training, co-operative trading and mutual aid, defence, the reception of immigrants and promotion of pioneer immigration from abroad, and the promotion of Hebrew language and culture'.[4] It was, in other words, one of the most important instruments of Zionist state-building. As such, it took on responsibility for the Haganah, also created in 1920, initially as a small underground self-defence force, which became the nucleus of an army. By means of these institutions, Ben-Gurion built up his power base. He initially worked hand in hand with Weizmann, but over time was to become his principal rival. Weizmann regarded him as headstrong; he in turn saw the older man as too cautious, too ready to compromise with the British.

Palestine's first High Commissioner, from 1920 to 1925, was Sir Herbert Samuel. A liberal politician and former cabinet member, Sir Herbert was a Jew and a Zionist who had been instrumental in the issuing of the Balfour Declaration. He was accordingly regarded with apprehension by the Arabs and by some British officials. But he bent over backwards to be even-handed. One of his first acts was to appoint Hajj Amin al-Husseini to the important post of mufti of Jerusalem. Hajj Amin, a striking figure with blue eyes, reddish hair, and a trimmed beard, belonged to one of Jerusalem's most illustrious Arab families. He had been convicted *in absentia* of helping instigate riots in 1920, and was later to become militantly anti-British. But in the early days of the mandate he showed signs of wanting to co-operate with the colonial power and to pursue Arab demands by non-violent means. Samuel and his advisers favoured him because, although still in his mid-twenties and possessing relatively weak religious credentials, he carried the prestigious Husseini name and seemed to have the backing of Arab public opinion.

The new mufti encouraged Arab dignitaries to set up a Supreme Muslim Council with control over Palestine's Muslim affairs, and he himself was duly elected as its head. The position gave him the considerable revenue of £50,000 a year and great powers of patronage. He built up a network of schools, orphanages, and other institutions, and oversaw the restoration of the Haram al-Sharif (Noble Sanctuary), the most important Muslim holy place in Jerusalem's Old City. Before long, he was Palestine's pre-eminent Arab leader.

As Jewish immigration continued, and with it the purchase of land (often from absentee Arab landowners), Arab resentment grew. Keith-Roach began to detect a tendency among British policy-makers to drift from crisis to crisis. As an administrator, he took pride in the fact that Britain was introducing electricity and paved roads, and combating locusts and malaria, in a country which had been left to languish under Turkish rule. He admired the energy of the young Jews who arrived from Russia and Poland 'bursting with enthusiasm'—men such as the former Russian revolutionary Pinhas Rutenberg, who was granted a concession to harness the waters of the Jordan and the Yarmuk rivers for electricity. This became the biggest industrial enterprise in Palestine. (Fadwa Tuqan's home town, Nablus, boycotted the Rutenberg project, and for many years relied on naphtha lamps.) But Keith-Roach was not alone in seeing that Zionist state-building was bound to provoke an Arab backlash. At a meeting at which Keith-Roach was present, Weizmann revealed privately to British officials what he was careful to hide in public: 'The Arabs must go elsewhere.'[5]

Despite the efforts of Herbert Samuel and successive High Commissioners, the story of Palestine between 1920 and 1948 was one of starkly unequal development. The Jewish settlers built up an impressive and largely autonomous network of schools, established Tel Aviv as a modern city, and revived the Hebrew language to replace the babble of tongues the immigrants had brought with them. The opening of the Hebrew University in Jerusalem, in April 1925, was their crowning cultural achievement. Balfour himself, now elderly and frail, was the guest of honour.

The Arabs, in contrast, lived for the most part in remote villages with limited access to healthcare, sanitation, and education. British administrators opened schools in the towns and villages, but kept a tight rein over what was spent and what was taught. They had no budget for mass education and, besides, wanted to encourage the peasants to stay on the land rather than migrate to the towns, where they feared they were more likely to catch the virus of nationalism.

Despite much talk of founding an Arab university to match the Hebrew University, this never happened. Instead, from 1918 until the end of the mandate in 1948, the Arabs had only one first-class institution of higher education—the Arab College in Jerusalem. Initially a teacher-training college, it was run for most of its life by a remarkable scholar and educationalist, Ahmad Samih al-Khalidi. Born in 1896 to an eminent Jerusalem family, Khalidi was educated at the American University of Beirut, served in the Ottoman army during the First World War, and then joined the Palestine mandate's education department. His Lebanese wife Anbara, a noted scholar and feminist, produced the first Arabic translation of Homer's *Iliad* and *Odyssey*. She described him, at the time of their marriage in 1929, as a tall man with 'blond hair, blue eyes, and a white and perpetually reddish face ... he was highly-strung, very lively in his movements and speech, and paid little attention to his personal appearance'.[6]

Khalidi personally supervised the selection of the brightest boys from the government schools throughout Palestine. Ranging, as one of the teachers put it, 'from the scions of wealthy landowners to the sons of stone-cutters and camel-drivers',[7] they entered the college at fifteen, stayed for two or three years and then, if they were lucky, won a scholarship to study in Beirut or at a university in Britain. After graduating, they would become teachers or work for the mandate government. The number of students was small—never more than a hundred in any one year—but Khalidi's success as a 'maker of men' was impressive.

The Arab College was a boarding school that charged little or nothing for its services. The language of instruction was Arabic, and the teachers were all Arab except the teacher of English. From 1927 to 1929, this was Stewart Perowne, the son and grandson of English bishops who in later life was known as an authority on Jerusalem and, briefly, as the husband of the travel writer Freya Stark. (When they first met, in a government office in Aden, Stark described how he 'swooped in and out, long-necked and bald-headed like a young vulture'.) Perowne enjoyed his three years' teaching at the Arab College, even though, as he later recorded, 'The buildings were primitive. We had neither electric light nor running water.' As for the students, he was shocked by 'the absolute squalor, filth, degradation and poverty, almost starvation, from which the majority of our boys come'.[8]

For students like Jabra Ibrahim Jabra, entry to the Arab College was a passport to a new life. Born in 1920 into a Christian Arab family in Bethlehem, Jabra grew up in abject poverty. His father had been conscripted into the Ottoman army in the First World War; then, dogged by ill health, had taken a variety of jobs as a construction worker, self-taught cobbler, and odd-job man. The family kept moving house to save money. The young Jabra went to a succession of local church schools, where he excelled, and eventually gained admission to the Arab College. Much later, living in exile in Baghdad as one of the most widely acclaimed Palestinian writers and critics, he recalled Khalidi's 'stentorian voice', 'strong presence', and rigorous régime: 'We read and studied with passion and perseverance all day long, and then all night to the point of sickness.'[9]

He was scarcely exaggerating. One of Jabra's contemporaries described a day in the life of the college. The students were woken at 6 a.m. by a bell. Breakfast was at seven and classes began at eight. Each class lasted 45 minutes, with a short break in between. The students had five classes before noon, and two after lunch. Between 3:30 and 6 p.m. there was football and basketball. Dinner was at six and at seven there was a two-hour study period. Shortly after nine, the students collapsed into their beds.[10]

When Herbert Samuel left Palestine in June 1925, there was a period of calm. He was succeeded by Lord Plumer, a military man with a distinguished reputation, a love of cricket, and a walrus moustache. (He was said to be the model for Colonel Blimp, the cartoon character of the 1930s later made famous in a Powell and Pressburger film.) But despite his Blimpish appearance Plumer succeeded, uniquely among High Commissioners, in winning the respect of Arab and Jew, and of his own officials. (Keith-Roach described Plumer's tenure as his happiest years in Palestine; Perowne revered him as a 'Christian gentleman'.) In some respects he was lucky. Political tension eased because of a slowdown in Jewish immigration, caused by the economic depression in Europe.

The calm did not last. In the summer of 1928, a fierce dispute erupted in Jerusalem when a British policeman, acting on Keith-Roach's orders, demanded the removal of a screen put up at the Wailing Wall to separate male and female Jewish worshippers. (Anything that affected the wall, however trivial, was sensitive because of the proximity of Muslim and Jewish holy places.) The dispute was still simmering when Plumer's successor, Sir John Chancellor, arrived a few months later, and it continued into the following year, finally exploding in August 1929 in a wave of violence which began in Jerusalem and quickly spread to other parts of the country. Perowne witnessed the unrest in Jerusalem from the roof of the education department, which looked down on the Montefiore Quarter, a Jewish area of the city:

> I heard a confused dull buzz as of angry bees somewhere near. Then I saw what it was, Arabs hurling stones against the windows of the [Jewish] houses. There were about 20 of them at first, but they were soon joined by others, attracted by the noise and shouting and whistling ... Soon they began using guns, and at least three grenades were thrown. I had suggested telephoning the police, which was done. At last they arrived. By this time the firing was fairly continuous, one old man ... firing a cut-down rifle from the road beneath us. The British police fired a volley, and the place was soon clear.

The riots jolted Perowne out of his charmed life as a young Englishman abroad who, when not teaching his students Shakespeare or taking them on picnics, enjoyed the social round of parties at Government House, open-air concerts at the Hebrew University, and expeditions to shoot duck and quail. The tone of his letters home changed abruptly. 'It was not pleasant,' he wrote, 'to have to stand there and watch savages break the windows of innocent old women.'[11]

The violence was not confined to Jerusalem. In the Jewish quarter of Hebron, in southern Palestine, sixty-seven Jews were massacred by Arabs from outside the town, incensed by rumours of the trouble in Jerusalem. The death toll would have been even higher but for the actions of the town's British police chief, Raymond Cafferata, and of local Arabs who protected their Jewish neighbours. Chancellor, who had been on leave during the riots, returned to take stock. In all, 133 Jews had been killed. He concluded that the Arabs were to blame, and responded by ordering hundreds of arrests. Three Arabs were hanged in Acre jail.[12]

For the young Fadwa Tuqan, growing up in Nablus, the events of 1929 marked the first glimmerings of political awareness. A girl of independent spirit, she languished under the stern authority of her father, while inwardly yearning to go to university and write poetry, like her brother Ibrahim. She could not bear the double standards practised by the dominant men of her society. They 'dressed in European style; they spoke Turkish, French, and English; they ate with knives and forks; they fell in love'—yet they kept their women in seclusion and servitude. In 1929, when Fadwa was twelve, Ibrahim returned home after graduating from the American University of Beirut. His poem *Al-Thulatha al-Hamra* (Red Tuesday), written to honour the hanged prisoners, won instant acclaim. For Fadwa, the dream of personal liberation became intertwined with that of national liberation.[13]

British officials suspected that Hajj Amin had fomented the unrest. For most of the 1920s, their investment in him had seemed to pay off, as he had on several occasions helped to maintain calm. But now, caught between the British and an increasingly radicalised Arab public opinion, he was forced to choose sides.

Ben-Gurion sought to initiate a political dialogue with the Arab leaders. In March 1934 he met privately in Jerusalem with a respected nationalist, Musa Alami, hoping through him to arrange a meeting with

Hajj Amin. The initiative came to nothing, but it produced a memorable exchange. When Ben-Gurion tried to convince Alami that Zionism would be a 'blessing to the Arabs of Palestine', bringing progress and development, Alami replied bluntly, 'I would prefer that the country remain impoverished and barren for another hundred years, until we ourselves are able to develop it on our own.'[14]

Chancellor was succeeded by Sir Arthur Wauchope, a wealthy Scottish bachelor and the only High Commissioner to serve two terms, from 1931 to 1938. It was during his watch that tensions between Arab and Jew came to a head.

Throughout the 1930s, as Hitler rose to power in Germany, Jewish immigration to Palestine increased inexorably, from 9,000 in 1932 to 42,000 in 1934 and almost 62,000 in 1935. The size of the Jewish community more than doubled from 180,000 to nearly 400,000. Finally, in the spring of 1936, Arab patience snapped. The Arab revolt of 1936–39 represented the most sustained challenge to British rule since the start of the mandate, and finally shattered British complacency.

Its harbinger was a charismatic preacher, Sheikh Izzedin al-Qassam. Born in the 1880s in a village near the Syrian town of Latakia, Sheikh Izzedin had studied in Cairo and then joined the Ottoman army. He fought the French during the mandate period in Syria, but was forced to flee, first to Beirut and then to Haifa, on the coast of Palestine. There, as imam of the Istiqlal Mosque, he built up a large following, especially among Arabs who had left the land to seek work. He went from village to village, calling on people to resist the British and the Jews. In November 1935, he took refuge with a group of armed men in the hills around Jenin, in northern Palestine. British soldiers tracked him down to a cave, and in the gun battle that ensued Sheikh Izzedin was killed. But his legend outlasted him, and for several years afterwards his followers, the Qassamiyun, kept up the fight.[15]

The Arab revolt began in April 1936 when, after a number of incidents of inter-communal violence, the newly-formed Arab Higher Committee, under Hajj Amin, ordered a general strike. The revolt had three aims: to bring about a halt to Jewish immigration, a ban on land sales to the Jews, and the establishment of an independent Arab government. Arab shops closed; cars, trucks, and buses stopped running;

Arab trade came to a standstill; and at the ports Arab workers stopped loading and unloading cargo. Issa Boullata, growing up in a Christian family in Jerusalem, remembers how his father, who worked in the telegraph office, had to walk five miles to work, while his mother struggled to feed their family:

> Once in a while, a butcher appeared in our neighbourhood, slaughtered a sheep clandestinely deep in Karm Karimeh, a grove of olive trees on the incline by the main road next to our home, hung the carcass on a tree, and was swarmed by neighbours wanting to buy fresh meat; and he had to finish his business in a short while before he was discovered by the roving members of the 'national committees' who enforced the strike.[16]

The insurgency was directed at the Jews and Jewish settlements, as well as at the British. It began as a peasants' revolt, with a grass-roots leadership, but soon turned into a nationwide rebellion that threatened Britain's grip on the country. No part of Palestine was unaffected.

Ibrahim Abu-Lughod—later to become a university professor in the United States—witnessed his first demonstration during the general strike. He had grown up in Jaffa, a prosperous and multicultural coastal city (known as the Bride of the Sea) where Muslims, Jews, and Christians mixed freely. The young Ibrahim had been sent to an Islamic school before attending a government one, since his father suspected the British were out to undermine their Arab and Muslim identity. He and his brothers had gone to the Al-Hambra cinema in Jaffa to watch Egyptian films and Laurel and Hardy. When he heard a demonstration was under way, Ibrahim went with his younger brother to see it. He was seven, his brother two years younger. 'Nobody pushed me to go,' he recalled; every child knew that the British were their main enemy.

> It was a huge demonstration and I saw ... for the first time the British army and police mounted on horseback with big batons, beating the head of one of the demonstrators. I saw blood streaming from [his head] ... I remember ... the chants of 'Down with the Balfour Declaration!' and 'Down with Zionism!' We did not hear any 'up'.

Ibrahim's father Ali had set up a foundry in Jaffa in 1929 to make water pumps, stone crushers, and olive presses. When, during the Arab revolt, the British found out he was using the foundry to produce mines, they shut it down. Ali was constantly in and out of prison, and young Ibrahim became skilled in finding out where his father was and bribing officials to give him food and messages. Like most of Jaffa, Ali Abu-Lughod supported Hajj Amin.[17]

The mufti had not initiated the rebellion, but sought to take charge of it. There was a plethora of local commanders, among them Fawzi al-Qawuqji, the Lebanese soldier of fortune who had taken part in the Great Revolt against the French in Syria in the 1920s, and thereafter became a kind of roving mercenary in the Arab nationalist cause. When he turned up in Palestine, he was at first immensely popular. Fadwa Tuqan wrote a poem about him ('Hero of heroes, flower of all young men') which later, when the personality cult had waned and Qawuqji was revealed as a braggart, she found foolish.[18]

But the revolt did throw up one outstanding commander, Abdul-Qader al-Husseini. A cousin of Hajj Amin, Abdul-Qader had first come to prominence as a student at the American University in Cairo. On receiving his graduation certificate, he launched into an impassioned attack on Western imperialism, denounced the university's complicity in the colonial project, and then, to the audience's astonishment, tore up his certificate.[19] Now, in this crucial phase of the Palestinian struggle, he was to prove himself a tough and decisive soldier and a born leader.

The Arab revolt was first and foremost a challenge to British rule. But it also challenged Palestine's traditional Arab leadership, calling into question their attempts to co-operate with the British and to cling to non-violent means to defend Arab rights. For them, and for Hajj Amin in particular, the choice now was to adopt a more militant approach, in line with popular sentiment, or risk being marginalised and discredited.

The rebellion had a darker side: lawlessness, banditry, and the settling of scores. Hajj Amin employed hit squads to eliminate rivals. But the rebellion was nevertheless a significant expression of the strength of nationalist feeling. Even Ben-Gurion was struck by its sustained and disciplined character, realising that there really was an Arab nationalism, and that Arab resistance could not simply be dismissed as the work of a few agitators and malcontents.[20]

British officials, forced out of their complacency, invited a Royal Commission under Lord Peel to examine the roots of the problem. In his report, issued in 1937, Peel punctured the myth that wise British rule could foster inter-communal harmony. He advocated the partition of Palestine into a Jewish state, an Arab state (joined with Transjordan), and an international zone remaining under British control. Zionist leaders were ambivalent but decided to keep their options open. The Arabs rejected what they saw as the dismemberment of their country.

The insurgency flared up with a new intensity. The mandate authorities declared the Arab Higher Committee illegal; Hajj Amin was dismissed and escaped into exile. An increasingly rattled colonial power resorted to harsh measures to suppress the unrest. There was martial law in all but name. Soldiers imposed collective punishments on villages suspected of harbouring rebels. Homes were destroyed and scores of insurgents hanged. One of the grim duties of Edward Keith-Roach, who was now the governor of Jerusalem, was to supervise executions. He was struck by their futility:

> One week, at hourly intervals, there were three executions one day, two the next and three on the third ... The irony of the whole process was that not a single execution made the slightest difference to public security, to Arab opinion, to Arab fears, to Arab respect for law, or to Arab action.[21]

At the height of the revolt, in October 1938, the rebels gained control of the Old City of Jerusalem for five days until, after fierce fighting, the British managed to take it back. The young Issa Boullata watched the battle:

> From my home in al-Thawri, I could see small British reconnaissance airplanes flying over the Old City repeatedly, and pinpointing the centres of rebel resistance in it by sending down signals of silver flashes that descended like shooting stars to direct and guide the British forces in the maze of the Old City.[22]

Fadwa Tuqan, now twenty, watched British soldiers enter her home town, Nablus, and separate the menfolk from the women and children. Their house was looted and ransacked. For a while, the British lost control of the town, as it lived up to its reputation as the 'mountain of fire'. Then one day there was a knock on the door at midnight and her father was taken to Acre prison, where he fell ill. According to Fadwa's account, the family had to bribe a British official to get her father released. Instead of being allowed to go home, he was again deported to Egypt.[23]

Even at its most violent, Palestine had an intoxicating beauty. For some visitors, the landscape had a uniquely biblical resonance; for others, especially those arriving from the furnace of Egypt, its hills were refreshingly cool and verdant. Almost every memoir from the period comments on what one British officer, Gawain Bell, called 'the Solomon's Glory of spring in Palestine'. The fields and hillsides, he wrote, 'became covered with white, purple and pink cyclamen and scarlet anemones'.[24] The Arabs called the anemones *hannoun*: for the young Jabra Ibrahim Jabra, growing up in Bethlehem, their arrival was magical:

> There were yellow anemones, blue anemones, violet anemones. And there were those anemones of deep red that have the colour of blood: poppies, which lifted their heads to the sun, their petals shining with dew ... In the shade of mulberry trees, apple trees, apricot trees, almond trees, and pomegranate trees, the poppies burst out of the brown soil like laughing wounds.[25]

In old age, living in exile, Jabra remembered the landscape of Palestine, with its springtime and harvest, its weddings and festivals, as a paradise lost.

By 1939 the Arab revolt had been crushed, with the loss of some 4,000 Arab lives. Now, as the Second World War loomed, British officials dropped the notion of partition and issued a White Paper proposing that Palestine should be independent in ten years—and that Jewish immigration should be limited to a total of 75,000 over the next five years. The proposal, although ostensibly about Palestine's future, was 'in fact a plan for a peaceful Middle East and safe oil supplies in the likely event of a European war'.[26] The Zionists were aghast. But their hands were tied: a British victory over Nazi Germany was their prime concern. The war brought about an undeclared truce in Palestine, as the local conflict between Arab and Jew was temporarily subordinated to the bigger battle. There was an influx of people and money into the country, which served (second always to Egypt) as the hub of Britain's Middle East campaign.

Among the flood of soldiers and civilians who arrived in war-time Jerusalem was Monica Dehn, a lively and attractive young British woman who, after studying journalism at London University, had spotted an advertisement in *The Times* for typists to work in one of the newsrooms of the BBC. The BBC transferred her to the Middle East, and in December 1943, at the age of twenty-three, she found herself on a long journey, by ship and plane, to Palestine. Here she worked for the British Mediterranean Service, a clandestine war-time radio station broadcasting to the occupied countries of south-east Europe and the Balkans.[27]

Monica fell in love with Palestine—and with her boss at the radio station, Roy Elston. Roy was a charismatic British journalist, twenty years her senior, and an ardent Zionist. Under the pen-name David Courtney, he wrote a column for the *Palestine Post*—the principal English-language Zionist newspaper in the Middle East (forerunner of the *Jerusalem Post*)—for which he was adored by the Jews and reviled by British officials. Monica and Roy immersed themselves in the Jewish life of Jerusalem. They got to know the senior Zionist officials— Weizmann, Ben-Gurion, Golda Meir, Moshe Dayan—and many of the leading Jewish intellectuals. The writer Arthur Koestler offered Monica marriage and a cottage in Wales. (She might have been flattered, but moments later saw him say the same thing to the next woman who caught his eye.)

They were also caught up in the propaganda war in the Middle East, as Britain vied with the fascist powers in a battle for Arab hearts and minds. Aiding the Germans, from exile in Iraq, was Hajj Amin, who continued from afar to wield influence in Palestine and the wider Middle East. British radio broadcasting was both covert and overt. Officials had set up the Palestine Broadcasting Service in 1936—on the eve of the Arab revolt—to broadcast in the mandate's three official languages—Hebrew, Arabic, and English. (One of its senior Arab staff was Fadwa Tuqan's brother, Ibrahim, later dismissed for alleged nation- alist bias.) But the PBS's audience was confined to Palestine. To reach a wider Arab audience, the British set up in 1941 the Near East Arab Broadcasting Station (Sharq al-Adna). Based in Palestine and notionally independent, Sharq al-Adna was in fact run by the Special Operations Executive (SOE)—the body Churchill had created to undermine the Axis powers through covert operations and propaganda.[28]

At the end of the war, when the British Mediterranean Service was closed down, Monica was offered a job with Sharq al-Adna. She was initially hesitant. 'I'm a bit nervous,' she wrote to her parents. 'Arabs scare me and maybe I shan't be so good at this type of work.' But she wanted to stay in Palestine with Roy, so she took the job.[29]

With the end of the war, the mandate entered its last, fateful phase. By now, the Zionists had split into two camps. Both wanted the British out; but while the mainstream Zionists under Ben-Gurion, were more cautious, especially about the use of violence, their right-wing rivals, the Irgun and the Stern Gang, were ready to resort to terrorism. Even before the war was over, in November 1944, the Stern Gang—after an unsuccessful attempt to assassinate the High Commissioner, Sir Harold MacMichael—succeeded in killing Lord Moyne, the British Minister of State in Cairo. This caused profound shock in London. Even Churchill, hitherto a staunch supporter of Zionism, began to have second thoughts:

> If our dreams of Zionism are to end in the smoke of the assassins' pistols [he declared] and our labours for its future to produce a new set of gangsters worthy of Nazi Germany, many like myself will have to reconsider the position we have maintained so consistently and so long in the past.

When a post-war Labour government came to power in Britain in 1945, Zionist hopes initially rose since the Labour Party and the British trade unions had a track record of support for Zionism. But these hopes were dashed when the new Foreign Secretary, Ernest Bevin, a former trade-union leader, committed himself to an even-handed approach. Zionists were soon denouncing him as an anti-Semite. He was not; but he could be crudely insensitive to Jewish feelings. His approach, supported by the military chiefs and the Foreign Office, was based on the time-honoured defence of British political and economic interests in the Middle East. He favoured the creation of a single bi-national state in Palestine, believing partition, however logical in principle, would be an admission of failure—and impossible to implement without a massive infusion of additional troops.

Monica disapproved of the actions of the Jewish extremists but was deeply disenchanted with British policy. She watched the arrival of immigrant ships with their pitiful cargo of Jewish refugees from Europe. Britain's policy of turning back illegal refugees was a propaganda disaster for Bevin, and one the Zionists exploited to the full. Monica was uncomfortable working for a British radio station that was pro-Arab and anti-Zionist. She found it far more congenial to moonlight at the *Palestine Post*, where she worked as a sub-editor in the evenings, after finishing her day-time shift at Sharq al-Adna.[30] In the event, her life in Arabic radio lasted only seven months. After going home to see her anxious parents in London, she returned to Jerusalem and for the last two years of the mandate worked for its press department, the Public Information Office, as a junior spin doctor for the administration of which privately she was so critical.

Her new boss was Richard Stubbs. After a pre-war career in advertising, Stubbs had worked with SOE in the Middle East. Now he had the thankless task of news management in Palestine at a time when the local and foreign media were increasingly critical of British policy. To woo the press away from the *Palestine Post*—which journalists found a useful and congenial place for gathering information—Stubbs refurbished the PIO, with the addition of a comfortable bar, and attempted to improve the often lacklustre public-relations skills of the mandate authorities. As he recalled in a memoir, the press office became affectionately known as the 'snake pit'. Few who saw Stubbs walking to work, immaculately dressed in an elegant suit and silk tie with a flower in his buttonhole, would have guessed that in his youth he had been a communist.[31]

'My new boss, Dick Stubbs, seems A Good Thing,' wrote Monica to her parents, 'and provided the work is impersonally non-political, I think I shall settle down well.' It was a naïve hope. But if this new job was scarcely more congenial to her than the last, it gave her a ring-side seat for the final act of the Palestine drama.[32]

The British now found themselves under pressure from within and from without: from the pro-Zionist Truman administration in Washington, and in Palestine from the increasingly assertive Irgun and Stern Gang. Having crushed the Arab revolt of the 1930s, they now found themselves struggling to crush a Jewish revolt. This was to prove a much tougher challenge.

On Saturday, 29 June 1946—a day that became known as Black Sabbath—Monica's breakfast was interrupted at 7:30 a.m. when her landlady summoned her to the phone. It was Dick Stubbs: 'Monica, come to the office at once. The army has taken over the Jewish Agency.' She arrived to find the Public Information Office guarded by tanks and armoured cars—and an unshaven Stubbs working on a statement to be issued by the High Commissioner. 'I went down to the press room to deal with the rush of phone calls with a heavy heart.' The British had decided to crack down on the mainstream Zionist organisations—the Jewish Agency and the Haganah—believing them to be hand in glove with the extremists. For Monica, the land of her birth was now at war with the people whose cause had become her own.[33]

Operation Agatha, as it was called, involved the arrest of over 2,000 Jewish suspects—including VIJs (Very Important Jews), as the British dubbed them—and raids on Jewish settlements, in one of which a large arms cache was discovered. Tensions between the British and the Jewish community reached a new intensity.

A few weeks later, on 22 July 1946, Barbara Board, a young British journalist who had been reporting from Palestine for a decade, was walking into the King David Hotel in Jerusalem when a huge explosion shook the building:

> The boom of exploding ammonal roared out over the city like a giant thunderclap; the six storeys of the southern wing bulged, swayed and crashed in a ghastly mountain of crumbling cement, twisted girders and snapped-off blocks of masonry out of which the screams of the dying rose in a piercing chorus of agony. A vast mushroom of sepia smoke climbed up into the sunlit sky and rolled away in the awful silence which followed.[34]

The young journalist was lucky to survive. A military policeman 'threw me to the ground and covered me from danger with a cool courage to which I owe my life'. The bombing was the Irgun's most notorious exploit. A group of its members, disguised as Arabs, had smuggled seven milk churns filled with explosives into the basement of the hotel. The explosion destroyed the south wing, which housed the civilian and military headquarters of the British administration, killing ninety-one people, including forty-one Arabs, twenty-eight Britons, and seventeen Jews.[35]

Monica Dehn's parents initially thought she was among the casualties. She was nearby but unhurt, and described the grim work of looking for survivors.[36] In the aftermath of the bombing, Jerusalem came to resemble a war zone. Official buildings were encased in barbed wire. Movement around the city became hazardous. Women and children and 'non-essential personnel' were evacuated—among them Barbara Board—and those that remained found life barely tolerable. For two weeks Tel Aviv was placed under martial law, as British security forces hunted for extremists thought to be hiding there.

In propaganda terms, the Zionists were on the defensive—until the commander of British forces in Palestine, General Sir Evelyn Barker, scored a spectacular own-goal. He gave a 'non-fraternisation' order to his troops: they should have no dealings with Jewish shops or businesses, thereby 'punishing the Jews in a way the race dislikes—by striking at their pockets'. Monica's letters, always opinionated, now blazed with fury at Barker's anti-Semitism and Bevin's policy. In her eyes, Britain had turned on the Jews at the very moment when they needed Palestine as a refuge from the horrors and devastation of Europe.[37]

With Palestine becoming ungovernable and a political solution nowhere in sight, Bevin announced in April 1947 that Britain would refer the issue to the United Nations. His aim at this stage was not to withdraw from Palestine but to force others to share responsibility for the problem. British public opinion increasingly viewed the territory as a liability. Between 1945 and 1947 the number of British troops in Palestine doubled from 50,000 to 100,000. One-tenth of the armed forces of the British empire now occupied a territory the size of Wales. Palestine was costing the British exchequer close to £40 million a year.[38]

In July 1947, in an incident which further inflamed British public opinion, the Irgun kidnapped and hanged two British sergeants in retaliation for the execution of three of its members. The *Daily Express* splashed a gruesome picture of the men across its front page, under the headline 'Hanged Britons: Picture that will Shock the World'. As the Palestine media were subject to censorship, Dick Stubbs had done his utmost to prevent the photographs leaving the country; but no spin doctor could prevent the horror of such events from entering British living-rooms.

In September 1947, despairing of a solution, Bevin declared that Britain would withdraw the following year. Even now, with the clock ticking, the United Nations responded slowly and uncertainly to the new responsibility thrust upon it. After a five-week investigation on the spot, a UN special committee (UNSCOP) recommended the partition of Palestine. But with Britain washing its hands of the problem, it was unclear how this could be implemented. In November, after intense American and Zionist lobbying, the UN General Assembly passed by a narrow majority a resolution calling for Palestine to be partitioned into a Jewish and an Arab state.

At the news, the Jews of Jerusalem poured onto the streets in a mood of jubilation. Monica and Roy had spent the evening, like most of their friends, glued to the radio listening to the votes being cast. Now they joined an ecstatic crowd that had gathered outside the Jewish Agency. They were greeted by the agency's acting head, Golda Meir. 'Fat, motherly Golda,' wrote Monica, 'was in the crowd shaking hands.' When she saw Roy, she put her arms around him, kissing him on both cheeks, and declared in her broad twang, 'My friend, you have helped towards all this.'[39]

The Arabs were angry and despondent, and their leaders declared a three-day strike. If the likelihood of the emergence of a Jewish state had increased, so too had the chances of war. The following month Arab foreign ministers, meeting in Cairo, agreed to set up what they optimistically called the Arab Liberation Army, under Fawzi al-Qawuqji, tasked with saving Palestine from a Zionist takeover.

A cycle of violence began. In January 1948, the Haganah attacked the Hotel Semiramis, in the Katamon district of Jerusalem, mistakenly believing it was being used as the headquarters of local Arab forces. Twenty-six people were killed, including the Spanish consul. A few weeks later, as Monica and Roy were sitting in the Atara café in the Jewish part of the city, a huge explosion shook the area. They rushed into the street to discover there had been a bomb attack on the offices of the *Palestine Post*.

'The sky was blood-red and blazing stars were drifting over the buildings,' wrote Monica to her parents. 'The flames were pouring out of the ground-floor windows and the crackling of wooden frames sounded like the crunching of bones.' The newsroom had been spared, as had their friend Gershon Agronsky, the paper's editor-in-chief, who was away in Tel Aviv. But eight of the compositors had 'dreadful face wounds from flying machinery or glass'. Two were blinded. In an act of defiance, the journalists worked through the night to help produce the next morning's edition of the paper. Roy's column—beginning with the ringing words 'Truth is more powerful than TNT'—was one of his most acclaimed.[40]

After the attack came the recriminations. Zionists suspected that British soldiers or policemen had somehow been involved. Dick Stubbs issued a furious denial. In fact the bombing had been carried out by Abdul-Qader al-Husseini's men, aided by two British deserters. Abdul-Qader wanted to show that his forces could strike at the heart of Jerusalem. Three weeks later, his men bombed Ben Yehuda Street, the city's main Jewish residential and shopping district, this time using four British deserters and killing fifty-four people.[41]

Abdul-Qader's most notable achievement, however, was to cut Jerusalem's lifeline—the road that linked it to Tel Aviv. With the city under siege, supplies of food, water, and ammunition ran low. 'It is cold as winter,' wrote Monica in early April 1948. 'The electricity has been off all morning, so there is no heating and not a drop of kerosene for cooking ... Worse than the cold ... is the absence of food.' Those on the Arab side of the city could get food from the surrounding Arab villages. Those, like Monica, on the Jewish side lived out of tins or were reduced to boiling a weed which tasted rather like spinach.[42]

Ben-Gurion, anxiously following events from his headquarters in Tel Aviv, was desperate to open the road to Jerusalem, so that convoys carrying food (and smuggled weapons) could get through to the city. Gradually, the Zionists' superior organisation and motivation began to tell. On 8 April 1948 the Arabs lost their most outstanding commander when Abdul-Qader was killed in the battle of Qastel, a strategic hilltop village near Jerusalem. Thousands flocked into Jerusalem for his funeral, abandoning the village, which quickly fell to the Zionists. They had been willing to fight for a god, wrote one chronicler of the conflict, but not for a hill.[43]

Even while the funeral was under way, news began to filter through that the Irgun and the Stern Gang had entered Deir Yassin, a hitherto peaceful Arab village near Jerusalem, and killed over a hundred people, including women and children. Ben-Gurion was furious. (Although he had not known about the attack, a senior Haganah official had in principle approved it.)[44] As news of the massacre spread, it provoked panic among the Arabs of Palestine and gave added impetus to their flight from their homes and land. In retaliation, seventy-four Jews were killed—most of them doctors and medical personnel—when their convoy was attacked on its way to Jerusalem's Hadassah hospital.

Among the Palestinian professionals who fled were Ahmad Samih al-Khalidi, the head of the Arab College, and his wife Anbara. As the tit-for-tat violence escalated, Anbara recalled, 'we began to think seriously of leaving—an absence we imagined would be temporary'.

> When we finally decided to leave, our hearts were very heavy and our nerves near breaking point. No sooner did the car arrive to carry us to Beirut than tears filled my eyes. I would go out of the door, then walk back again to examine the rooms, bathrooms, kitchen and garden, as if to bid them farewell and promise them I would soon come back.

They arrived in Beirut on 12 April 1948, but Khalidi's exile was short-lived. A heart condition led to his death in 1951, at the age of only fifty-five.[45]

In the countdown to the British departure, there were scenes of chaos, and flashes of black humour. Dick Stubbs' car was stolen, a not uncommon occurrence in the disorder of the time. It was a maroon Ford saloon which he was fond of. When he made enquiries through Arab contacts to see if he could recover it, he received an unexpected reply from Fawzi al-Qawuqji in Nablus. He could have the car back in return for advice on how to improve Arab propaganda. While readily acknowledging that Arab public relations left much to be desired, Stubbs declined the offer.[46]

In Jaffa, the 19-year-old Ibrahim Abu-Lughod volunteered to work with the local committee trying to defend the city against attack by the Irgun and the Haganah. They were an amateur bunch, mostly schoolteachers, shopkeepers, and a few students. Their commander, a Bosnian loyal to Hajj Amin, spoke no Arabic. Ibrahim had a gun that didn't fire.

The committee urged people to stay, assuring them (mistakenly) that Arab reinforcements would soon arrive. But as the fighting intensified, the exodus from the city gathered pace. Those who remained hid in their houses and struggled to get food and water. Ibrahim's family left at the end of April, but he and his friend Muhammad stayed to fight. On 3 May, they heard that a Red Cross ship, the *Princess Alexandra*, was about to leave; it was their last chance to escape. They joined dozens of others crowded onto a small *jarrem* (dinghy) taking people out to the ship. Even now the two of them hesitated, unwilling to leave. But when they went back ashore, they found there was no one left; the battle was lost.

Around 3 p.m. we saw smoke coming out of the smoke-stack of the [Red Cross] boat. The boat was about to leave. Muhammad and I left our guns and ran to catch the last *jarrem*. We were the last to board the *Princess Alexandra*. We were sitting in the corridor and a Belgian sailor passed. He looked at us and asked: 'Why did you leave your country?' I didn't have an answer.[47]

The ship took them to Beirut, and the Abu-Lughod family eventually settled in Amman, to a life of exile.

Fadwa Tuqan, in Nablus, watched as the refugees fled eastwards, finding shelter in the city's mosques and schools and in caves in nearby hills. In all, some 700,000 refugees, more than half the Arab population of Palestine, either fled or were driven from their homes.

On 14 May 1948, the last British High Commissioner, Sir Alan Cunningham, left Jerusalem to board a waiting ship in Haifa. Later that day, in a museum in Tel Aviv, Ben-Gurion proclaimed the birth of the state of Israel. It was, wrote one historian, a Jewish triumph, an Arab tragedy, and a British failure.[48] Thirty years, five months, and four days after General Allenby had entered Jerusalem in triumph, British rule ended in ignominy.

5

ABDULLAH'S LITTLE KINGDOM

In March 1921, at a meeting in Jerusalem between a British official and an Arabian prince, the oddest of all the new states of the Middle East was born. The official was the Colonial Secretary, Winston Churchill; the prince was Abdullah, of the Hashemite family of the Hijaz; and the new state was Transjordan—the country we know today as Jordan. For the most part desert, with no resources and a sparse population, Transjordan had no obvious reason to exist. Unlike Palestine, it had no strategic value. Unlike Iraq, it had no oil. It was the place in between: a vacant lot which Churchill decided to fill, in order to complete a swathe of British-controlled territory from the Mediterranean to the Gulf, to give a role to a protégé—and to keep out the French. He would later boast that he had created Transjordan with the stroke of a pen one Sunday afternoon.[1]

Abdullah was not yet forty. He had been born in Mecca in 1882, the second son of the Sharif Hussein, whose family, the Hashemites, claimed descent from the Prophet Muhammad. The Hijaz was then part of the Ottoman empire. While the Ottoman sultans cared little for Arabia as a whole, they did care about the Muslim holy places of Mecca and Medina—and the annual revenue from the pilgrims who travelled there. In 1891, as a result of a dispute, Hussein earned the displeasure of Sultan Abdul-Hamid and was summoned to Istanbul. Abdullah was only nine when he and his brothers set off to join their father in exile in the Ottoman capital:

> On 7 February 1891 [he recorded in his memoirs] we sailed from Jedda in the fine paddle-steamer *Izzeddin*. We three brothers, Ali, Faisal and myself, were under the care of our grandmother ... Passing through the Suez Canal we spent one night on the lake near Ismailia, then sailed on to Port Said where we saw something quite new and strange to us, namely, Christian women unveiled.[2]

After a long, storm-tossed voyage, they finally reached Istanbul, where the three brothers were greeted by their father. The sprawling cosmopolitan city was an exciting place for a young prince who'd grown up in the sheltered world of Arabia. It was here, during the sixteen years he spent in the Ottoman capital, that his education began in earnest. He and his brothers began lessons 'in a new style'. 'We were forbidden to speak Arabic ... The subjects were the Turkish language, Turkish grammar, reading aloud in Turkish, geography, arithmetic and Ottoman Muslim history.'[3] No less important, Abdullah gained an initiation into the life of the Ottoman court, and learned what drew Arabs and Turks together and what kept them apart.

In 1908 his father, now rehabilitated, was made emir of Mecca and the family returned home—though Abdullah was to retain his links with Istanbul as a deputy in the Ottoman parliament. The turning-point in their lives, and in Hashemite fortunes, came with the outbreak of the First World War in the summer of 1914. Hussein and his sons played a key role as allies of Britain when they launched the Arab Revolt against the Turks in 1916. Hussein believed he would be rewarded by becoming the ruler of a post-war Arab kingdom. His hopes were raised when his son Faisal became king of Syria—then quickly dashed when the French ousted him in July 1920.

Undaunted by his brother's defeat, Abdullah found an unusual way to thrust himself onto the post-war stage. In September 1920, with a few hundred followers, he journeyed by camel from Mecca to Medina, and then by train to Ma'an—traditionally part of southern Syria but now part of British-controlled territory. His avowed aim, which he pronounced to all who would listen, was to drive the French from Syria and restore Hashemite rule. He remained in Ma'an for three months, waiting to see what the British would do.

The British did nothing. They had received a mandate from the League of Nations to govern Palestine and Transjordan as a single entity, but had not decided what to do with Transjordan. As a stopgap measure, they had established a limited presence there. Alec Kirkbride, a big jovial Scot still in his early twenties, was one of a handful of political officers sent to take charge of three districts of the country. Captain Kirkbride had been born in 1897, the son of a lithographer. In 1906 his father had taken up a job in the Egyptian customs service and had sent his son to Jesuit schools in Alexandria and Cairo, where he learned French and Arabic. During the First World War, Kirkbride had fought alongside Faisal and T. E. Lawrence in the Arab Revolt, and had entered Damascus with them.[4]

Now he found himself, virtually without soldiers or money, running part of a newly-acquired territory. His domain—to which he gave the wry title the National Government of Moab, with himself its reluctant president—was Kerak, a district south of Amman, populated by 'the wildest tribesmen in the country'. The Scotsman relished the challenge. 'The place had many advantages from my point of view. No motor-road, no telephone or telegraph and no other British: I was, in fact, truly my own master.'[5]

Kirkbride's splendid isolation was interrupted by Abdullah's unexpected arrival, which put him in an awkward position. He had received no instructions from London as to whether he should receive the presumptuous Hashemite, ignore him, or eject him. But with only fifty policemen at his command, his options were limited. So he decided to ride out to welcome his Arabian visitor. He found Abdullah charming but mischievous. Was Captain Kirkbride there, he asked, to welcome him on behalf of the British government? Kirkbride hesitated. He was there to welcome the emir on behalf of the National Government of Moab. Abdullah was gracious. 'I could not wish to be welcomed by anyone more acceptable than yourself,' he declared, before asking innocently, 'By the way, has the National Government of Moab ever been recognised internationally?' Thus began a close association between two of the makers of modern Jordan which was to last for the next thirty years.[6]

Gradually Abdullah built up support in the country, and eventually the British came round to the view that they should accept his *fait accompli*. In March 1921 Churchill summoned the emir to Jerusalem. After some negotiation it was decided that he should rule Transjordan for a probationary period of six months. Conditions were attached: he should accept British guidance, and do nothing to upset the French. In return, he would get a British subsidy of £5,000 a month, and Churchill promised, disingenuously, to do what he could to further the emir's claim to Syria.

Abdullah accepted Transjordan as a stepping-stone to something bigger and better. For a man of his vaulting ambition, it had little to offer. With a population of some 300,000, it was short of land, short of water, and short of money. It had only one main link to the outside world—the Hijaz railway, built by the Turks and partially blown up during the war by T. E. Lawrence and his Arab fighters—and virtually no roads. Its capital, Amman, was a small, dusty town of fewer than 5,000 people. Since the country lacked trained officials, the emir was obliged to rely, in forming his first government, on Syrian, Iraqi, and Palestinian nationalists who began flocking to Amman to support him. Before long, he was openly bewailing his predicament:

> I came over to Trans-Jordania determined to make a bid for Syria [he complained to British officials in August 1921]. In Jerusalem I agreed to Mr Winston Churchill's policy, because I did not wish to do anything to cause trouble to Great Britain ... I understood that there was a good chance of means being found by the end of the six months to install me in Damascus. I have now lost everything ... I have had enough of this wilderness of Trans-Jordania where I am surrounded by these hateful Syrians who think only of themselves.[7]

The early period of Abdullah's rule was not a happy one. His administration was spendthrift and incompetent. It had weak control of the country's borders, which upset the French in neighbouring Syria as they grappled with unrest. Friction developed between the Transjordanians and the Arab nationalists who dominated the government. In 1924, with the country on the verge of bankruptcy, the British gave the emir an ultimatum—accept tighter imperial control, or be replaced. Abdullah had no choice but to agree. The British Resident, Henry Cox, took charge of political and financial affairs, and a British officer, Frederick Peake, assumed command of the defence force, the Arab Legion.

Abdullah chafed at the bit. But however much he might resent it, he was acutely aware that he needed British money and British protection. A new threat came from Ibn Saud, who was consolidating his hold on most of the Arabian peninsula. In 1924 his Ikhwan warriors conquered the Hijaz, ejecting Abdullah's family from their ancestral fiefdom. An Ikhwan raid into Transjordan, reaching the outskirts of Amman, was held back only by British planes and armoured cars.

What sort of man was Abdullah? He was short, shrewd, mercurial, and possessed of an impish sense of humour. Kirkbride declared him to be the only Arab he had met capable of laughing at himself. He 'spent his money as fast as it came in, sometimes faster'.[8] He was devout but not fanatical. He loved chess and was a good shot, but was not the military strategist he fancied himself to be. He was, above all, driven by restless ambition—a 'falcon trapped in a canary's cage', never content with being ruler of Transjordan, believing his destiny, and that of his family, required a grander setting for its fulfilment.[9]

Abdullah's relations with Britain were enshrined in a treaty in 1928. This gave him a notional independence but in fact underlined his complete dependence on his colonial masters, who controlled finance, foreign affairs, and defence (through their funding and training of the Arab Legion). The treaty also obliged the emir, against his will, to take halting steps towards constitutional rule. The first political parties were formed, and the first elections held, producing an acquiescent parliament. A nationalist party, the Istiqlal, emerged as an articulate voice of opposition, but with little popular support.[10]

After the award of the mandate, the British had taken two crucial decisions regarding Transjordan—to separate it from Palestine, and to declare that the provisions of the Balfour Declaration did not apply there. In other words, there would be no Jewish settlement east of the river Jordan. Zionist leaders of both left and right strongly opposed these decisions. Nevertheless they did their utmost to cultivate relations with Abdullah, and for his part he stayed in touch with senior Jewish figures in Palestine, either directly or via intermediaries, throughout his thirty-year rule. The Zionists were able to provide Jewish expertise in developing his backward country. In 1926 they won a concession to exploit the mineral resources (chiefly potash) of the

Dead Sea, and the following year a concession to start a hydroelectric project harnessing the waters of the rivers Yarmuk and Jordan. The Zionists discovered that Transjordanian landowners, including Abdullah himself, were willing to lease them land. But their efforts were blocked by the British, and caused Abdullah embarrassment when they were made public. This did not stop him pocketing sums of money paid by the Jewish Agency to secure land transactions which never materialised. These became, in effect, a regular subsidy.[11]

But in Palestine itself, despite Abdullah's efforts to cultivate support, the rising star of the nationalist movement was the mufti, Hajj Amin al-Husseini. While Abdullah remained steadfastly loyal to the British, Hajj Amin turned against them and soon became Abdullah's bitterest enemy.

In 1930 a young British officer called John Glubb arrived, tasked with ending tribal raiding, a mission he had pioneered among the bedouin of Iraq. He was to remain in Transjordan for a quarter of a century. Born in Lancashire in 1897, the son of an army officer, Glubb was outwardly unprepossessing. He was shy, spoke in a high-pitched voice, and had a crooked jaw—the result of a wound in France during the First World War. He was a devout Christian who, living among the bedouin of Iraq, had taught himself Arabic. Over the next two years, Glubb built up a force known as the Desert Patrol, which was part of the Arab Legion. Despite the scepticism of those who believed the bedouin could not be tamed, he persuaded them to police themselves—and did so, as he later remarked with pride, without a shot being fired. Glubb did much more than establish law and order in lawless parts of the country. He 'absorbed the tribes into the state, giving [them] a material stake in arguably its most important institution'. He cemented his relations with the bedouin by becoming their benefactor, regularly helping members of the Legion and their relatives gain access to education and medical treatment.[12]

The Arab Legion developed into a praetorian guard loyal to the Hashemite throne. Recruits flocked to join it not just from Transjordan but from neighbouring states. There was soon a waiting-list. But while the country was internally secure, it could not insulate itself from the growing unrest in next-door Palestine. When Arab grievances there exploded in the rebellion of 1936–39, Transjordan felt the impact. There were small-scale strikes and demonstrations in solidarity with the Palestinians. As time wore on, the destiny of the two countries became fatefully intertwined.

In late 1936 a young British journalist, Barbara Board, crossed from Palestine into Transjordan seeking an interview with the emir. She was to cover Palestine for British newspapers over the next decade and was, as we have seen, nearly killed in the bombing of the King David Hotel in 1946. For journalists as for politicians, Transjordan was something of a sideshow. But the desert kingdom offered colour—and a chance to escape the stifling political atmosphere of Palestine. As Board waited at the palace in Amman, she admired the emir's Circassian bodyguard with their 'tall kalpaks of black astrakhan, rows of cartridges across their chests, flowing black coats ... and high Russian boots'. Finally Abdullah arrived in 'a blood-red limousine'— she discovered he loved cars, and had a fleet of about twenty—and they shook hands. A photograph shows a small, smiling prince in long flowing robes and a tall, confident Englishwoman with a polka-dot dress and broad-rimmed hat. The emir asked an aide who her husband was, and was surprised to discover she was unmarried. (Abdullah learned to deal with Western women when the need arose, but retained an old-fashioned view of women's place in society.) When she asked if she might visit the royal harem, he agreed, provided she returned after Ramadan, the month of fasting.

In January 1937, Board travelled by car from Jerusalem, crossed the Jordan valley, and ascended into the hills of Moab with their 'tiny patches of red anemones ... white sweet-scented narcissi and—rarer still, but more beautiful—scarlet and white tulips'. She watched young kingfishers 'flash along the wadis', their brilliant blue plumage 'out of place amongst the tawniness and dust of the bleak hillsides'.

On arrival at the palace, she entered the harem—the first Western journalist to do so—and met the emir's first wife, his Hijazi cousin Misbah, whom he'd married in 1902. (He also had a second, younger wife, and a black mistress.) Misbah was dressed in a white robe and purple cloak. Board was struck by her smooth skin, lovely eyes, and long white hands—and by the tiny scented cigarettes she smoked.

When finally a translator arrived, the journalist discovered that Misbah's life revolved almost entirely around her family. One of the few occasions she left the palace was, once a week, to see films in Jerusalem. She was a fan of Clark Gable and Marlene Dietrich. Her grandson, Hussein—who in less than two decades was to become king—was now two years old. As she left, Board saw the little prince with his German nurse, and blew him a kiss.[13]

In 1937 the Peel Commission—charged by British officials to examine the roots of the Palestine problem—issued its report. It recommended the partition of Palestine into a Jewish state and an Arab state linked to Transjordan. For Abdullah this was a godsend, opening up the prospect that his kingdom might be expanded, and some part of his regional ambition fulfilled. But the word 'partition' was poison to Arab ears. Abdullah was the only Arab leader who favoured the idea, and was widely reviled for doing so. After initially backing partition, however, British officials backed off as they contemplated its implications. The idea would not resurface until after the Second World War, and then in an altogether new context.

On the eve of the war, Transjordan remained a backwater, and Amman's population had grown to only 20,000. There was no political opposition to speak of, and the parliament was malleable. The country was ruled by the powerful triumvirate of Abdullah, as emir; Glubb, who had taken command of the Arab Legion; and Kirkbride, who had succeeded Cox as British Resident. Their grip appeared secure. But beneath the surface the seeds of future trouble were germinating. Kirkbride was widely viewed as the power behind the throne. Glubb controlled every detail of the Legion's life, including the sensitive issue of who was promoted. The dominant British role in the country's affairs was bound to arouse growing resentment.[14]

The Second World War, like the First World War, transformed the fortunes of the Middle East. Many Arabs hoped Hitler's Germany would prevail and oust the British from the region. But Abdullah remained Britain's most dependable Arab ally and was quick to put the Arab Legion at its disposal. In the dark days of 1941, when the Germans advanced on several fronts in the Middle East, the Legion played a role in pushing them back—first in Iraq, where it helped crush a pro-German coup, and then in the Allied operation to oust Vichy forces from Syria and Lebanon.

After the war came Abdullah's reward. In 1946 he went to London to negotiate a new treaty under which the mandate was brought to an end, the country became independent, and he became king. Britain's main interests were safeguarded: the treaty allowed it to station troops in Transjordan for the next twenty-five years. The war had witnessed a significant expansion of the Arab Legion, which Britain funded with an annual subsidy of £2.5 million. This was paid, not into the exchequer in Amman, but into a bank account in London.[15] After signing the treaty, Abdullah returned home to great fanfare. Kirkbride, now British ambassador, may well have thought things would go on much as before. But in reality everything had changed. In the post-war Middle East, nationalism was in the ascendant—and Abdullah's little kingdom, subservient to a hated colonial power, looked increasingly like an anachronism.

Abdullah had never been a puppet, even though his Arab critics constantly depicted him as one. He had a mind and a will of his own, and never gave up his dream of ruling a Greater Syria—a goal the British saw as both quixotic and deeply damaging to his relations with other Arab leaders. But if the end of the war gave him greater room for manoeuvre, it also left him tied to a declining power. Britain was no longer in control of events. An anti-British nationalism was taking root among the new educated class—even among the officers of the Arab Legion, despite Glubb's best efforts to insulate the army from political infection. And the issue which did most to keep nationalist sentiment burning was the struggle for Palestine.

The Palestine trio—Britain, the Arabs, and the Jews—now became a Palestine quartet, as Transjordan became increasingly involved in its destiny. In 1947 Britain's post-war Labour government, and its Foreign Secretary Ernest Bevin, announced they were handing the problem over to the infant United Nations. In August of that year, a UN committee recommended that the territory should be partitioned, and in November its proposal was due to be put to a vote at the UN General Assembly. In this radically new situation, Abdullah sensed both danger and opportunity. Unlike most other Arab rulers, he did not underestimate the power and determination of the Jews of Palestine. On the contrary, he saw a risk that the Arabs might lose Palestine altogether, and in the chaos that followed he might lose his throne. But if part of Palestine could be saved he was determined to absorb it into his kingdom, however unpopular this might make him in the Arab world.

With the stakes so high, a secret meeting was arranged between Abdullah and Golda Meir. It was an odd choice of envoy: she was a woman sent to negotiate with a conservative Muslim leader; and she spoke no Arabic. Nevertheless they met on 17 November 1947 at a house near the river Jordan. The king proposed the creation of a Greater Transjordan, embracing the whole of Palestine, in which the Jews would have an autonomous 'Hebrew Republic'—a proposal Mrs Meir quickly rejected. But, referring to the imminent vote at the UN, she said the Zionists would accept his takeover of the part of Palestine the UN had allotted to the Arabs, provided he did nothing to prevent the establishment of the Jewish state. Here were the makings of a deal. While there was much to divide them, the two sides had a shared interest in avoiding conflict between them—and in preventing the birth of a Palestinian state under their common enemy, Hajj Amin al-Husseini.[16]

Ten days later, the UN General Assembly passed its historic resolution in support of partition, providing Zionism with a charter of international legitimacy, much as the Balfour Declaration had done thirty years earlier. This set the stage for the division of Palestine, either peacefully or by force of arms. But if Abdullah were to take over part of Palestine, he needed a green light from Britain—and at a secret meeting in London, in February 1948, Bevin supplied it. Provided the king's forces kept out of the areas the UN had allotted to the Jews, he told Abdullah's prime minister, Tawfiq Abul Huda, he had no objection to military intervention by the Arab Legion.[17]

Arab leaders, meeting under the auspices of the Arab League, decided that, once the British had left, five Arab states—Egypt, Iraq, Syria, Lebanon, and Transjordan—would send forces into Palestine to defend it from the Zionists. Abdullah was notionally commander-in-chief. But in reality the Arab states were weak and divided, motivated by their own rivalries and jealousies rather than a concerted commitment to help the Arabs of Palestine. Abdullah despised the Arab League, referring to it as 'seven heads thrust into a sack'. As pressures mounted on them to act, Arab leaders were haunted by fear of their own public opinion. 'We must invade [Palestine],' remarked one Arab foreign minister, 'otherwise the people will kill us.'[18]

Such was the tension in the run-up to Britain's withdrawal from Palestine that Kirkbride feared Abdullah was close to a nervous breakdown. On the eve of war, Ben-Gurion sent Golda Meir for a second round of talks with the king. They met, amid elaborate security precautions, at a house in Amman on 10 May 1948. Mrs Meir thought Abdullah looked depressed and nervous. He was, he told her, more constrained than before, since Transjordan was now one of five Arab states involved in the struggle for Palestine. The meeting was friendly and lasted about an hour, but without agreement.[19]

As all sides prepared for war, Glubb was wracked by anxiety. He had no illusions about the balance of forces. He had only 4,500 men at his disposal, and was deeply reluctant to throw them into a battle he feared they might lose. Nevertheless, at a few minutes to midnight on 14 May 1948, Abdullah and members of his staff stood at the eastern end of the Allenby Bridge across the river Jordan, waiting for the formal end of the Palestine mandate. Kirkbride was there to witness the scene:

> At twelve o'clock precisely the King drew his revolver, fired a symbolic shot into the air and shouted the word, 'forward'. The long column of Jordanian troops which stretched down the road behind the bridge, already had the engines of their cars ticking over and, as they moved off at the word of command, the hum of their motors rose to a roar.[20]

As the Legion took up positions in the West Bank, Glubb was well aware that, for Arabs and Jews alike, the great prize was the Old City of Jerusalem with its holy places. He was extremely reluctant to advance towards the city, but after repeated orders from Abdullah had no choice but to do so. What followed was a ten-day battle for Jerusalem, from 18 to 28 May, with heavy casualties, which ended with the Arab Legion in control of the Old City. Abdullah—so often reviled in the Arab world as a stooge of the imperialists—was, for a brief and heady moment, riding high.

There followed a four-week truce, from 11 June to 9 July, engineered by the UN's Swedish mediator, Count Folke Bernadotte. The Israelis used the truce to re-arm with weapons from the United States and the Eastern bloc. But, under strong American pressure, Britain announced it was removing British officers from the Legion and stopping arms supplies to Transjordan. The first of these steps proved only temporary, but the second left the Legion desperately short of arms and ammunition.

Having done well in round one, Abdullah and the Legion fared badly in round two. The focus of the fighting was in the area between Jerusalem and Tel Aviv, and in particular the towns of Lydda and Ramleh. When Glubb decided he had no choice but to withdraw his forces from the area, these towns fell to the Israelis and tens of thousands of refugees were expelled. Shmarya Guttman was an Israeli intelligence officer who witnessed the exodus from Lydda:

> Women walked burdened with packages and sacks on their heads. Mothers dragged children after them ... Occasionally warning shots were heard ... Occasionally you encountered a piercing look from one of the youngsters ... in the column [of refugees], and the look said: 'We have not yet surrendered. We shall return to fight you.'[21]

There was uproar in Transjordan over the abandonment of the towns, with strikes and demonstrations. Glubb was a convenient scapegoat; his car was stoned and spat at. When a large crowd of refugees from Lydda and Ramleh protested outside Abdullah's palace, the king went out, in white robes and headdress, to confront them. He pushed his way through the crowd and struck one of the ringleaders on the head. 'So you want to fight the Jews, do you?' he roared. 'Very well, there is a recruiting office for the army at the back of my house.' Those who wanted to fight should go and enlist; the rest should clear off. The crowd dispersed. Kirkbride, who observed the scene, was impressed by the king's bravery but concerned at his disregard for his own security.[22]

As the Israelis gained the upper hand, a wave of Palestinian refugees swept eastwards. The population of the West Bank doubled. (Others fled west to Gaza, whose population quadrupled.) By 1949 there were about 400,000 Palestinians in the West Bank and another 100,000 in the East Bank. Amman's population grew from 50,000 in 1948 to 120,000 in 1950.[23]

The first Arab-Israeli war ended, not with a peace settlement, but with a series of armistice agreements signed in Rhodes between January and July 1949. Jerusalem remained divided, the western part controlled by the Israelis, the eastern part—the Old City—by the Transjordanians. The two sides glared at one another across the armistice line which separated them. The Arab College, which Ahmad Samih al-Khalidi had built up so lovingly during the mandate years, stood forlornly in no man's land, looted and derelict.[24]

The war left the West Bank ravaged and traumatised:

> [It] was suffering the shock of amputation, its heart—Jerusalem—divided, its economic arteries cut, its roads to the west running nowhere … its frontier farms were ruined, its countryside swarming with exiles … and its town life clogged with not only these refugees but its own ever mounting ranks of unemployed.[25]

Abdullah embarked on a policy of gradual integration of the West Bank into his kingdom. In February 1949 all Palestinians were offered Transjordanian citizenship (a step no other Arab host country has taken, then or since). Three Palestinians were named as ministers. In April 1950, closely-fought elections were held in which both East Bankers and West Bankers took part. Henceforward, Palestinians were to play an altogether new role in the country's affairs, as politicians, businessmen, doctors, lawyers, teachers, and journalists. The new parliament voted to unite the two banks of the Jordan under Abdullah's rule. To Transjordan's population of 476,000 were now added almost a million Palestinians. The new country was named the Hashemite Kingdom of Jordan.

Abdullah had succeeded in putting his enlarged kingdom on the map, and giving it an altogether new significance in the Middle East and the wider world. But the cost was high. In ways he seems not to have foreseen, the absorption of a large new population—for the most part destitute and filled with hatred of both Israel and Britain—had profoundly destabilising consequences for Jordan. What was under way, Kirkbride reported to London, was nothing less than a revolution. He did not share Abdullah's confidence that future tensions between Palestinians and Jordanians could be avoided. The king had taken on a good deal more than he'd bargained for.[26]

On Friday, 20 July 1951, as he entered the Al-Aqsa mosque in the Old City of Jerusalem, the 69-year-old Abdullah was shot dead by a young Palestinian. For a moment, it seemed East Bankers might turn on West Bankers to exact revenge; but the tensions were contained. Abdullah was succeeded by his son Talal—who suffered from schizophrenia and after just over a year was declared unfit to rule—and in 1953 by his young grandson Hussein, who remained on the throne until 1999.

All the other Hashemite states were overthrown (Syria in 1920, the Hijaz in 1924, Iraq in 1958). Jordan alone endured. The improbable state, contrived by Churchill with the stroke of a pen one Sunday afternoon, survived.

6

OIL AND EMPIRE

In 1953 the United States and Britain joined forces to overthrow the elected prime minister of Iran, Muhammad Mossadeq. The Americans acted because they thought, mistakenly, that he was driving his country into the arms of the Soviet Union; the British because he had nationalised the Anglo-Iranian Oil Company, on which they and their empire depended for cheap and abundant fuel. Neither understood that by removing a popular nationalist and restoring an unpopular monarch they were sowing the seeds of hostility to the West which, two and a half decades later, exploded in the Islamic revolution of 1979. The events leading from Mossadeq's election in 1951 to his overthrow two years later were a brief episode in the making of the Middle East. But the fallout from them has been felt in Iran, the Middle East, and the West to this day.

Mossadeq was an unlikely revolutionary. He was born in 1882 in Ahmadabad, a village eighty-five miles from Tehran, into an aristocratic family. His father, a senior government official, died of cholera when he was only thirteen, and he grew up under the influence of his formidable mother, Najm al-Sultaneh, a princess of the Qajar dynasty which had ruled the country for almost a century. He studied law, receiving his doctorate in Switzerland, and embarked on a career as a provincial administrator. He soon acquired a reputation for opposing corruption and nepotism.

Mossadeq's political apprenticeship took place at a time when Persia (as the country was then called) was weak, divided, and the plaything of foreigners. It had become a battleground in the 'Great Game' for regional influence played out by the British and Russian empires. For Britain, Persia was an extension of India; for Russia, an extension of its southern territories. A succession of feckless Shahs sold concessions to each of them, as a means of playing off one against the other and as an easy way to raise cash. In 1901 a British businessman, William Knox D'Arcy, paid the Shah £50,000 for a concession to prospect for oil; its duration was sixty years and it covered three-quarters of the country. A solicitor from Devon, D'Arcy had made his fortune from a gold mine in Australia. But searching for oil in Persia proved far more difficult and costly than he'd anticipated, and in the early years the project seemed destined to fail.

Resentment of the power of foreigners, and of the Shahs' kowtowing to them, was one of the principal factors behind the Constitutional Revolution of 1905–06, the first successful constitutional movement in the Middle East. Each of the protagonists had external backing: the monarchists from Tsarist Russia; the revolutionaries—an alliance of intellectuals, merchants, and mullahs—from Britain. In 1906 the Shah reluctantly acquiesced to the revolutionaries' demand for a new constitution and an elected assembly. It was a turning-point in the country's destiny—and the formative moment in Mossadeq's career, when he emerged as a champion of reform and a committed constitutionalist. Although staunchly opposed to British imperialism, he was a fervent admirer of British democracy. 'In many ways,' writes the historian Ervand Abrahamian, 'he was an Iranian version of a nineteenth-century English Whig.'[1]

The Constitutional Revolution provided a benchmark for what the country wanted to be. But living up to its ideals was another matter. Successive Shahs, accustomed to unfettered autocracy, had no intention of succumbing to the new constitutional order. Members of the parliament, or Majlis, were all too often corrupt. And the two rival powers, Britain and Russia, had no intention of ending their intervention in a country both regarded as vital to their strategic interests. In 1907 they formally divided it between them, with Russia dominating the north and Britain the south.

It was Britain's influence, however, which was to prove decisive. In 1908 William Knox D'Arcy's men finally struck oil in significant quantities, and the following year a new enterprise, the Anglo-Persian Oil Company, was set up to take over his concession. It was to be no ordinary company. On the eve of the First World War, at the instigation of the First Lord of the Admiralty, the young Winston Churchill—who was committed to converting the Royal Navy from coal to oil—the British government took the unusual step of acquiring a controlling stake in it. In return for investing £2.2 million in the company, the government received fifty-one per cent of the shares and the Admiralty an assured supply of Persian oil for twenty years, at a heavily discounted price (this last part was kept secret). The agreement gave D'Arcy a lifeline.

The First World War enhanced the importance of both Persia and its oil. After the war the British Foreign Secretary, the arch-imperialist Lord Curzon, drew up the Anglo-Persian treaty of 1919, which was designed to formalise the country's new subservient status. Persians showed their opposition to the treaty in strikes and demonstrations, and eventually the Majlis refused to ratify it. But much of its substance survived. For much of the first half of the twentieth century, although never formally colonised, Persia was a British protectorate in all but name.

Two notions, held as articles of faith by Curzon, took root in official British thinking. One was that Persian oil was really British oil—the fruit of British labour and the lifeblood of British power. The other was contempt for what Curzon called 'the incomparable, incurable and inconceivable rottenness of Persian politicians'. Of Persian government ministers, he declared: 'they come and go these puppets—like performing dogs on a music-hall stage'.[2]

Such sentiments were to colour the crisis of 1951–53.

Manucher Farmanfarmaian was born in Tehran in 1917, a prince of the Qajar dynasty. His long life, recorded in a vivid memoir, witnessed the country's transition from the Qajars to their successors, the Pahlavis, and from feudal aristocracy to Islamic revolution. His father, Prince Farma Farman, a powerful landowner and politician, had a household of more than 700. They lived in a huge compound in Tehran with its own supply of water and electricity, and 'a fairyland of pools and garden hideaways' where the young Manucher could escape from his father's stern supervision. Prince Farma Farman was married eight times and by the time of his death, at the age of eighty-one, had fathered thirty-six children. A military man, with 'piercing steel-blue eyes', he ruled his household and his harem with iron discipline. 'When you are alive,' he told his children, 'fire should come out of your mouth. When you are dead, fire should come out of your grave.' The prince's sister, Najm al-Sultaneh, was Muhammad Mossadeq's mother. Though they were cousins sharing a similar aristocratic background, Muhammad and Manucher were very different characters and took very different political paths.[3]

The Qajars had grown accustomed to power and wealth based on their substantial land holdings. But their power was to be shaken and ultimately destroyed by the ascent of a new and very different dynasty. In 1921 an army officer, Reza Khan, marched into Tehran at the head of a small army. At first he left the ruler, the weak and ineffectual Ahmad Shah, on the throne. But his rise to power was unstoppable. He became minister of war in 1921, prime minister in 1923, and in 1925, after pushing Ahmad Shah into exile, he forced the Majlis to proclaim him the new Shah, thereby ending the long rule of the Qajars. Throughout, he had the quiet backing of the British, who had lost faith in the Qajars and believed the country needed a strongman.

A tough, barely literate soldier, six foot four inches tall, Reza Khan had been born in a small northern village in 1878, the son of a soldier. At the age of fifteen he had joined the Persian Cossack Brigade as a stable boy, and rose to become its commander. Now, as Reza Shah Pahlavi, he aspired to be a Persian Atatürk—a ruthless secular reformer who would drag his country into the modern world. And to some extent he was. His signal achievement was to regain control of the country from the British, the Russians, and the tribes. During his sixteen-year rule, he crushed those who stood in his way, suppressed unrest, curbed the power of the *ulema* (scholars of Islam), whom he despised, and banished Mossadeq— one of the few politicians ready to stand up to him—to his home village. In a largely illiterate country of some sixteen million, he built schools and founded the University of Tehran. He overhauled the justice system and the bureaucracy, and told women to stop wearing the veil and men the fez. (As in Turkey, the introduction of the European-style hat provoked riots.) Among his reforms, he changed the country's name from Persia to Iran. Anglo-Persian followed suit and renamed itself the Anglo-Iranian Oil Company (AIOC).

Among those who were crushed by Reza after the coup of 1921 were Prince Farma Farman and his family. The prince and his eldest son were jailed—and, according to Manucher, were only released after paying him a substantial bribe in money and land. This was a particular indignity since Reza had been employed as a soldier in the prince's personal guard.[4]

Although the British had supported his rise to power, Reza Shah was no puppet. He was a nationalist. He deeply resented the fact that Iran's oil was in the hands of foreigners. Furious to discover his revenues had slumped precipitately, he demanded negotiations with the AIOC. But, in 1932, finding the company inflexible, he startled his cabinet by announcing the cancellation of the concession. In alarm, the British government took the issue to the League of Nations, but then decided to send the company's chairman, Sir John Cadman, to Tehran. After difficult negotiations, some of them conducted face-to-face by Cadman and the Shah, a new concession was agreed in 1933. This extended the life of the concession to 1993, gave Iran higher royalties, and reduced the concession area from 500,000 square miles to 100,000. The company pledged to accelerate the 'Persianisation' of its workforce, something that would be a recurring bone of contention in the future. Despite these apparent concessions, the agreement left the company in a dominant position; indeed many Iranians wondered whether the Shah had been coerced or bribed into accepting it. The country's oil revenues nevertheless grew from £500,000 in 1920 to £4 million in 1940, enabling him to press ahead with his programme of 'slash and burn' modernisation.[5]

The Second World War enhanced Iran's strategic importance. Reza Shah proclaimed his country's neutrality. But as he had German advisers and had built up trade with Germany, in British eyes his loyalty was suspect. When the German army attacked the Soviet Union, British apprehension grew. If the Russians succumbed, Hitler's next target might be Iran and its oil. If they held out, Iran would be the vital corridor for their re-supply. So, in August 1941, Britain and the Soviet Union invaded Iran, with British forces entering from the south and the Russians from the north. They met little resistance.

The chief diplomat at the British legation—a huge, fifteen-acre compound with high walls overlooking the centre of Tehran—was Sir Reader Bullard. He had arrived in 1939 and was to stay throughout the war. He found the country and its climate a refreshing change from the torpor of Jeddah, his previous posting. His long letters, written to his wife and family back in England, reveal a man with a prodigious command of languages, a passion for correct English, and a wry sense of humour, who was devoted to the legation, its staff, and its much-admired wisteria. But they also reveal an intense, almost obsessive, dislike of Iranians, whom he castigated for 'inefficiency, corruption, and a complete lack of public spirit'.[6]

Manucher Farmanfarmaian was not alone in regarding Bullard as blunt and bullying. He had a soft spot, however, for the legation's hard-working press attaché, Ann Lambton—a woman with 'sensible opinions and sensible shoes'.[7] (Lambton was later to become, as a professor at the University of London, one of Britain's leading authorities on Iran.) It was Bullard's and Lambton's task to pave the way for the Anglo-Soviet invasion. War-time propaganda was an important weapon. 'The Persian public,' wrote Bullard, 'is much influenced by the broadcasts in Persian from Berlin ... they want to see a strong Germany as a counterweight to the Soviets, and ... they admire the Hitler sort of man.'[8] The legation used the new-born BBC Persian Service to counter German propaganda and to highlight Reza Shah's repressive and rapacious behaviour.[9] Bullard was particularly alarmed that the Shah tolerated the presence of hundreds of Germans in the country, whom the British minister regarded as a fifth column. But despite repeated demands, the Shah refused to expel them. In August 1941, Bullard and his Soviet counterpart delivered an ultimatum. 'We hammered at the Prime Minister's door at 4:15 a.m. to give him the note which told him that the two Governments could not wait any longer for the removal of the Germans.'[10]

The Shah was left in no doubt that the British were out to remove him. He was forced to abdicate, sent into exile, and died in South Africa a few years later. For Iranians, it was a moment of national humiliation. Reza Shah had been a harsh dictator but he had imposed law and order and set the country on a new path. Now they watched aghast as he was toppled—by the very power which had helped install him twenty years earlier—and their country was invaded and split into zones of occupation by their two traditional enemies. It remained occupied throughout the war.

Time and again in his letters, Bullard dwelt on the acute bread shortages that afflicted the country during the war and the occupation. The Iranians blamed the British, but Bullard held hoarding landowners and corrupt officials responsible. 'I wonder how many Persians concerned in food distribution are honest: perhaps one in a thousand.' When the shortages led to riots, he wrote despairingly: 'I do not see how the country can escape the choice between anarchy and despotism.'[11]

Once the United States entered the war, American forces arrived in Iran, too. In 1943, the leaders of the Big Three—Churchill, Stalin, and Roosevelt—chose Tehran for their famous war-time summit. (Bullard thought the Russian leader looked like a 'benevolent church-warden'.)[12] At the end of the war, British and American forces withdrew, but Stalin's did not. The Russians sought to assert their influence through the Tudeh (Masses) Party, the loyally pro-Moscow Iranian communist party which had been established in 1941. But although the party evolved into an organised and disciplined force, the Russians were never able to dominate the country, and their efforts to win an oil concession in the north were unsuccessful. In 1946 Stalin withdrew his troops, leaving Britain as the principal master of Iran's destiny.

Having removed Reza Shah, the British decided after some hesitation to accept his young son, Muhammad Reza, as the new Shah. Muhammad Reza Pahlavi, who was to remain on the throne until the Islamic revolution of 1979, was twenty-two. He was nervous and inexperienced. His father had bullied and dominated him, and he never felt equal to the task of succeeding him. Although a natural autocrat, he lacked his father's ruthlessness in controlling the country and in dealing with foreign powers.

The war brought a young British poet to Iran. Born in Northumberland in 1900, Basil Bunting had a Quaker upbringing, and in his youth led a bohemian and nomadic life as a gregarious and usually penniless writer. In 1930 he became fascinated by Persian poetry and, encouraged by his friend Ezra Pound, set out to learn classical Persian so that he could

107

translate it. ('It didn't take long,' he wrote blithely. 'It's an easy language if it's only for reading that you want it.')[13]

Bunting's knowledge of the language, albeit in its classical form,
enabled him to get a job as an interpreter with the Royal Air Force. The
RAF sent him to Iran in 1942 to help counter German influence in the
south-west of the country, near the oilfields, where the British and the
Germans were both trying to win over the dominant local tribe, the
Bakhtiaris. He came to absorb the country's culture and history, and
translated fragments of its poetry.

> The thundercloud fills meadows with heavenly beauty,
> gardens with plants, embroiders plants with petals,
> distils from its own white pearls brilliant dyes,
> makes a Tibet of hills where its shadow falls,
> San'a of our fields when it passes on to the desert.
> Wail of the morning nightingale, scent of the breeze,
> frenzy a man's bewildered, drunken heart.
> Now is the season lovers shall pant awhile,
> now is the day sets hermits athirst for wine.[14]

Bunting's work with the RAF took him to north Africa and Sicily,
but in 1944 he managed to return to Iran when, at the instigation of
the British intelligence service, MI6, the Foreign Office offered him a
job as vice-consul in Isfahan. The city instantly captivated him. He was
now diplomat, poet, and spy. As such, he lived in some style, travelled
around the country in an old Ford, smoked opium, hunted deer and
ibex, and kept an eye on what the Russians were up to. He was to
return to Iran after the war to witness the run-up to the overthrow of
Mossadeq, and perhaps play his own part in that drama.[15]

The issue which, during and after the war, most inflamed nationalist
passions and anti-Western feeling was the struggle for control of oil.
The Anglo-Iranian Oil Company was high-handed and secretive. It kept
the lion's share of profits, refused to disclose its accounts, and treated
Iranians as servants who should know their place. Its oil refinery at
Abadan, on a remote and swampy island at the northern end of the
Gulf, was Britain's biggest overseas investment. It was a little piece of
England. The flower boxes, the gardens, the cars and buses—all were
quintessentially English. The company employed 30,000 workers—

mostly Iranians and Indians—yet all the senior managers were British. Few Iranians were promoted.

For British expatriates, Abadan, for all its remoteness and the harshness of the climate, was, as one of them put it, a 'little dream world'. They formed a self-contained community. Since their servants did the shopping in the local bazaar, they had little contact with Iranians—and virtually none with the poorest of them, the workers who lived in nearby shantytowns without electricity or clean water. The British, in contrast, had swimming pools, cinemas and air conditioning. There were dinner parties, bridge evenings, amateur dramatics. They played cricket in temperatures of 120 degrees Fahrenheit. The centre of their social life was the Gymkhana Club. In its restaurant, one expatriate recalled, 'you dressed properly: white trousers, white shirt and of course in summer one always wore a topi. That was *de rigueur*.' This was the Persian Raj.[16]

Manucher Farmanfarmaian spent a week at the refinery in 1941 after returning from Europe. His father, determined to see his sons educated abroad, had sent him away at the tender age of nine; he didn't return until he was twenty-four. He went to school in France and then, at his own request, enrolled to study petroleum engineering at the University of Birmingham. The course had been established by Sir John Cadman, the AIOC chairman. Each year the company sent five or six young Iranians to Birmingham, and usually took them on after graduation. As a student of oil and a proud Iranian, Manucher was impressed by Abadan's technical marvels:

> The refinery was awe-inspiring. It was the biggest in the world and was shipping 300,000 barrels a day ... it sprang from the earth in a plethora of smokestacks and piping ... Gas burned off in towering flames ... I breathed in the heavy smell of sulfur and kerosene and felt transported ... the heat from [the] metallic sides [of the great holding tanks] shivered the air, turning the whole vast, smoking, spitting complex into a wavering mirage.

But he was shocked by the company's blatant discrimination. Even the buses were segregated. 'Not this bus, mate,' a driver shouted to him when he tried to board it. 'Mine's a British bus. No Persians allowed.' He turned down the company's offer of a job.[17]

When Cadman died in 1941, he was succeeded by his deputy, the tough autocrat Sir William Fraser. Fraser's twin characteristics were stubborn intransigence and a complete disdain for Iran and Iranians. Between 1945 and 1950 the company—the world's fourth-largest oil producer—made £250 million in profits, while in the same period Iran received £90 million in royalties.[18] What's more, it didn't hesitate to interfere in the country's internal affairs, running its own intelligence service, bribing politicians, Majlis deputies, and newspaper editors, and doing its utmost to influence Iranian government policy in its favour. Like Aramco in Saudi Arabia, it became a state within a state—and, like Aramco, successive governments back home found it difficult to rein in. Fraser's attitude was simple: he knew the oil business, and bureaucrats in Whitehall and Washington should keep their noses out of the company's affairs.

The pattern of events in the late 1940s and early 1950s was one of increasing pressure from Iranian nationalists for the country to take over its most precious natural resource—and of constant efforts by both the British and the Americans (not always in harmony) to keep that resource in Western hands. While British thinking was dominated by imperial interests, the Americans increasingly saw Iran through the prism of the Cold War. Their abiding fear was that the Soviet Union would take over the country and its oil, creating a domino effect leading to Soviet domination of the Middle East. This fear, however exaggerated, was fuelled by the rise of the Tudeh Party.

On May Day 1946, the Tudeh led an oil workers' strike at Abadan. It was the biggest industrial action yet seen in the Middle East. The government declared martial law, ordered troops to fire at demonstrators, and arrested over a thousand 'troublemakers'.[19] The company, under pressure, made a few concessions on working conditions. The strength of the communists' influence, among oil workers and increasingly among students and intellectuals, alarmed the Shah. His chance to curb them came in February 1949, when he survived an assassination attempt. Proclaiming he had been saved by divine intervention, he used the incident to assert his authority, declaring martial law and outlawing the Tudeh. The communists were driven underground, but their influence in factories, schools, and on campuses remained considerable.

Opposition—fuelled above all by the oil issue—could not be bottled up for long. In May 1949 Sir William Fraser arrived in Tehran and presented the Iranians with what was called a Supplemental Agreement—one that would supplement, but not replace, the oil concession of 1933. It offered Iran the inducement of 20 per cent royalties instead of 15 per cent. Manucher Farmanfarmaian, now a young man in his thirties, had just taken up a senior post in the finance ministry, and was involved in the meetings with Fraser. He did not warm to the 'dour Scotsman, with his baleful glare and white wispy eyebrows'. Rather than offering to negotiate, Fraser simply presented his offer as a *fait accompli*.[20]

The country badly needed the money, and the Shah badly wanted a settlement. But such was the strength of nationalist sentiment that the government delayed putting the agreement before the Majlis. Mossadeq was by now the undisputed leader of the nationalist opposition. He headed a loose coalition known as the National Front, created in October 1949 to bring together groups that wanted honest elections, a free press, and constitutional government. The front included nationalists, leftists, and mullahs, notably Ayatollah Abul-Qassem Kashani and his Islamist group, the Assembly of Muslim Warriors. Kashani, the son of a cleric, had been brought up in Najaf, in southern Iraq. Father and son had both taken part in the Iraqi revolt of 1920 against the imposition of a British mandate. The alliance between Mossadeq, a secular nationalist, and a conservative Muslim cleric was one of convenience, but while it lasted it was highly effective. Kashani derived his support, as Khomeini was later to do, from the Tehran bazaar. He was also thought to be linked to a shadowy militant group called the Fedayan-e Islam (Devotees of Islam), which assassinated those it regarded as enemies of God.

The Tudeh remained outside the National Front, and Mossadeq's relations with it were ambivalent. There was mutual mistrust. He was opposed to communism and wary of Moscow. The Tudeh, for its part, saw him as a bourgeois liberal eager to foster good relations with the United States. But on the issue of the day—the struggle for oil—the party was to throw its considerable weight behind him.

Given such opposition, the Supplemental Agreement was doomed to fail. When it was belatedly debated in the Majlis in June 1950, it was clear there was no chance it would be approved. In response, the Shah appointed a new prime minister, the former army chief of staff General

Ali Razmara. The British and the Americans backed the appointment, hoping the general would be able to push through the agreement.

But the global oil business was undergoing dramatic change, as even Fraser was forced to realise when, in the autumn of 1950, Aramco negotiated what became known as the 'fifty-fifty' agreement with the government of Saudi Arabia. The author of the deal was an American State Department official, George McGhee, himself a wealthy Texan oilman, who did not disguise his view that the AIOC's approach was badly out-of-date. When he visited London for talks with the company's officials shortly before the fifty-fifty deal was announced, he found them obdurate. 'Their reaction was very cool,' he told the BBC years later. 'Pretty much—"Mind your own business. We've had more experience of dealing with the Iranians than you. If you give them an inch, they take a mile." They turned me down.'[21]

Events in Iran were now spinning out of the control of the Shah and his foreign allies. In March 1951, after General Razmara came out against nationalisation of the oil industry, he was assassinated by a Muslim extremist. The following month the Majlis chose as prime minister Muhammad Mossadeq, now nearly seventy, but the man who had come to embody the country's desire for independence from foreign influence. His first act was to table a bill for the nationalisation of the AIOC. It was passed unanimously, and a few weeks later, on May Day 1951, the Shah felt obliged to sign it into law.

Iranians were ecstatic. It was a moment of national liberation. Manucher Farmanfarmaian, although convinced his cousin Mossadeq was being wildly reckless, shared in the glow of euphoria. 'The British Empire had been slapped in the face,' he wrote in his memoir, 'and Iran felt a triumph it had been awaiting for fifty years.' His excitement was eclipsed, however, when he discovered he had been fired from his post at the finance ministry. Although Mossadeq was a relative and a fellow aristocrat, they were politically far apart: Farmanfarmaian was regarded as too close to the Shah and to the British. A friend warned him to leave the country. He went to Venezuela, where he would later become the Shah's ambassador, and which he chose as his place of exile after the Islamic revolution.[22]

For British officials, the nationalisation of the AIOC was an act of theft and an intolerable affront. For them, it was irrelevant—although inconvenient—that Britain's Labour government was itself carrying out a programme of post-war nationalisation. Iran's actions were seen as a grave challenge to Britain's power and wealth and its position in the Middle East. The government's response was to prevent the Iranians from exporting their oil. It warned foreign tankers, whatever their nationality, not to take from Abadan what it termed 'stolen oil'. At the same time it froze Iran's assets in London (worth £25 million), restricted British exports to Iran, and sent warships to the Gulf. Hawks in the Labour government, notably the Foreign Secretary, Herbert Morrison, favoured military action. A plan to seize Abadan was drawn up, codenamed Operation Buccaneer. But the cabinet found itself split. The operation posed military risks and was liable to alienate both the United States and the Soviet Union.

The Americans were determined to head off military action. Dean Acheson, President Harry Truman's Secretary of State, asked an old friend, the veteran diplomat Averell Harriman, to go to Tehran to mediate a settlement. He did so in July 1951. It was the first of several missions, by Americans and others, designed to defuse the crisis. All failed. A series of negotiators found themselves both charmed and maddened by Mossadeq, who would receive them lying in bed in his pyjamas (he was, it was true, ailing; but he was also an incorrigible political showman). In these talks, conducted in French since the prime minster spoke little English, it quickly became apparent that he had no idea of how the oil business was run. It didn't interest him. He cared about the 'moral aspect' of the problem, he insisted, not the economic aspect. In practice, it all boiled down to control, which Britain was unwilling to cede, and without which nationalisation would be a sham. His interlocutors left exasperated.

The National Iranian Oil Company (NIOC) was set up to take the place of the AIOC. But the physical takeover of the oil facilities proceeded slowly. Mossadeq would have preferred British technicians to stay on under new management. But the AIOC told most of its British staff to leave, and its general manager, Eric Drake, did his best to disrupt Iranian efforts to keep the oilfields and the refinery operating. When the Majlis accused him of sabotage, Drake hurriedly left the country. Back in London, he was summoned to a meeting of the cabinet and gave the ministers a prescient warning: if Iran was allowed to get away with nationalising the AIOC, within five years Britain would lose the Suez Canal.

In late September 1951 Mossadeq gave the remaining British staff a week to leave. There were fewer than 300 left in Abadan, and on 4 October they gathered at the Gymkhana Club. A British cruiser, the *Mauritius*, was waiting to receive them.

> The oilmen arrived at the Gymkhana Club, spreading their luggage of suitcases, travelling bags, golf clubs, fishing rods and tennis rackets in a square for Customs inspection ... The Customs check was perfunctory, for the Persian Government had told the officials to clear the British as quickly as possible.
>
> At 1:30 p.m. the cruiser's engines began to throb, and the ship slowly glided up river, with the Royal Marines Band playing the 'Colonel Bogey' march.[23]

It was a significant moment not only for Iran and Britain but for Middle East oil. In the words of the historian Daniel Yergin, 'The first of the great Middle Eastern oil concessions was also the first to be summarily cancelled.' For the companies, it was an uncomfortable precedent.[24]

Later that month, when Britain took its case to the UN Security Council, Mossadeq decided to respond in person. In a masterly speech, he mocked the British contention that Iran's actions were a threat to world peace. It was Britain, he declared, that had sent warships to the Gulf. 'Iran has stationed no gunboats in the Thames.'

While he was in the United States, he went to Washington to see President Truman and Dean Acheson, in the hope that he could drive a wedge between the Americans and the British. Acheson has left us one of the most vivid portraits of the Iranian prime minister: 'He was small and frail with not a shred of hair on his billiard-ball head; a thin face protruded into a long beak of a nose flanked by two bright, shoe-button eyes. His whole manner and appearance was bird-like, marked by quick, nervous movements as he seemed to jump about on a perch.'[25]

Mossadeq had extensive talks with George McGhee. The two men got on. McGhee came up with a complicated formula for resolving the oil dispute, to which Mossadeq seemed to agree. But the British government shot it down as 'totally unacceptable'.[26]

British warnings that the Iranians lacked the expertise to keep the oil industry going proved unfounded. But because of the embargo, they were unable to export their oil for the next two years. Mossadeq had difficulty paying salaries. He was forced to print money, fuelling inflation, and introduced a programme of austerity. The country was not crippled, but austerity gave his critics plenty of ammunition.

In the autumn of 1951, Churchill returned to power in Britain. The old imperialist was now seventy-seven. Having attacked Labour's policy over Abadan as one of 'scuttle and run', he favoured a more robust approach to Iran and its recalcitrant prime minister. Negotiating with Mossadeq was by now viewed as futile. There was a growing feeling he had to go.

The two key figures in the planning and execution of the coup—Christopher Montague ('Monty') Woodhouse of MI6 and Kermit ('Kim') Roosevelt of the CIA—have left their own rather different accounts of what happened.[27] Woodhouse, from an aristocratic English background, had fought alongside the Greek resistance during the Second World War, and afterwards joined MI6. When he visited Iran in August 1951, he found a country 'on the brink of catastrophe'. He concluded that, with a weak Shah and a strong communist party, it would be easy prey for the Soviet Union. His object was accordingly to build up a network of supporters committed to Mossadeq's removal. In this task, his chief allies were the three Rashidian brothers, who were wealthy, ardently pro-British, and fiercely anti-Mossadeq. Manucher Farmanfarmaian had encountered two of the brothers during the Second World War, when they were well known as British agents. 'Assadollah was broad, fat-faced, and jovial; Nasrollah was a heroin addict, thin to the extreme, with yellow eyes.' With their flaunted wealth and flashy Chryslers, they looked like 'a pair of peacocks'.[28]

British agents paid the brothers £10,000 a month to build up their extensive web of contacts among the merchants of the bazaar, the clergy, the army, and among politicians, newspaper editors, and gang leaders. Woodhouse became convinced they could mobilise a coalition of forces to support the planned coup, but thought it vital to secure the active co-operation of the Americans. With Truman in the White House, and Acheson as Secretary of State, that looked unlikely.

Mossadeq returned from the United States to a hero's welcome. But in reality a number of factors were starting to work against him. His attempts to win over the Americans had failed. Though Truman and Acheson were charmed by him, they were frustrated by the failure of every attempt to resolve the crisis, for which they held him largely to blame—though, privately, they also fumed at the AIOC's stubborn refusal to compromise.

Meanwhile in Iran, as the embargo continued to bite, the political scene was becoming increasingly chaotic. Mossadeq, the committed constitutionalist, began acting in a thoroughly unconstitutional way, spurning both the Majlis and the Shah, and appealing directly to the people to get his way. In July 1952 he triggered a constitutional crisis by insisting that he should name the minister of war. This was traditionally the Shah's prerogative, and he saw the move as a direct challenge to his authority. Mossadeq's resignation, followed by the short-lived premiership of the elderly, pro-British Ahmad Qavam-Sultaneh, sparked a wave of protest that became known as the July Uprising. Mossadeq's supporters—the National Front, Kashani, and the Tudeh—united in outrage against the Shah. There were several days of strikes and demonstrations in which at least twenty-nine people were killed.

The British embassy reported that the Shah seemed 'paralysed with fear'. Qavam resigned and went into hiding. Mossadeq returned, triumphant, to the premiership. Riding high, he took steps that had previously been unthinkable. He reduced the royal budget and forced the Shah's domineering twin sister, Ashraf, to leave the country. He cut the military budget, retired over a hundred senior officers, and named a new and more sympathetic chief of the general staff. Finally, in October 1952, he broke off diplomatic relations with Britain and expelled the remaining Britons from the country. It seemed his popularity, and his powers, had no limits.

But this was illusory. Mossadeq was beginning to alienate many of his key supporters by his high-handed and undemocratic behaviour. The National Front began to crumble. Especially crucial was the defection of Kashani. The Shah and the Americans had done their utmost to win him over, partly with bribes and partly with the argument that they, not Mossadeq, represented the only viable bulwark against godless communism.

As Mossadeq's relations with the West grew more tense, so too did his relations with the Western media. Among the correspondents in Tehran in the early 1950s was the poet Basil Bunting. In 1947 MI6 had sent him back to Iran as chief of political intelligence for Persia and the Gulf at the Tehran embassy. (Bullard's legation had been upgraded to an embassy in 1944.) He had met and married the beautiful Sima, a peasant girl from a Kurdish village who was more than thirty years his junior. The embassy job was cut short by the scandal caused by his marriage to a teenager, but in 1949 *The Times* agreed to appoint him as its Tehran correspondent on a salary of £350 a year. It is likely he was still working for MI6.

In a long article for the paper in January 1950, entitled 'Persia as a Modern State', Bunting expressed sympathy for Iranian nationalism, arguing that the West had little understanding of what animated it. But following the nationalisation of the AIOC, Mossadeq became increasingly suspicious of Western coverage, and took a dislike to Bunting's reporting. He certainly did nothing to ingratiate himself with 'Dr Moussadek', describing him on 22 August 1951 as an essentially timid man who 'when he can speak for Persia ... has a martyr's temerity, marred by nervous instability and the tears he sheds as a result of it'. When a crowd gathered outside the Ritz Hotel in Tehran calling for his death, he went out and joined them in shouting 'Death to Mr Bunting!'[29]

On 7 December 1951, in a piece entitled 'Fixed Bayonets in Tehran', he described how he had seen 'more than 20 policemen beating a boy of 14 with rubber truncheons in a main street'. Soldiers arrived in trucks and drove into the crowd of students and schoolchildren, many of whom were badly hurt.

Although several Western journalists had by now been expelled, Bunting stayed on, despite efforts by the authorities to deny him residence papers and limit his movements. His last article for *The Times* was written in March 1952. The following month he was expelled—on the grounds that he had once been a consul and, by implication, was not a legitimate journalist. The Iranians probably knew of his MI6 connection. One of Bunting's biographers speculates that he may have fomented unrest among the Bakhtiaris—who, not long after his expulsion, initiated a short-lived insurgency against Mossadeq's government.[30]

It was not just journalists who left. When Mossadeq broke off relations, the British embassy staff had to go, and with them the undercover spies of MI6. The British wanted a coup, but now needed the Americans to carry it out. At this point Woodhouse and his colleagues had a stroke of luck. In November 1952, Harry Truman lost the presidency and a Republican, the war-time general Dwight Eisenhower, entered the White House. Woodhouse went straight to Washington to argue his case:

> Not wishing to be accused of trying to use the Americans to pull British chestnuts out of the fire, I decided to emphasise the Communist threat to Iran rather than the need to recover control of the oil industry. I argued that even if a settlement of the oil dispute could be negotiated with Musaddiq, which was doubtful, he was still incapable of resisting a coup by the Tudeh Party, if it were backed by Soviet support. Therefore he must be removed.[31]

The British knew that an appeal based on imperialist self-interest would not work; but an appeal to Cold War paranoia might. The Americans seemed sympathetic. But obstacles remained. There were those in the State Department who thought it better to work with Mossadeq, rather than against him, to keep out Soviet influence. At one point Churchill's Foreign Secretary, Anthony Eden, got cold feet and decided to stop funding the Rashidians (he soon changed his mind). But while the mandarins wavered, the spies kept the plot alive. The task Woodhouse had begun was now handed over to a resourceful young American, Kim Roosevelt. Roosevelt, the head of CIA operations in the Middle East, was only thirty-seven. The grandson of President Theodore Roosevelt, he'd been born in Buenos Aires, where his father had worked as a banker. After graduating from Harvard, he'd worked during the Second World War for the Office of Strategic Services, forerunner of the CIA.

In July 1953, using an assumed name, Roosevelt entered Iran by car from Iraq to take charge of what the Americans called Operation Ajax—and the British, more prosaically, Operation Boot. Among his immediate challenges was to persuade the Rashidians, who were anti-American, to work with him. At the same time he had to persuade a nervous Shah to play his part. Muhammad Reza seemed frozen in indecision, unsure whom to trust. Could he rely on the British, who had overthrown his father? Could he trust the Americans, a new and untested force on the Iranian scene? When it came to the crunch, could he be sure the people and the army would back him? He was told all he had to do was issue two decrees—one to dismiss Mossadeq and another to appoint his successor. The chosen candidate was General Fazlullah Zahedi, who was considered reliable and credible, even though the Shah didn't trust him. (He always preferred weak prime ministers to strong ones.) Ironically, the general had been kidnapped by the British during the Second World War for his pro-German sympathies and interned in Palestine. [32]

Operation Ajax began on 15 August 1953. There were in reality two coups. The first failed. When a convoy of military vehicles arrived at Mossadeq's house in Tehran at 1:30 a.m., the army officer who had come to arrest him found himself arrested instead. The prime minister had been tipped off. When news of the coup was announced, his supporters and members of the Tudeh Party took to the streets of Tehran and other cities. Crowds smashed statues of the Shah and his father. Muhammad Reza and his wife fled the country, first to Baghdad and then to Rome. It looked unlikely they would return.

Fury at the Shah for conspiring to remove the prime minister reached fever-pitch. Some of those closest to Mossadeq urged him to declare a republic. But this was something he had never sought. He was committed to a constitutional monarchy. His slogan was that the Shah should reign but not rule. Besides, the formal abolition of the monarchy risked alienating many of those who had rallied to his cause.

At this critical moment, the American ambassador, Loy Henderson, rushed back to Tehran after an absence of almost three months. (He had stayed away to distance himself from the government—and from the coup.) He went to see Mossadeq and issued him with an ultimatum: clear the streets and restore law and order, or he would advise all Americans to leave the country. He added for good measure that he could no longer recognise Mossadeq as head of government, as he understood the Shah had dismissed him. Mossadeq assured him order would be re-established, and on 18 August banned all demonstrations. Some see this as a fatal mistake. For while his supporters complied with the order, his opponents did not. [33]

After the failure of the first coup, Roosevelt had been ordered to return home. He had refused, unwilling to accept defeat. Remarkably, the second coup succeeded. Pro-Shah demonstrations began—organised by the Rashidians and paid for with CIA dollars—and gathered momentum. A group of some 300 men—weight-lifters, jugglers, and muscle-men from local sports clubs—marched from southern Tehran through the bazaar towards the north of the city. They carried knives, clubs, and portraits of the Shah. Along the way, their numbers grew as they were joined by prisoners released from jail and prostitutes from the red-light district.

The marches gave hope to Mossadeq's enemies, and added colour to the scene. But the real action was elsewhere. A significant part of the army now rallied to the Shah, and proved better organised than their opponents. Doubters may have been swayed by the widespread distribution (by Roosevelt) of the Shah's decrees dismissing Mossadeq and making Zahedi—a respected military man—the new prime minister.

A two-hour tank battle took place outside Mossadeq's house, with heavy casualties. Inside he was huddled up with his colleagues. Despite urgent pleas from supporters and from the Tudeh, he refused to sanction the use of force against his opponents. He hated bloodshed and was appalled at the prospect of civil war. In the end, weak, demoralised, and exhausted, he fled, escaping over the garden wall with a group of associates, before eventually handing himself in at a police station. By the end of August 1953, the Shah was back on the throne.

Kim Roosevelt later bragged that the coup had been cheap. 'Well, damned little money was spent,' he told the BBC. 'We had a million dollars' worth of rials—a closet safe jammed to the ceiling with rial notes—but we only used about $70,000 worth.'[34] It is an implausible claim. The Americans and the British had invested heavily in the coup: money Eisenhower and Churchill considered well spent. Three hundred lives were lost, many of them in the fierce battle around Mossadeq's house. And then there were the political costs. The coup was the work of Roosevelt and the CIA, but it had, in McGhee's words, 'a British origin and a British purpose'.[35] The Americans had indeed pulled Britain's chestnuts out of the fire. Yet, as it turned out, the overthrow of Mossadeq marked the end of the British era in Iran. From now on, the Shah's chief ally and chief supplier of arms and aid was the United States.

The AIOC's monopoly was broken. American officials decided the solution to the Iranian oil problem was to put together an international consortium in which 'Anglo-Iranian was camouflaged in the midst of a number of companies, several of them American'.[36] This wasn't straightforward. The American oilmen took a lot of persuading. In their eyes, Iran was unstable—and, besides, the world had plenty of oil. But they were browbeaten by the American government into joining forces with the AIOC. Sir William Fraser invited six of the big companies for talks in London, where a deal was finally reached in October 1954. The Iranians would in principle own the oil, but the consortium would manage the industry and buy and sell all the oil. The AIOC—now renamed British Petroleum—did well under the circumstances to emerge as the largest partner in the consortium, with a forty-per-cent stake. Another forty per cent was shared by five of the big American companies. Of the remainder, Royal Dutch/Shell got fourteen per cent, and a French company, CFP, six per cent. Fraser had driven a hard bargain; he even managed to obtain compensation for the company's losses.

Mossadeq was put on trial and defended himself with eloquence, humour, and occasional histrionics. He was sentenced to three years in solitary confinement, after which he spent the rest of his life under guard at his home in Ahmadabad, until his death in 1967 at the age of eighty-four.

The period from Mossadeq's election to his overthrow lasted a mere twenty-eight months. But it marked, writes Ervand Abrahamian, 'a defining fault line not only for Iranian history but also in the country's relations with both Britain and the United States'.[37] The coup safeguarded the West's short-term interests, but in the longer run Mossadeq survived as a nationalist icon, a symbol of Iran's rejection of Western tutelage. The coup is chiefly remembered as proof that Western powers, when confronted by a troublesome Third World leader, believed they were entitled to resort to 'régime change'. The Mossadeq episode was thus the natural precursor of the Suez crisis of 1956.

7

THE PIGEONS OF DENSHAWAI

On 13 June 1906, five British officers went pigeon-shooting in Denshawai, a village in the Nile delta. As the pigeons were not wild but domesticated, their owners objected, and attacked the officers with sticks and stones. In the ensuing confusion, one of them tried to grab one of the officers' rifles. It went off, wounding some of the villagers. Another of the officers went to get help from the British military camp some miles away, but collapsed and later died from a combination of sunstroke and concussion. Soldiers arrived and randomly arrested some seventy villagers. British officials decided an example should be made of them. Fifty-two defendants were put on trial before a special tribunal of five judges (three British and two Egyptians). Four were condemned to death for the alleged murder of the officer, two were sentenced to life with penal servitude, and eighteen others were ordered to be flogged or imprisoned.[1]

The punishments were carried out in Denshawai, and the men, women, and children of the village were made to witness the spectacle. A report in *The Times* described the scene:

> The prisoners were conveyed on carts from Shibir el Kum [the town where the trial had been held] early today, guarded by a detachment of infantry. The gallows and the whipping post followed. The cavalcade arrived at Denshawai at 7:40 ...
>
> The prisoners arrived at half-past one o'clock. One man was first hanged, and then left hanging while two others were being whipped.

Another was then hanged and two more were whipped. The remaining men sentenced to death were then hanged and the other culprits flogged. Troops were posted round the enclosure and hundreds of natives stood in a wide circle 200 yards distant. The women wailed dismally as the lash was applied and the prisoners hanged. All the condemned men met their death with calm. The executions were over at half-past four.[2]

In both Britain and Egypt the incident provoked a storm of protest. It was taken up by Bernard Shaw. Questions were asked in parliament. The Denshawai affair was a formative moment in the growth of Egyptian nationalism and cast an enduring shadow over British imperialism in the Middle East.

Britain occupied Egypt for three-quarters of a century, from 1882 to 1956. It was never a colony, and its status—technically part of the Ottoman empire, but actually part of Britain's—was ambiguous. A succession of British statesmen promised to end what they insisted was a temporary occupation. Egyptians could be forgiven for their scepticism.

The intrusion of European colonialism into the Middle East had begun with Napoleon's expedition to Egypt in 1798—an act of French expansion which directly challenged Britain and its control of the route to India. The French occupation left a cultural and intellectual legacy— French became the language of the élite, and Napoleon remained a figure of fascination—but it lasted only three years. The country was governed for most of the nineteenth century, and the first half of the twentieth, by the dynasty established by a remarkable Albanian soldier, Muhammad Ali. Although illiterate, Muhammad Ali was a man of drive and ambition widely regarded as the creator of the modern Egyptian state and a modern Egyptian identity. He ruled the country for forty-four years, during which he reorganised the army, the government, and the economy, which began to profit from the export of cotton. He introduced the railway and the telegraph, and Cairo acquired its first modern hospital. In a series of wars, he and his son Ibrahim expanded their domain into Sudan and even threatened Ottoman control of Syria—until the European powers grew alarmed and intervened to rein them in.

Muhammad Ali's successors proved distinctly less capable. His French-educated grandson Ismail, who became ruler in 1863, had himself proclaimed khedive (a Persian word for ruler), and embarked on a series of grandiose schemes—including the completion of the Suez Canal, begun in the 1850s under his predecessor, Said—which relied on punitive taxation and forced labour on a massive scale. The canal was built by a French company using Egyptian workers, many thousands of whom died during its construction. In preparation for the grand opening of the canal, Ismail turned Cairo into a vast building-site. He ordered the construction of new roads, street lighting, gardens, and an opera house—all in record time—and built Abdin Palace, an Italian-style structure with 500 rooms, set in twenty-four acres. The canal was finally inaugurated in 1869, amid great fanfare and in the presence of European royalty. But Ismail's delusions of grandeur bankrupted the country and put it in thrall to European creditors who charged exorbitant rates of interest on their loans. Desperate for cash, he sold his 44 per cent stake in the canal to the British government of Benjamin Disraeli for a paltry £4 million.

The devastating impact of Ismail's projects on the bulk of the population—the *fellahin* (peasants) who worked the land—was witnessed by Lucie Duff Gordon, an aristocratic Scottish writer and traveller who spent seven years in Egypt in the 1860s, recording in her letters a vivid impression of the country and its travails. Diagnosed at the age of thirty with tuberculosis, she moved to Egypt for her health and settled beside the Nile in Luxor, in a house on top of a ruined temple. 'Egypt,' she wrote, 'is one vast plantation where the master works his slaves without even feeding them.' Nearly one-third of Luxor's male population was carried off into forced labour, and many subsequently died of disease or exposure. 'We are eaten up by taxes,' she wrote, 'every day some new tax. Now every beast, camel, cow, sheep, donkey, horse is made to pay.' Her efforts to arouse public opinion in Britain against Ismail's 'wholesale extortion and spoliation' were unsuccessful. But they alerted him to her activities, and he had her watched and her letters intercepted. She died in Cairo in 1869, at the age of only forty-eight.[3]

The British and French governments eventually lost patience with Ismail and persuaded the Ottoman sultan to depose him in favour of his more amenable son Tawfiq. But popular resentment grew, and in 1881 found expression in a movement within the armed forces led by Colonel Ahmad Urabi. Urabi's demands—for an end to foreign interference, the promotion of Egyptians in the Turkish-dominated army and government, and the creation of a parliament and constitution—made him a national hero. They also made him a threat to the European powers. Violent riots in Alexandria, in which some fifty Europeans were killed, gave the British a pretext to intervene to crush Urabi's movement and restore power to the khedive. In 1882 their ships launched a ferocious bombardment of the city, and a few weeks later they landed troops which defeated Urabi's forces at the battle of Tel al-Kabir. The Egyptian army was disbanded, and Urabi was tried and exiled to Ceylon (present-day Sri Lanka). Thus began, without plan or intent, the British occupation of Egypt.

For a quarter of a century, from 1883 to 1907, the country was ruled by Sir Evelyn Baring (later to become Lord Cromer) under what was dubbed the 'veiled protectorate'. Tall, aloof, and impassive, Cromer was born into wealth—his grandfather had established Barings Bank in London in 1762—and he had begun his imperial career in India. During his first appointment in Egypt in the 1870s, he was a member of the Anglo-French debt commission charged with restoring order to the country's chaotic finances. But when the commission proposed drastic cuts in expenditure, it came into collision with the Khedive Ismail. Cromer resigned and returned home. When he came back with far greater authority in 1883, he did so convinced that thorough-going reform required curbing the power of the khedive. He established a system whereby, formally speaking, the khedive ruled—Tawfiq and after him his son Abbas Hilmi—and Cromer, as the British agent and consul-general, merely gave advice. But behind this façade, real power lay in the hands of Cromer and a network of British officials and advisers who, between them, ran the government, the economy, the police, and the army. He was a man who enjoyed power: 'his progresses through Cairo were of almost viceregal splendour: an elegant carriage accompanied by running grooms with white wands and flying sleeves'. A servant would run ahead shouting his name, telling people to get out of the way.[4]

Cromer effectively ruled Sudan as well as Egypt, and for much of his tenure Sudan was an unwelcome distraction. When he took up his post in 1883, the revolt of a charismatic Sudanese preacher, the Mahdi, was under way, leading to the death of General Charles Gordon ('Gordon of Khartoum') in 1885. Sudan's loss was a humiliation for the British empire, and its reconquest was not achieved until the battle of Omdurman in 1898, when the Mahdist forces were defeated. Cromer—who was what we would now call a control freak—was irked by Sudan because he could not easily subdue it and because it was a drain on his time and resources. Egypt, on the other hand, he felt he could control. Though offered other, more senior, positions elsewhere, he showed no inclination to leave.

Egyptians were conscious that the wealth and power of their country were in the hands of foreigners. In the big cities of Cairo and Alexandria, Greeks and Italians as well as British and French owned the banks, the factories, the hotels, and the department stores. By the early twentieth century, Cairo was a city of 700,000, an eighth of whom were foreigners enjoying the consular protection of the Capitulations— measures introduced by the Ottomans in the sixteenth century which gave foreigners immunity from the law and from taxation. The benefi- ciaries were not merely officials and businessmen but criminals and prostitutes who, legitimately or otherwise, had foreign passports. The abuse of the Capitulations was deeply resented.[5]

In the eyes of his admirers, Cromer was a brilliant administrator who saved the country from bankruptcy and rescued the *fellahin* from the worst aspects of exploitation. He reorganised the army, the econ- omy, and the civil service, priding himself on introducing honest and efficient administration. But his plan of modernisation was skewed. It gave no priority to education, which was allocated a mere one per cent of the budget, and favoured agriculture at the expense of industry. Egypt's cotton was used to feed the mills of Lancashire, not to develop a local textile manufacturing base. (A significant expansion of educa- tion and industry did not occur until the 1930s.)

In the eyes of Egyptians—and of British anti-imperialists of the day, such as Wilfrid Scawen Blunt—Cromer embodied the worst aspects of colonial domination and condescension. He broke the power of the khe- dives and instituted a form of one-man rule with distinct shades of mega- lomania. He regarded Egyptians as entirely unfit to govern themselves, and Islam as reactionary and unreformable. The controversy that flared up in 1906 over the pigeon-shooting incident at Denshawai—and the grotesque official over-reaction it prompted—cast a pall over his last months in Egypt. After the verdicts were handed down, he realised that a mistake had been made, but nevertheless defended them. In March 1907, in poor health, he resigned and returned to England.[6]

The outbreak of the First World War in 1914 led Britain to cast aside all pretence and declare Egypt a protectorate. The notion that the country should formally remain a sovereign part of the Ottoman empire became unthinkable once the Turks had entered the war on the side of Germany. The British reinforced their presence and imposed martial law. Cairo and the area around the Suez Canal became a huge military base. Throughout the war Egypt played a central role in Britain's Middle East campaign against the Turks.

On a bright autumn day in 1916, a young British diplomat, Laurence Grafftey-Smith, went for a stroll through the streets of Cairo. He listened to the 'raucous cornering of tramcars' and observed 'the bronze lions guarding the Kasr-el-Nil bridge' over the Nile and the nearby barracks 'where British troops paraded and kicked footballs about to the admiration of urchins'. Grafftey-Smith, who had two spells in Egypt between 1916 and 1925, was struck by the impact of the war on the growth of Egyptian nationalism. Of a population of fourteen million, over 80 per cent were *fellahin*, from whom the British recruited a war-time labour corps: 55,000 workers (the figure later rose to 125,000) who were employed in Palestine, Syria, and Iraq, as well as in Egypt itself, building roads and railways, loading and unloading goods, and performing other tasks for the British army. The recruitment, carried out by unscrupulous village headmen, left families without breadwinners. Many of those who survived the war returned home maimed and angry. The British added to these grievances by requisitioning land, cereals, and livestock. As a result, anti-British sentiment was not confined to the towns and cities but spread throughout the countryside.[7] The *fellahin* directed their resentment at Sir Reginald Wingate, the High Commissioner:

Woe on us Wingate
Who has carried off corn

Carried off cotton
Carried off camels
Carried off children
Leaving only our lives
For love of Allah, now let us alone.[8]

In Egypt as elsewhere, the end of the war and the collapse of Ottoman power raised hopes of independence. Urabi's successor, almost forty years on, was Saad Zaghlul. Of *fellah* origin, Zaghlul was born in 1859 in a village in the Nile delta and trained as a lawyer. Cromer made him minister of education in 1906. In November 1918, Zaghlul and two other prominent nationalists went to see Wingate to argue that Egyptians were entitled to a say in the post-war reordering of the Middle East. They wanted to send a delegation—or *wafd*—to present their case at the Paris peace conference. This was the origin of the Wafd Party, which, despite being led by wealthy landowners, became immensely popular as the standard-bearer of the national movement. Wingate was sympathetic to their demands, but his superiors in London, who regarded Zaghlul as an extremist, were not.

Months passed without progress. Wingate began to despair. Zaghlul was warned not to stir up nationalist sentiment. He ignored the warning. Soon afterwards, on 7 March 1919, the young Grafftey-Smith was entrusted with an envelope addressed to the British military headquarters in Cairo, giving instructions for Zaghlul and three other nationalists to be arrested and deported to Malta. 'Next morning,' he recorded, 'the Egyptian Revolution began.' There was a wave of strikes and demonstrations. Crowds attacked trains, burned railway stations, and assaulted British soldiers and civilians, as well as Greek and Armenian shopkeepers. Thirty-six British and Indian soldiers were killed and four British civilians, and perhaps a thousand Egyptians. Students were in the forefront of the protests, and also, for the first time, women.

'Long-hoarded photographs of the poor Denshawai dead, swinging by the neck in 1906, were brought out of hiding,' records Grafftey-Smith, 'and reproduced by the thousand.' The violence shook the confidence of officials in London. The prime minister, Lloyd George, sent the war hero General Allenby to take charge as High Commissioner. Within days, Allenby reversed Cromer's policy and insisted, in the face of objections from London, on an accommodation with the national-

129

ists. He called for Zaghlul and his companions to be released. As soon as they were freed, they travelled to the Paris conference.

General Edmund Allenby, nicknamed 'the Bull', was reputed to have a violent temper. But he soon earned the affection of Grafftey-Smith and his colleagues. Like all High Commissioners (and, later, ambassadors), he lived in the British residency, a grand Victorian mansion beside the Nile built by Cromer in the early 1890s. Its fine gardens stretched down to the banks of the river. Here he kept a stork. 'This morose bird was devoted to its master and would even gently unlace his shoes, but for some reason it viewed the rest of the world with vengeful animosity ... Its long beak was painful through a summer dress, and sometimes, to Allenby's amusement, visitors' hats were suddenly tweaked from their heads as they were having tea in the residency garden.'[9]

The British government despatched to Egypt a mission of enquiry under Lord Milner which arrived at the end of 1919 and stayed for three months. The nationalists boycotted its proceedings. In the end, its central recommendation—for an Anglo-Egyptian treaty which would end the protectorate and declare Egypt independent—was not implemented. Churchill and other senior figures in London regarded control of Egypt and the Suez Canal as non-negotiable. The outcome might have been different, according to Grafftey-Smith, had Zaghlul not rejected the mission's findings in public while accepting them in private.

Faced with deadlock, Allenby acted unilaterally. He introduced what has been dubbed Egypt's 'liberal experiment'—a period when the outward trappings of elections, a parliament, and a constitution were established—which was to last for thirty years. This new era began in 1922 when Allenby, using the force of his personality and the threat of resignation, persuaded the Lloyd George government to approve a declaration ending the protectorate and proclaiming Egypt independent. Four conditions were attached to safeguard British interests with regard to the Suez Canal, Sudan, the defence of Egypt against external aggression, and the protection of minorities and foreign residents. While for officials in London the declaration was a shockingly novel break with colonial tradition, for Egyptian nationalists it was vitiated by its unilateral character and by the broad scope of the conditions attached. Instead of a treaty followed by independence, there was no treaty and only nominal independence.

Egypt's ruler, Fuad, the great-grandson of Muhammad Ali, was proclaimed king. Fuad was autocratic and aloof, speaking Italian, French, and Turkish, but barely any Arabic, and holding Egyptians ('*Ces crétins!*') in low esteem. He kept a copy of Machiavelli's *The Prince* beside his bed. According to Grafftey-Smith, he had 'a pro-Italian bias in matters of opera, investment, and mistresses'. He had been shot in the throat by an aggrieved brother-in-law, and as a result would utter 'a high sporadic bark' which visitors found disconcerting. He was also rapacious, accruing land and money on a phenomenal scale.[10]

In 1923 Allenby took the next step and introduced a liberal constitution. This was followed by elections in which the Wafd achieved a resounding victory. Zaghlul became prime minister—the first native Egyptian to hold the post. But he held it for only ten months. In 1924 he visited London for talks with the new Labour government, led by his friend Ramsay MacDonald, but came away empty-handed. What finally destroyed his career was the assassination later that year of Sir Lee Stack, the British governor-general of Sudan and commander-in-chief of the Egyptian army. This was the work of a paramilitary organisation within the Wafd. Zaghlul had not ordered the killing, but Allenby held him responsible for it, arguing that his fiery speeches had stoked up a climate of violence. He presented Zaghlul with a set of punitive demands: the government was to pay a fine of £500,000; all Egyptian forces were to be withdrawn from Sudan (ruled since the turn of the century by an Anglo-Egyptian condominium); and Sudan would be allowed to increase its use of the waters of the Nile for irrigation, regardless of the (downstream) consequences for Egypt. Officials in London were unhappy at this excessive and arbitrary behaviour, and Allenby's offer of resignation, previously shelved, was now accepted. For his part, Zaghlul paid the fine, ignored the other demands, and promptly resigned. Allenby's successor, Sir George Lloyd, reverted to Cromer's policy and made sure Zaghlul never became prime minister again.[11]

Cairo was becoming a vibrantly cosmopolitan city. Its European quarter, on the right bank of the Nile, was dominated by three main communities—the Greeks, the Italians, and the Jews. The city was home to some 30,000 Jews, descendants of families who since the mid-nineteenth century had come from southern Europe and parts of the Ottoman empire to settle there.[12] Into this community Henri Curiel was born in 1914. His blind father Daniel was a wealthy banker, music-lover, and Francophile. Their home, the Villa Curiel, stood at the northern tip of the island of Zamalek, facing the European quarter. (Today it houses the Algerian embassy; later in life Henri Curiel donated it to the Algerian people as a tribute to their liberation struggle.) It had seventeen bedrooms and ten servants. The family also owned a large estate of some 250 acres in Mansouria in the Nile delta.

The young Curiel grew up among the *jeunesse dorée* of the Cairo élite. They went to foreign schools, held foreign passports (which, under the Capitulations, gave them immunity from Egyptian law), spoke French rather than Arabic, and spent their holidays in Lebanon or Syria or France. Their rich and privileged world was far removed from the lives of ordinary Egyptians. But the plight of the *fellahin* working on his father's estate—their poverty, disease, and harsh working conditions—led the young Curiel to rebel against his well-to-do upbringing. At the age of twenty-one, he scandalised his father by taking Egyptian nationality and learning Arabic. He opened a bookshop in Cairo, the Rond Point, which specialised in left-wing literature, and as the threat of Nazism grew in Germany, he and his friends became active in the anti-fascist cause.[13]

Zaghlul had died in 1927 at the age of sixty-eight. Such was the throng at his funeral that the centre of Cairo had to be shut down. The Wafd was taken over by Mustafa Nahas. He too was of *fellah* origin but lacked Zaghlul's calibre and charisma. It was Nahas who signed the Anglo-Egyptian treaty of 1936, which the Wafd portrayed as a nationalist victory. Under its terms, British troops would withdraw from the main cities, Cairo and Alexandria, and be confined to a zone around the Suez Canal; and in 1956 they would withdraw altogether. Britain would support Egypt in its bid to join the League of Nations. British advisers would be removed, leading to the Egyptianisation of the government and the armed forces. In addition, the treaty paved the way for the end of the Capitulations.

All these were gains, and some nationalists accepted the treaty as a step in the right direction. But others denounced it. Among them was an 18-year-old student, Gamal Abdul-Nasser, who castigated the Wafd for its 'calamitous decision'. Born in Alexandria in 1918 to a father whose roots were in Upper Egypt, Nasser had acquired his first taste of politics in student demonstrations. A British policeman's bullet had left a scar on his forehead. His upbringing had been unsettled. His mother, to whom he was close, had died when he was eight. The family was constantly on the move as his father, a post office clerk, was transferred from one town to another. By 1936 Nasser—a serious, reserved young man, fascinated by the French revolution—had become an ardent nationalist, although uncommitted to any particular party. He and like-minded activists demanded nothing less than a complete and unconditional end to the occupation. Nevertheless the treaty, however objectionable, was to change his life. By opening up the officer corps—hitherto dominated by a Turkish élite—to young Egyptian men of lower-middle-class background, it enabled him to enter the military, which in turn became his springboard to power.[14]

In that same year, 1936, Fuad died and was succeeded by his son Farouq. Young, good-looking, and at first immensely popular, Farouq had the advantage of speaking passable Arabic and, outwardly at least, was respectful towards Islam. What ensued was a three-cornered contest between the king, the Wafd, and the British. Farouq had a continually strained relationship with the British ambassador, Sir Miles Lampson. Six foot five, a bulky and domineering figure, Lampson held sway in Cairo for more than twelve years, from 1933 to 1946. (The treaty abolished the post of High Commissioner, and Britain's representative henceforth became an ambassador.) Lampson referred disparagingly to the king as 'the boy'; Farouq, for his part, called the ambassador the 'water buffalo'.

The outbreak of the Second World War dispelled any idea of a British withdrawal. Cairo experienced a massive invasion of British and Commonwealth soldiers and civilians. This stimulated a war-time boom and enabled a new class of profiteers to make a killing. It also created new tensions between Egyptians and Britons, many of whom treated their (unwilling) hosts with undisguised contempt. The suburb of Garden City was chosen as the headquarters of Britain's Middle East Command. The canal zone grew into a 750-square-mile network of roads, railways, encampments, and storage depots. War-time Cairo became a byword for pleasure and intrigue, and the setting for a series of novels—Olivia Manning's *Levant Trilogy*, Len Deighton's *City of Gold*, and a host of others—which captured the contrast between the bright lights of the city and the harsh reality of the war in the desert.[15]

In 1941, as German tanks drew dangerously close to Alexandria, Farouq chose Ali Maher as his prime minister, a man Lampson regarded as unacceptably pro-German. On 4 February 1942, the ambassador sent the king an ultimatum: replace the prime minister by 6 p.m. that evening, or abdicate. At 6:15 p.m. the king rejected the demand. At 9 p.m. Lampson arrived at Abdin Palace, which had been ringed with British troops, tanks, and armoured cars, to enforce his compliance. The king dithered, but eventually caved in. Lampson's diaries make it clear he thoroughly enjoyed himself.[16]

For Britain, securing a dependable government in Egypt was a war-time imperative. But the brutal manner in which Lampson imposed his authority ensured it was a moment Egyptians never forgot or forgave. The impact was especially pronounced on proud military men such as Nasser and Muhammad Neguib, who were to lead the Free Officers' coup of 1952.

> We seized power [wrote Neguib in his memoirs] because we could no longer endure the humiliations to which we, along with the rest of the Egyptian people, were being subjected ... My own breaking point was reached in 1942, when King Farouk surrendered to the then British ambassador, Sir Miles Lampson ... I was then a lieutenant-colonel of infantry. The King refused to accept my proffered resignation, and from then on I remained in the Army more or less against my will.[17]

The king duly brought in the Wafd leader, Mustafa Nahas, as prime minister. This damaged the party's credibility. Once famously anti-British, it now stood accused of coming to power on the back of British tanks. To make matters worse, Nahas and his young wife were soon tainted by allegations of corruption.

For months, Egypt's fate—and Britain's position in the Middle East—hung in the balance, as the desert war ebbed and flowed. In the tense summer of 1942, the British embassy burned its files: wags dubbed the occasion 'Ash Wednesday'. Meanwhile the owner of a patis-serie in Alexandria hedged his bets, making two cakes for display in his window: one with the words 'Viva Mussolini' and the other 'Long live

Montgomery'. He alternated them, according to the shifting fortunes of war.[18]

Among the British soldiers who frequented Henri Curiel's Rond Point bookshop was Dave Wallis, who in 1939 had abandoned an office job in London to join the army. In 1941 he was shipped out to Egypt, where he was to stay for the remainder of the war. He was twenty-four and a member of the Young Communist League, though by his own account his politics had been shaped more by Bernard Shaw than by Karl Marx. Shortly after their arrival at a military camp, he and his colleagues were addressed by a 'fatherly old sergeant-major':

> Now then, especially you drivers, just a word of advice. Traffic's very chaotic in Cairo—so, if you happen to knock down a wog, stop and back over him and finish him off. It's much the best thing to do. The British will pay compensation to his widow—more than she would ever earn in a hundred years ... It saves a lot of form-filling ... If you injure a fellow ... you wouldn't believe the paperwork you've got to go through, and you might end up on a charge anyway. So my advice is, if you knock a wog down, stop, back over him and finish him off.

Wallis later recalled the episode, in an interview, as a decisive moment in his life. His first response had been one of boiling anger at such casual racism. But then he reached the conclusion: 'This is the face of the enemy. The enemy is not some kind of Eichmann or ... sadistic lunatic brooding in a black uniform with a whip. No, this is the face of the enemy—the acceptance of received ideas, even by kindly, defeated men—this is what's got to be altered.'[19]

Corporal Wallis was wounded and transferred to the Cairo suburb of Maadi, where friends introduced him to Curiel and his circle. In the interview—and in his novel *Tram-Stop by the Nile*—he describes how local communists in Cairo, and their sympathisers in the British army, were able to carry on their political work under war-time conditions. In the novel, Hafez, an Egyptian railway worker, walks across Cairo to the European quarter, where he has never set foot, to attend a party meeting in the very bourgeois flat of one of the local communists. Meanwhile Wallis and other soldiers produced propaganda leaflets, printed on the army's Roneo machines, and took part in a mock parliament which held lively debates until it was shut down for proposing that Britain abolish the monarchy and become a people's republic.[20]

135

Curiel founded his own party, the Egyptian National Liberation Movement, in 1943. Whereas other communists took an internationalist line and downplayed national issues, Curiel correctly saw that the slogan which animated Egyptians was not 'Workers of the World, Unite' but 'Egypt for the Egyptians'. The communist movement was quarrelsome and fractured, and constantly watched by the British and Egyptian authorities. Yet Curiel managed to run a clandestine Marxist training school on his father's estate and to build up an Egyptian following—despite the inherent difficulty that working-class Egyptians were not naturally attracted to a movement led by wealthy Jewish intellectuals. What's more, Curiel spoke Arabic atrociously and had the un-Egyptian habit of wearing shorts.[21]

After the German defeat at the battle of El Alamein in October 1942, the threat to Egypt receded. But the end of the war brought fresh demands for Egyptian independence. Britain's post-war Foreign Secretary, Ernest Bevin, tried a new approach. He removed Lampson, and in October 1946—in the aftermath of a series of strikes and protests in Egypt in which the communists had played a part—reached an agreement with the prime minister, Ismail Sidqi, whereby British troops would withdraw from the towns by March 1947 and from the canal zone by September 1949. But the Wafd, now in opposition, scuppered the deal by demanding that the British withdraw from Sudan, too, and this they refused to do. (Many Egyptian nationalists favoured the union of the countries of the Nile; many Sudanese, however, wanted to be independent of both Britain and Egypt.)

Farouq was no longer the popular young king he'd been in the 1930s. Ten years into his reign, he was fat and dissolute. He had 200 cars—all of them red—as well as four palaces and innumerable mistresses. He had around him a coterie of aides who enhanced the palace's reputation for sleaze. Typical among them was Antonio Pulli, an Italian who in King Fuad's time had been the court electrician. He had mended the young Farouq's train set and befriended him to the point where they became inseparable. Once Farouq was king, he became the royal pimp.[22]

Farouq hoped an assertive foreign policy would enable him to regain his old popularity. In the run-up to the emergence of the state of Israel in 1948, he tried to put himself at the forefront of the Arab leaders calling for intervention to save Palestine from the Zionists. But in the event, the first Arab-Israeli war badly tarnished his reputation. Egyptian soldiers—among them Gamal Abdul-Nasser, by now a young army officer—blamed him and his cronies for the army's poor leadership and hopelessly inadequate weapons. The war radicalised and embittered Nasser and his fellow officers, and led them to believe it was their mission to save the Egyptian nation from weakness and humiliation. At the same time, it reinforced their belief that Egypt had an Arab destiny. A pan-Arab body, the Arab League, had been established with British support in 1944, with its headquarters in Cairo. Its raison d'être was the harnessing of Arab solidarity to solve the region's pressing problems. Egyptians increasingly felt themselves part of an awakening Arab world whose priorities were to drive out the colonialists and confront the new and unwelcome reality of Israel.

For Egypt's Jews, meanwhile, the birth of Israel marked a turning-point. Until then, as one of Curiel's colleagues remarked, 'Jerusalem simply meant the 9.45 train from Cairo station.' But after 1948 they were seen, however unjustly, as a fifth column. To make matters worse, Curiel's movement, following the line laid down by Stalin, recognised the Jewish state. Not for the first time, he was arrested and spent two years in prison. On his release in 1950 he was stripped of Egyptian nationality and deported to Italy. He eventually settled in Paris and never saw Egypt again.[23]

The communists were not the only movement to emerge in the 1930s and 1940s to rival the Wafd. There were a number of small right-wing parties, such as Misr al-Fatat (Young Egypt), some of them openly fascist. Meanwhile Egyptians who felt threatened by Westernisation, with its implicit secularising tendency, were drawn to the Muslim Brotherhood. This was a movement of revivalist Islam founded in the late 1920s by an Egyptian schoolteacher, Hasan al-Banna. The Brotherhood enjoyed great success in recruiting among the lower and middle classes. But it came into sharp conflict with the Egyptian authorities through its use of violence as a political weapon. Its covert paramilitary wing was responsible for the killing of government ministers, including at least one prime minister. In retaliation, Hasan al-Banna was assassinated in Cairo in 1949.

Anti-British sentiment grew, and with it hostility to an old order widely regarded as corrupt and decadent. In 1950 the Wafd returned to power, and the following year parliament abrogated the 1936 treaty and declared Farouq the king of Sudan as well as Egypt—declarations the British government disdainfully ignored. Since negotiation had failed, the prime minister, Nahas, tried a different tack. He covertly encouraged a guerrilla war—waged by an assortment of volunteers ranging from nationalists and Muslim Brothers to communists and gangsters—against British forces in the canal zone. This in turn provoked British reprisals. On one occasion, British tanks demolished a village, Kafr Abdou, where the fighters—the *fedayin*—were hiding. In January 1952, suspecting that Egyptian police had been helping the *fedayin*, British soldiers surrounded a police station in the canal town of Ismailia. They urged those inside to surrender, but the government in Cairo ordered them to fight on 'to the last bullet'. In a three-hour battle, between forty and fifty police were killed in what many Egyptians regarded as a massacre.

The following day, 26 January 1952—Black Saturday—furious crowds took to the streets of Cairo. The riots began spontaneously but were soon taken over by instigators. Mobs set fire to department stores, cinemas, clubs, restaurants, and the famous Shepheard's Hotel—symbols, for the most part, of foreign influence—while the police looked on. Some 700 buildings were damaged or destroyed or looted, and scores of people were killed. Soldiers did not move in to restore order until the early evening, by which time much of central Cairo was a charred ruin. Why was Farouq so slow to call in the army? One possible explanation is that he was not sure of its loyalty. As to who instigated the rioters—the palace, the communists, right-wing groups, the Muslim Brotherhood?—debate has continued to this day.

The events of Black Saturday drew a line under the thirty-year 'liberal experiment'. As the Egyptian historian Afaf Lutfi al-Sayyid observes, all the main elements of constitutional politics—the palace, the parliament, and the political parties—were by now thoroughly discredited. In 1952—as in 2013, in the aftermath of the Arab Spring—the army was seen as the saviour of the nation, a patriotic force untainted by the corruption and inadequacy of the main political actors.[24]

The burning of Cairo led directly to the decision by Nasser and his fellow officers to seize power. The Free Officers carried out their virtually bloodless coup in the early hours of 23 July 1952. Farouq and his family were sent into exile. The officers set up a Revolutionary Command Council under General Neguib. But it soon became apparent that the real power in the land was Colonel Nasser. His coup inaugurated a new era. It was the first time Egypt had been ruled by Egyptians since the days of the Pharaohs. Nasser set about ousting the old élite and creating a régime which introduced sweeping reforms in health, education, and the economy. He crushed all dissent, whether from the Wafd, the communists, or the Muslim Brotherhood. At the time of the coup, he was only thirty-four.

The new régime took a pragmatic approach to two sensitive issues. Abandoning the slogan of the 'unity of the Nile valley', it reached agreement with Britain in 1953 to let the Sudanese decide for themselves whether they wanted union with Egypt or complete independence. They opted for the latter, and Sudan became an independent republic three years later. The second and most crucial challenge to be confronted was that Britain still had 80,000 troops in the canal zone. It took more than a year to negotiate a settlement. But finally, in July 1954, agreement was reached for their phased withdrawal. The scene appeared to be set for an improvement in Anglo-Egyptian relations.

Nasser had achieved a remarkable amount in a mere two years. A political novice, he had consolidated his position at home and reached two important accords with his country's traditional enemy, Britain. He had come to power without a plan. ('It was necessary to improvise,' he remarked candidly in his book, *The Philosophy of the Revolution*.) He had shown no marked ideological preference, and was far from being militantly anti-Western or obsessed with the question of Israel. Nor had Nasser yet acquired the confidence and charisma which were his later hallmarks. As a public speaker he was nervous and lacklustre. At this stage in his career, he had every reason to focus his attention on urgent issues at home—above all, the poverty, disease, and illiteracy which scarred the lives of the majority of the Egyptian people. At the time of the coup, per capita income stood at £42 a year; the life expectancy of an Egyptian male was thirty-six; and 77 per cent of the population was illiterate.[25]

But, in the event, it was foreign policy which consumed—and almost destroyed—him, as a series of crises culminated in the great drama of 1956 over control of the Suez Canal.[26]

The first crisis was over Israel. Since the truce that had ended the first Arab-Israeli war in 1949, the border with Israel had been relatively quiet. Now it grew increasingly tense, as Egyptian *fedayin* launched raids which provoked heavy Israeli retaliation. In February 1955, an Israeli attack on Gaza killed thirty-six Egyptian and Palestinian soldiers and two civilians. Nasser could not remain passive. The incident helped fuel an arms race between the two countries. Israel had not yet established a special relationship with the United States; its main source of weapons was France, which provided it with tanks and fighter planes. Nasser cast around for an arms supplier. He would have preferred Britain or the United States. But both set conditions—a peace settlement with Israel, and membership of the Baghdad Pact, a regional alliance designed to contain Soviet influence—which he was unwilling to accept.

So he turned to the Soviet Union. His bold decision to secure arms supplies from the Eastern bloc was the result of the contacts he made at the Bandung Conference in April 1955, where he rubbed shoulders with Nehru, Tito and other champions of the new movement of the non-aligned. The so-called Czech (in fact, Soviet) arms deal boosted his standing in the Arab world. At the same time it enabled the Soviet Union to become a significant player in the Middle East, thereby aggravating Cold War tensions. Henceforth the Middle East was no longer exclusively in the West's sphere of influence.

It was in this context that the dispute over the Baghdad Pact played out. Nasser sought to counter Western efforts to draw Arab states into the pact, using as a weapon his new radio station, Voice of the Arabs. When he helped persuade Jordan not to join the pact, Anthony Eden—who had succeeded Churchill as prime minister in the spring of 1955—was furious. His antagonism grew when in March 1956 Jordan's young monarch, King Hussein, sacked Glubb, the long-serving British head of the Arab Legion. Eden, mistakenly, blamed Nasser—and vowed to destroy him.

Meanwhile Egypt sought foreign aid to build a giant dam on the Nile at Aswan, near the border with Sudan. (The first dam had been built by a British company in 1902.) This ambitious ten-year project would regulate the flow of the Nile, generate electricity, and provide an important source of irrigation. The World Bank estimated the cost at $1.3 billion. The United States and Britain initially supported the project as a means of earning Egyptian goodwill and pre-empting Soviet influence in the region. For his part, Nasser, anxious to balance his relations with East and West, was eager for Western aid.

The pace of events now quickened. On 13 June 1956, in fulfilment of the 1954 agreement, the last British soldiers left their bases in Egypt. Nasser described it, at a ceremony in Port Said, as 'the most memorable moment of a lifetime'. But the following month, the United States withdrew its support for the Aswan dam and did so in a manner which Nasser found insulting. Shortly afterwards, Britain followed suit. A week later, on the evening of 26 July 1956, he delivered his response. In a long, defiant, and brilliantly delivered speech before a packed throng in Alexandria, he asserted Egypt's right to take over the company which operated the Suez Canal. This would not only be an act of national pride; the company's revenues of $100 million a year would be used to fund the dam. Even as he spoke, under cover of night, the takeover of the company and its operations was under way.

The Suez crisis—one of the most extraordinary dramas of the end of empire—pitted a young political novice from an impoverished Third World country, facing his first big international crisis, against a shrewd veteran of British imperial policy, widely regarded as being at the height of his powers. Eden was Churchill's chosen successor and the darling of the British Conservative Party. What's more, he knew Arabic and Persian and understood, or thought he understood, the Middle East. But he faced two handicaps in the crisis that now unfolded. The first was that he was deeply ambivalent about Britain's withdrawal from empire, seeing it as in the long run unavoidable, yet acutely aware of an old guard of imperialists (Churchill prominent among them) ready to pounce on any hint of weakness. The second was that, to a greater extent than most people realised at the time, he was a sick man.

Eden immediately saw the nationalisation of the canal company as a direct threat to Britain's position in the Middle East, and set in train military action to overthrow an Egyptian leader he chose to depict, with increasing irrationality, as an Arab Hitler. But an invasion of Egypt would take time to prepare, and in the meantime his great fear was that international—and in particular American—opinion would turn against him. President Dwight Eisenhower and his Secretary of State, John Foster Dulles, were not against (in their words) 'cutting Nasser down to size'. They felt he had snubbed their earlier overtures and was now moving dangerously close to Moscow. But they thought control of the canal—on which Egypt's legal position was strong—was not the issue on which to confront him. The canal company's main shareholders were British and French, but in law it was an Egyptian entity. Egypt was accordingly entitled to nationalise it, provided it compensated the company and kept the canal open to international traffic—both of which Nasser was careful to do.

In the months that followed, as Britain prepared for military action, Dulles used a variety of devices to forestall it. One international meeting on the future management of the canal was followed by another, leading Eden to feel with mounting fury that he was being denied a credible pretext for intervention. Yet somehow convincing himself the Americans would in the end come round to supporting him, he pressed ahead with his military plans.

On 21 October 1956, at a house in Sèvres on the outskirts of Paris, a secret plot was hatched between Britain, France, and Israel for a concerted attack on Egypt. The three parties had their own reasons for collusion. For Britain, the issue was the maintenance of its position in the Middle East, and hence the preservation of its status as a great power. For the French, it was Algeria, where Nasser was supplying arms to the rebels; officials in Paris convinced themselves that by removing Nasser they would solve their Algerian problem. For Israel, the aim was to defeat its largest and most powerful Arab enemy.[27]

The invasion began on 29 October. As soon as Israeli forces had entered the Sinai peninsula, Britain and France delivered a pre-prepared ultimatum to Israel and Egypt, calling on them to cease fire and withdraw their forces ten miles from the canal. This paper-thin stratagem was designed to provide cover for the next stage of the operation, on 31 October, when British and French planes attacked Egypt's airfields. The ostensible purpose of the intervention was to separate the supposed combatants (Israel and Egypt); the real aim was to regain the canal and overthrow Nasser.

Barely a week later, on 6 November, amid international uproar and after sustained economic and diplomatic pressure from the United States, Eden was forced to accept a UN ceasefire. The grand old duke of York had marched his men half-way up the hill before marching them down again. British and French troops had advanced only a quarter of the way along the canal before being halted in their tracks.

In Iran in 1953, an act of nationalisation had led Britain and the United States to co-operate in the overthrow of a Middle East leader. In Egypt in 1956, an act of nationalisation produced a very different outcome. The Eden government colluded with France and Israel to seize back the canal and topple Nasser, but achieved neither of these aims and in the process alienated its most important ally, the United States—and distracted attention from the Soviet Union, at the very moment when it was engaged in crushing the Hungarian uprising.

Eden's career was over; Nasser's was only beginning. He had kept his nerve throughout the crisis, and now enjoyed a moment of triumph which established him as the pre-eminent Arab leader and one of the champions of a resurgent Third World. His biographer, Robert Stephens, describes Suez as 'the culminating point of modern Egyptian nationalism, making the Egyptians for the first time for seventy-five years fully masters of their own country'.[28]

For Britain, Suez has cast a long shadow. The very word connotes blunder and duplicity. Analogy with 1956 seemed apt when, in 2003, the Blair government in Britain joined the United States in invading Iraq. In its historical context, however, the crisis had another meaning. For Britain and France, it marked the demise of empire. As Nasser's confidant Muhammad Heikal remarked, the pigeons of Denshawai had come home to roost.

8

REVOLUTION ON THE TIGRIS

On 14 July 1958, Lamia Gailani, who had returned from Cambridge for her summer vacation, was sleeping with her family on the roof of their home in Baghdad. Suddenly shots rang out. Unwilling to stir herself, she turned to her brother, remarking that it must be some quarrel between two tribes. 'This is Cambridge education,' he retorted angrily. 'The idea that there are tribes on the streets of Baghdad!' In fact, as they quickly discovered, these were the first shots of a revolution which toppled the British-backed monarchy that had ruled Iraq since the end of the First World War.[1]

Britain's occupation of Iraq was a classic case of mission creep. When a 5,000-strong force of British and Indian troops landed there in November 1914, the country was under the rule of the Ottoman Turks. The force's limited aims were to weaken the Turks, who had sided with Germany in the war, impress the Arabs with a show of force, and guard the nearby oilfields of southern Persia.

The country that the invaders encountered, and of which they knew little, was a land of desert, marsh, and mountain. Its twin rivers, the Tigris and the Euphrates, gave it life, but took it too when periodically they burst their banks. The population of fewer than three million was a complex tapestry, divided ethnically between an Arab majority and the Kurds of the north, and in religious terms between a Shi'a majority and a Sunni Arab élite. There were eight or more Christian sects and a long-established Jewish community.

At first, the force made headway. Strengthened with reinforcements from India, it captured Basra, the main town in the south, and began to advance up the Tigris, facing resistance from the Turks and local Arabs, as well as sand storms, disease, and ferocious heat. But the mission was dogged by inept planning and organisation. When the Turks successfully counter-attacked, British and Indian forces retreated to Kut, a small town on the Tigris between Basra and Baghdad. Here they endured a siege of almost five months. As attempts to relieve them failed, they were reduced to eating horsemeat. In April 1916 the garrison surrendered. Of the 13,000 men who survived the siege, many died of hunger, thirst, and disease on the long march to captivity. Kut, like Gallipoli, became an emblem of British humiliation at the hands of the Turks.[2]

Yet within a year the tide had turned. In March 1917 British forces under Sir Stanley Maude captured Baghdad. Once most of the country was conquered and the Turks were in retreat, British officials had to decide what to do with a territory they had acquired almost by accident. It was not clear what form British rule would take, how long it would last, or what borders the new state would acquire. There were rival claims to the oil-rich, mainly Kurdish, province of Mosul in the north. Should it be part of Iraq, part of Turkey, or enjoy some form of Kurdish autonomy? (It was not until 1925, eight years after the fall of Baghdad, that the League of Nations awarded the area to Iraq.)

In the meantime, while foreign chancelleries debated the future of Iraq as part of the post-war settlement, on the ground the process of governing it got under way. The challenge of nation-building—creating a single entity out of three provinces of the old Ottoman empire—fell to a diverse trio of colonial officials: Sir Percy Cox, a tall, taciturn figure with fluent Arabic and a long nose, dented in a football accident; his deputy, the young Captain Arnold Wilson, a workaholic administrator steeped in the Indian Raj tradition; and Cox's Oriental Secretary, the accomplished, independent-minded, sharp-tongued Gertrude Bell.

When Bell had arrived in Baghdad in April 1917, she was already well known as a writer and traveller and as the only female member of an élite intelligence unit, the Arab Bureau in Cairo. Tall, thin, with auburn hair and piercing eyes, she had been born in County Durham in 1868, a child of the English industrial aristocracy (her grandfather, Sir Isaac Bell, was a steel magnate). She had proved herself a brilliant scholar at Oxford, a skilled mountaineer, and author of well-regarded books on the history and archaeology of the Middle East. But her parents had prevented her marrying a young diplomat whom they considered unsuitable, and the great love of her life—never consummated—was for a married man, Captain Dick Doughty-Wylie, who died heroically at Gallipoli.

Now, at the age of forty-nine, Bell was to devote the last decade of her life to the making of modern Iraq. From the first, she kept up a hectic pace:

> My programme [she wrote in April 1917] is to ride from 6 to 7.30, come in and have a bath and breakfast and then straight to the office. I don't get away until past 7 or sometimes nearly 8 ... My duties are of the most diverse kinds. We are very short-handed. I take on everything I can to spare Sir Percy—interview Bps and Aps [bishops and archbishops] of innumerable creeds, keep an open door for tribal sheikhs and messengers from the desert whose business I discover and send up in brief to Sir Percy, and then behind all this there's my real job, the gathering and sorting of information. Already the new tribal maps and tribe lists are getting into shape, and the first big batch of confidential notes on Baghdad personalities will be issued to our Political Officers tomorrow.[3]

Iraqis were not used to seeing a Western woman in such a role, especially one who went riding beside the Tigris early in the morning, sometimes stopping for a swim or for breakfast in the garden of her friend Hajji Naji, and who had her hats and dresses and fur coats sent from London and Paris. She was, it was true, a loyal servant of the *pax Britannica*, but the Iraqis warmed to her. They called her Al-Khatun (the Lady). She spoke Arabic, it was said, like a *bulbul* (nightingale), and was devoted to Iraq and tireless in reaching out to a wide range of Iraqis.

Under the post-war settlement, Britain was awarded the mandate for Iraq. This committed it, in theory, to self-determination. But there were two schools of thought among officials. Old-style imperialists, such as Arnold Wilson, favoured direct rule. Wilson underestimated the current of nationalism now entering the bloodstream of the Middle East. He believed the Arabs were incapable of self-government and that the choice lay between wise and efficient British administration and anarchy. Others, including Bell, came to favour indirect rule: the nurturing of an Arab state in which British influence would be exerted, in Cox's telling phrase, behind an 'Arab façade'.

Tension between Bell and Wilson grew after Cox was transferred to Persia, leaving Wilson in charge. Bell, caring little for official protocol, didn't hesitate to go over Wilson's head in making her views known to highly-placed friends in London. He wanted her dismissed, but knew she had Cox's backing. In the event, his rigid and old-fashioned approach to colonial rule was fatally undermined by a swelling tide of revolt. Resentment of British rule briefly united Sunni and Shi'a, who rallied at mosques to show their opposition to the mandate.

> We have had a stormy week [wrote Bell in June 1920]. The Nationalist propaganda increases. There are constant meetings in mosques ... The extremists are out for independence, without a mandate. They play for all they are worth on the passions of the mob and what with the Unity of Islam and the Rights of the Arab Race they make a fine figure. They have created a reign of terror; if anyone says boo in the bazaar it shuts like an oyster. There has been practically no business done for the last fortnight.[4]

The following month the Shi'a tribes of the south rose up in revolt. Soon much of the country was aflame. Suppressing the revolt, using British planes and reinforcements from India, cost £40 million, with a death toll of some 6,000 Iraqis and 500 British and Indian troops. Although the impulses behind the revolt were as much tribal and religious as nationalist, it shook British complacency and convinced officials they must find a different formula for governing the country. 'We had promised an Arab Government with British advisers,' reflected Bell ruefully, 'and had set up a British Government with Arab advisers.'[5]

In September 1920 Wilson was removed, and the following month Cox returned to take up the post of High Commissioner. His aim, energetically supported by Bell, was to build up, as the cornerstone of their 'Arab façade', an Arabian prince called Faisal. Faisal was a striking figure: erect and dignified, with a neatly-trimmed beard and an aura of melancholy. Born in Mecca in 1883 into the Hashemite family, which claimed descent from the Prophet Muhammad, he had spent his formative years, like his brother Abdullah, at the court of Sultan Abdul-Hamid in Istanbul. In 1908 he returned home to help his father, the

Sharif Hussein of Mecca, advance his political ambitions. During the First World War, as we have seen, Faisal led the Arab Revolt of 1916 against the Turks. After the war he was, briefly, king of Syria, until the French rudely ejected him—an experience which taught him the dangers of dependence on foreign powers. Now, a new throne awaited him. He was not Iraqi but he had the prestige of a war hero and an Arab nationalist, and the British saw him as a loyal ally.[6]

Faisal's installation was carefully stage-managed. It was thought essential to show that he enjoyed Iraqi support, so Bell helped organise a referendum which implausibly claimed that 96 per cent of Iraqis wanted him to govern them. In fact there was little warmth for him among the Kurds of the north or the Shi'a tribes in the south. And on the eve of the vote, a rival candidate was unceremoniously bundled off into exile.[7]

For Bell, king-making was a great adventure. Here is her highly-charged account of Faisal's reception at the house of the Naqib, the leading Sunni Muslim notable of Baghdad:

> The Naqib's family received us at the door and we climbed up two flights of stairs onto a roof overlooking the mosque ... A burning wind blew on us while we drank coffee and talked, till the clapping of hands in the street announced the arrival of Faisal. The Naqib got up ... and reached the head of the stairs just as Faisal's white-robed figure appeared. They embraced formally on both cheeks ... Faisal sat down between the Naqib and Sir Percy and, after a few minutes, dinner was announced ... It was a wonderful sight that dinner party. The robes and the uniforms and the crowds of servants, the ordered dignity, the real solid magnificence, and the tension of spirit which one felt all around one as one felt the burning heat of the night. For, after all, to the best of our ability, we were making history. But you may rely upon one thing—I'll never engage in creating kings again; it's too great a strain.[8]

Other British officials, in private at least, took a more jaundiced view of Faisal's grooming and elevation. Wallace Lyon had arrived in northern Iraq as a political officer in late 1917, at the age of only twenty-five, and was to remain in the country for the next twenty-six years. A soldier who had fought at the battle of the Somme, he was tough, honest, a good linguist—and tended to have a cynical view of officials in Baghdad. (He made an exception of Wilson, whom he admired, but regarded Cox as a 'cold-blooded diplomat'.)

In 1920 Lyon was based in the mainly Kurdish area of Arbil. When, like all the political officers, he received 'a top-secret coded telegram instructing us to use all our influence, personal and official, to persuade the people to elect Faisal', he was uncomfortable. He knew that it would not be a free election and that the Kurds he was supposed to persuade 'cared little for any Arab prince'. Indeed, independent-minded to the point of anarchy, they had no desire to be coerced into a predominantly Arab state. But Lyon did what he was told.[9]

His cynicism had not diminished by the time of Faisal's coronation in August 1921. For Lyon and some of the other younger officers, the solemnity of the occasion was somewhat deflated when it was discovered, during the dismantling of the throne and the platform, that they had 'been hurriedly put together from sections of Japanese beer crates with the stencil marks "Asahi" and "NAAFI" still showing on the seat'.[10]

After the coronation, an Arab government was formed, with two of Faisal's closest allies, both former officers in the Ottoman army, in key positions: Nuri al-Said as chief of staff of the new Iraqi army and Jafar al-Askari as minister of defence. A secular Arab nationalist from Syria, Sati al-Husri, took charge of the ministry of education. Of these men, all Sunni Arabs, Nuri had the most lasting influence. He was to serve as Faisal's right-hand man, and from Faisal's death to the demise of the monarchy in 1958 was the impresario of Iraqi politics.

Born in Baghdad in 1888, Nuri was of relatively modest middle-class origins. His father was a low-ranking official working for the Ottoman administration. At the age of fifteen, Nuri went to the military college in Istanbul. (The journey, by land and sea, took him forty-six days.) Here he was soon marked out as promising officer material. Jafar al-Askari, his close friend and future brother-in-law, has left an account of what life was like for young Arab officers in the dying years of the Ottoman empire:

> Supervision of the students was very strict, and we were monitored by Sultan Abdul-Hamid's notoriously suspicious spies. The mere act of reading a newspaper was deemed sufficient grounds for expulsion. Our military education absolutely excluded any training in leadership qualities. Live firing was forbidden and we were taught using obsolete rifles.

Worse was to come when the training ended and they embarked on active service. 'We young officers were to endure cruel treatment, wretched living conditions and the hardships and miseries of constant minor wars throughout our military careers in the Ottoman army.'[11]

Both men joined a secret society in Istanbul called Al-Ahd (the Covenant), which brought together Arabs critical of Ottoman rule and sympathetic to an as yet ill-defined Arab nationalism. (Branches were later formed in Baghdad and Mosul.) On the eve of the First World War, unwilling to fight for a cause he didn't believe in, Nuri deserted from the Ottoman army and later joined Faisal's forces in Arabia, where he played a prominent role in the Arab Revolt.

Nuri was gregarious, energetic, impulsive, resourceful. Early photos show a smartly-dressed, rather serious-looking army officer; later ones, a suited politician, short and stocky, with bushy eyebrows and a Charlie Chaplin moustache. Aptly described as a 'prodigious manipulator of men', Nuri was to become prime minister fourteen times; and even when not holding the office, he was adept at pulling strings. During the first decade of the monarchy, the British were not entirely sure they could trust him. But, after 1930, although occasionally exasperated by his love of intrigue (an 'imp of mischief', one official called him), they came to regard him as indispensable.[12]

Faisal had charm, dignity, and intelligence. But he was a tragic figure. He faced two inescapable dilemmas. He was tied to foreigners whose rule was deeply resented, and he had somehow to mould a new nation from the most unpromising materials. The British believed he would do their bidding, but in this they were mistaken. He instinctively understood that a monarchy imposed by an alien power had to put down roots if it was to have any hope of success. Tension between the monarch and his British backers was inevitable.

Before long there was fierce debate over a proposed treaty designed to formalise relations between Iraq and Britain. For Faisal and the Iraqis, it was a point of honour to secure a treaty between equals. For the British, what mattered was to safeguard their principal interests: above all, their military bases and access to them in time of war, and the political influence they exercised through the High Commissioner in Baghdad, the British advisers attached to government ministries, and the political officers scattered around the country.

By June 1922, the issue of the treaty had brought relations between Cox and Faisal to breaking point. Sir Percy even contemplated the king's removal. When Faisal was suddenly—and, from a British point of view, fortuitously—rushed to hospital with appendicitis, Cox took charge, arrested opposition leaders, muzzled the press, deported troublesome Shi'a clerics, and pushed through the ratification of the treaty.

For Faisal, it was an object lesson in power politics.

In March 1924, Ida and Calvin Staudt arrived in Baghdad and opened the American School for Boys. The Staudts, of German stock, were Protestant missionaries from Pennsylvania. They started the school in a large house formerly used by the British army, and quickly found that Iraqi families were eager to send their sons there. In those days the United States, lacking the stigma of a colonial power, was seen as the harbinger of science and progress. Soon the street rang to the sound of 'Work, for the Night is Coming', the hymn the boys sang at their morning assembly. The school had a Christian ethos—Bible classes were mandatory, despite some initial opposition—but it did not actively proselytise.

The Staudts were astonished at the boys' vitality as they recited Tennyson's *Idylls of the King*, put on plays in Arabic and English, performed in a chorus and orchestra, and played basketball (a novelty in Iraq). The school began with 174 students, a number that soon grew to 250. It enjoyed official support. One of the Staudts' early visitors was Jafar al-Askari, then prime minister; he returned to enroll two of his sons and a nephew.

The American School was proudly multicultural. Its language of instruction was English, but Arabic and Arab history were included in the curriculum. The students—Muslims, Christians, and Jews—included members of the Sunni Arab élite, the grandson of Baghdad's Chief Rabbi, the sons of Kurdish sheikhs, and the children of Armenian and Assyrian refugees (two Christian communities that had fled from Ottoman Turkey to take refuge in neighbouring countries). The Staudts catered for both primary and secondary students. King Faisal urged them to expand the school into a Baghdadi version of the prestigious American University of Beirut. This did not prove possible, but the Staudts were indefatigable in helping their boys find university places abroad, often in the United States.[13]

Having played her role in installing Faisal and helping create the new state, Gertrude Bell slipped into the shadows. Now in her late fifties,

Image 1: Istanbul in 1880, when the once-great Ottoman empire was already in decline; out of its ashes emerged modern Turkey–and the modern Middle East (Abdulhamid II Collection, Library of Congress)

Image 2: The Turkish nationalist and feminist Halidé Edib, addressing a crowd in Istanbul in 1919, at a perilous moment in her country's destiny (from her memoir, *The Turkish Ordeal*)

Image 3: The founder of the modern Turkish republic, Mustafa Kemal Atatürk, with his wife Latifé (Carpenter Collection, Library of Congress)

Image 4: The making of a special relationship: Ibn Saud with President Franklin Roosevelt at their war-time meeting in Egypt; on the left, translating, is Colonel William Eddy (Wikimedia Commons)

Image 5: American adventurer: Bennett Doty, who fought in Syria in the 1920s with the French Foreign Legion (from his memoir, *The Legion of the Damned*)

Image 6: Druze princess: Amal al-Atrash, who 'bowled over British officers with the accuracy and speed of a machine gun' (Wikimedia Commons)

Image 7: Damascus after the French bombed the city in 1925 to suppress an uprising: the two-day bombardment left 1,400 dead and destroyed whole quarters (Matson Collection, Library of Congress)

Image 8: The new occupiers: British soldiers guard one of the entrances to the Old City of Jerusalem in 1920 (Matson Collection, Library of Congress)

Image 9: Arab protest meeting in Jerusalem following the unrest of 1929: in the front row, second from left, is Palestine's pre-eminent Arab leader, Hajj Amin al-Husseini (Matson Collection, Library of Congress)

Image 10: Rioting in Jerusalem in 1933: as Jewish immigration increased, Arab anger grew, finally exploding in violent demonstrations (Matson Collection, Library of Congress)

Image 11: The principal leader of the Arab revolt in Palestine, Abdul-Qader al-Husseini, who was later killed in the Arab-Israeli war of 1948 (Wikimedia Commons)

Image 12: Repairing a railway line sabotaged during the Arab revolt: the revolt, lasting from 1936 to 1939, finally shattered British complacency over Palestine's future (Matson Collection, Library of Congress)

Image 13: Collective punishment: houses demolished by British troops in Jaffa during the Arab revolt (Matson Collection, Library of Congress)

Image 14: Zionist protest at the British White Paper of 1939: anxious to secure Arab good-will on the eve of the Second World War, the British limited Jewish immigration and proposed that Palestine should be independent in ten years (Matson Collection, Library of Congress)

Image 15: Jerusalem, 1946: the grim task of recovering bodies from the rubble of the King David Hotel; the attack on the hotel, in which ninety-one people died, was the most notorious exploit of the right-wing Zionist group, the Irgun (Matson Collection, Library of Congress)

Image 16: Emir Abdullah of Transjordan at a ceremony in Amman; at far left is the British officer who ran his army, General John Glubb (Matson Collection, Library of Congress)

Image 17: The Palestinian exodus of 1948: some 700,000 Arabs either fled or were driven from their homes (Wikimedia Commons)

Image 18: Oil and empire: British and Indian soldiers occupy the oil refinery at Abadan, after the Anglo-Russian invasion of Iran in 1941; the country remained under occupation for the remainder of the Second World War (Wikimedia Commons)

Image 19: The two Pahlavis: Reza Shah at the wedding of his son Muhammad, far right; when Reza, a ruthless autocrat, was removed by the British, his son found it hard to fill his shoes (Wikimedia Commons)

Image 20: Iran's combative prime minister, Muhammad Mossadeq, who challenged the might of the British empire by nationalising the Anglo-Iranian Oil Company (Wikimedia Commons)

Image 21: A pro-Mossadeq demonstration in Tehran in 1953: the overthrow of Mossadeq in a coup planned by MI6 and the CIA marked a turning-point in Iran's relations with the West (Wikimedia Commons)

Image 22: Saad Zaghlul, the immensely popular leader of the Wafd party, which challenged British rule of Egypt (Wikimedia Commons)

Image 23: The young King Farouq of Egypt: at first handsome and popular, he became fat and dissolute, and was eventually overthrown in the coup of 1952 (Library of Congress)

Image 24: Nasser with adoring crowds: after the Suez crisis of 1956, in which the British, the French, and the Israelis had sought to topple him, the Egyptian president became the unchallenged leader of the Arab world (Wikimedia Commons)

Image 25: King Faisal, the Arabian prince installed by Britain as ruler of Iraq in 1921: for all his charm and intelligence, Faisal was a tragic figure, unable to shake off the charge that he was a puppet of the British (Matson Collection, Library of Congress)

Image 26: The Iraqi regent, Abdul-Ilah, dressed in white, with his faithful minister Nuri al-Said: the two men effectively ran Iraq from 1939 until the revolution of 1958, in which the British-backed monarchy was finally swept away (Library of Congress)

Image 27: Emir Abdul-Qader, leader of one of the earliest and most sustained rebellions against French rule in Algeria (Library of Congress)

Image 28: Algerian soldiers who fought in the French army in the First World War: 25,000 lost their lives, and a further 100,000 were recruited to work in French munitions factories or in digging trenches (Bain Collection, Library of Congress)

Image 29: General Charles de Gaulle in north Africa during the Second World War: although a committed imperialist, he came to realise France had no choice but to relinquish Algeria (Library of Congress)

Image 30: Messali Hadj, leader of the first Algerian nationalist movement, which eventually lost out to its fierce rival, the FLN (Wikimedia Commons)

Image 31: Ahmed Ben Bella, the FLN leader who became the first president of independent Algeria (Wikimedia Commons)

Image 32: Sultan Ali Abdul-Karim of Lahej, one of the largest and wealthiest states in southern Arabia: the British came to regret overthrowing him (from June Knox-Mawer's memoir, *The Sultans Came to Tea*)

Image 33: End of empire: demonstrations in Aden's Crater district in 1967; Britain's humiliating withdrawal from Aden marked the virtual end of the British Raj in the Middle East (Wikimedia Commons).

unmarried, her health deteriorating, she devoted the last two years of her life to building up the new Iraq Museum, designed to house the country's archaeological treasures. She found the extremes of climate—the fiercely hot summers, the cold and sometimes wet winters—increasingly hard to bear.

> By day it's little above freezing point [she wrote in January 1925] with an excruciating north wind which cuts you like a knife. The sheep are dying like flies ... and all the young orange trees are dead. The people suffer horribly; the price of food has doubled and trebled, and they are not clad or lodged in a manner to resist cold. Lots of people in the desert and the villages have died. In the north we hear that there is deep snow. They say there has not been such prolonged cold for 40 or 50 years.[14]

Resisting pleas from her family to return to England, she insisted on staying but felt increasingly lonely and unfulfilled. 'Except for the Museum work,' she wrote to her parents in June 1926, 'life is very dull.'[15] The following month she took an overdose of sedatives and died in her sleep.

Gertrude Bell and her colleagues had invented Iraq and, against all odds, set it going as a modern state. But the period of the mandate, from 1920 to 1932, exposed inherent flaws in the structure. Under the British, just as under the Turks, the country was governed by a Sunni Arab élite. The Shi'a tribes in the south and the Kurds of the north had little reason to identify with the new state, and their deeply-rooted sense of alienation found expression in periodic revolts, put down by the new Iraqi army with help when needed from British troops and planes.

A second weakness was that relatively little was achieved in the way of economic and social development. The education system, in particular, remained stunted and the rural areas, where 70 per cent of Iraqis lived, were scarcely touched by modernisation. A third problem was that the two-stage electoral process which was introduced under the monarchy was open to manipulation. In the years to come, leading political figures—and here Nuri was the master—were able to fill parliament with their supporters. Finally, behind everything lay the inescapable reality of foreign rule. Even if the British brought with them the fruits of modernity—cars, planes, roads, the cinema, modern medicine—Iraqis were conscious that they were not masters of their own destiny.[16]

Their hopes were raised in 1929, when a Labour government came to power in Britain and pledged to support Iraq's admission to the League of Nations. This would mean that, in form at least, they would become independent. But once again there was the thorny matter of a treaty. The Anglo-Iraqi treaty of 1930 was only ratified after prolonged and heated debate. While it offered Iraqis an obvious inducement—the prospect of independence—the treaty preserved Britain's interests in all important respects; and by now these included not only its military bases but its dominant stake in the Iraqi economy. Oil had been found in substantial quantities in 1927, near Kirkuk in the north, and was jointly exploited by a group of British, French, and American companies. In the end it was Nuri, dependable as ever from Britain's point of view, who pushed through ratification of the treaty.

In October 1932, the Hashemite Kingdom of Iraq duly became the first of the mandated territories to become a sovereign independent state. But the successive political crises of the previous decade had taken their toll. In September 1933, Faisal died in Switzerland after a heart attack. Only fifty, he was worn out by the thankless tasks of nation-building. His much-quoted summing-up of the challenges he faced, set out in a memorandum addressed to the cabinet shortly before his death, is eloquent in its pessimism:

> ... with my heart filled with sadness, I have to say that it is my belief that there is no Iraqi people inside Iraq. There are only diverse groups with no national sentiments. They are filled with superstitious and false religious traditions with no common ground between them. They easily accept rumour and are prone to chaos, prepared always to revolt against any government. It is our responsibility to form out of this mass one people that we would then guide, train, and educate. Any person who is aware of the difficult circumstances of this country would appreciate the efforts that have to be exerted to achieve these objectives. [17]

Faisal's death left a void. He was succeeded by his 21-year-old son Ghazi, who lacked his father's charm and political skill and surrounded himself with a sycophantic coterie of nationalist army and air-force officers. The young king loved planes and fast cars. As war with Germany loomed, he broadcast anti-British propaganda from his own private radio station—and upset neighbouring Kuwait by claiming it as a historic part of Iraq. Among Iraqis, however, even those who disapproved of his dissolute lifestyle, Ghazi was widely admired for his nationalist spirit.

It was during his reign that, in 1936, Iraq experienced the first of many military coups, led by a Kurdish army officer, Bakr Sidqi. The British were apparently caught napping. Neither the British military nor the ambassador, wrote Wallace Lyon caustically, 'had an inkling of what was afoot'. Worse still, the British (and the monarchy) lost a staunch ally when the defence minister, Jafar al-Askari, was shot and killed while trying to mediate with the coup plotters.[18]

Under Ghazi, cabinets came and went with alarming frequency— Sidqi was ousted and killed in August 1937—and the military increasingly became the arbiter of Iraq's political life. At the same time, new and important political movements began to take root. These included a loose coalition of socialists and social democrats known by the name of its respected newspaper, *Al-Ahali* (The People). Leading figures of the Ahali group included a prominent lawyer and newspaper editor, Kamel Chadirchi, and Muhammad Hadid, an economist and graduate of the London School of Economics (and father of the award-winning architect Zaha Hadid). Also to become a significant force, although never legalised, was the Iraqi Communist Party, whose influence was at first confined to urban intellectuals but soon spread more widely.

In April 1939, Ghazi died after crashing his Buick sports car, when drunk, into an electricity pylon. Germany's shrewd and influential representative in Baghdad, Dr Fritz Grobba, put it about that the British had murdered him. In the north, Wallace Lyon witnessed the mood of hysteria—whipped up, he recorded, by a German agent—which led the British consul in Mosul to be stoned to death by an angry crowd.[19]

Since the Crown Prince, Faisal II, was only three years old, the country was ruled for the next fifteen years by his uncle, Abdul-Ilah. The 26-year-old regent sought to assert himself as a player in the political game, but he was never popular. He was famously indecisive—and besotted with all things British, including the pomp and pageantry of royalty. 'His cars, his aircraft, his clothes, his hunters, his fox-hounds, even his swans, are British, and so are many of his closest friends,' one British official remarked approvingly. Abdul-Ilah presided over an Iraqi version of the Royal Hunt, performed in full regalia, with jackals standing in for foxes.[20]

With the outbreak of the Second World War, Germany's desire for influence in Iraq acquired new significance. One day as Ida Staudt was walking across the Faisal Bridge over the Tigris, a car stopped beside her and the driver offered her a lift. It was Dr Grobba's wife. The Staudts, themselves of German stock, were uncomfortably aware of the Grobbas' well-funded propaganda activities. As they drove on, Mrs Grobba remarked with some pride, 'My husband is the most popular man in Baghdad.'

Mrs Staudt was not inclined to contradict her. The persuasive Dr Grobba was an Arabic speaker who entertained lavishly, built up close relations with the palace and with nationalist army officers, and would sit chatting with Iraqis in roadside cafés (something British officials would never dream of doing). He quietly subsidised some of Baghdad's newspapers. Bright young Iraqis were invited to Berlin, all expenses paid, where they would be reminded that Hitler was sympathetic to the Arab cause in the Middle East—and didn't like Jews.

'One evening in Baghdad,' recalled Mrs Staudt, 'we saw the house in which dwelt, openly, unmolested, and in state, the grand mufti of Jerusalem, Hajj Amin al-Husseini, brilliantly lighted and full of people as if for a special occasion.' This was not a special occasion, she was told, but a nightly occurrence. Hajj Amin, having fled from British-ruled Palestine, had taken refuge in Baghdad in October 1939. He was warmly received and for the next two years did much to foment pro-German and anti-British feeling. Ida Staudt couldn't understand why the British were doing so little to counter this blatant political offensive.[21]

In 1940 Rashid Ali al-Gailani, an ardent nationalist with pro-German sympathies, became prime minister, with Nuri as his foreign minister. When Italy joined the war on the side of Germany, the cabinet split, with Rashid Ali favouring neutrality and Nuri supporting Britain. In alarm, the British ambassador intervened with Abdul-Ilah to insist that Rashid Ali should go. He eventually resigned in January 1941, only to return to power in April, when four influential army officers carried out a successful coup.

For a full month, Iraq's fate hung in the balance. Nuri and Abdul-Ilah fled the country. The British ambassador, Sir Kinahan Cornwallis, invoking the treaty, demanded that British troops be allowed to land in Iraq, which Rashid Ali grudgingly accepted. Fighting broke out round the British base at Habbaniyah, in the desert west of Baghdad, and in the capital itself the Iraqi army placed a cordon round the British embassy. Here, for four tense weeks, Cornwallis and some 360 British residents and their staff were under siege—an episode recounted with characteristic verve by the writer and traveller Freya Stark.

> The Chancery [the political section of the embassy] is a bonfire, mountains of archives being burnt in the court, prodded by staff with rakes; black cinders like crows winged with little flames fly into the sunlight ... Petrol tins of sand everywhere for bombs; cars parked on lawn; men sprawling asleep round the blue-tiled fountain in the hall to be cool.[22]

Britain rushed reinforcements from Palestine and Transjordan, across 500 miles of desert. The rebellious army officers had been counting on German assistance, but little materialised. By the end of May it was all over. But it had been a close-run thing.

In the brief power vacuum between the fall of the Rashid Ali government and the reimposition of British control, two days of rioting broke out in Baghdad during which angry crowds made scapegoats of the long-established Jewish community. In what became known as the Farhud (the Pillage), Jewish homes and properties were robbed and damaged and some 200 Iraqi Jews were killed.

If Britain viewed the coup through the lens of war-time imperatives, Iraqis saw it very differently. There was widespread support for the dissident army officers and corresponding bitterness when, in the aftermath of the coup, a second British occupation began which was to last five years. Nuri and Abdul-Ilah returned and exacted retribution from their political enemies. Leading nationalists were arrested or deported. Up to a thousand people were interned during the remainder of the war. The four officers who had engineered the coup were executed at Abdul-Ilah's insistence—an act which shocked many Iraqis. To make matters worse, the war brought considerable hardship to ordinary people, while landowners and merchants hoarded grain and maximised their profits.

In the wake of the coup, British officials, forced to acknowledge the success of German propaganda, put new energy into public relations. Freya Stark was asked to set up an Iraqi branch of her Brotherhood of Freedom (Ikhwan al-Hurriya). Already established in Egypt, the Brotherhood sought to rally Arabs to Britain's cause under the guise of a campaign for democracy. She used her influence to get her friend (later, briefly, her husband) Stewart Perowne appointed director of publicity. But wooing Iraqi opinion was not easy. As Stark noted, 'The country was soaked in German doctrines; the Berlin radio blared from every coffee-house; the army was surly over its defeat ... and the worst of the Middle Eastern war was beginning.'

Stark was, as ever, indefatigable. She built up a following, even defying political sensitivities to recruit, by her own account, forty army officers. But some Iraqis were cynical about what they dubbed the 'Brotherhood of Freya'. According to Tamara Chalabi, whose wealthy family took part in some of its activities, its main achievement was to introduce young Iraqis to whisky.[23]

Stark and Perowne joined a colourful cast of characters drawn to war-time Baghdad as soldiers, diplomats, or spies. While Stark visited the holy places of Najaf and Karbala (as Gertrude Bell had done) to bring her message to turbanned Shi'a clerics, Perowne loved organising royal pageants, even obtaining a disused royal carriage from Buckingham Palace. For the Royal Hunt, he had bowler hats despatched by diplomatic pouch.[24] To influence opinion outside the capital, he sent out mobile cinemas. The vans would be preceded by posters announcing 'The People's Cinema is Coming Tomorrow'. At dusk 'the silver screen was unfurled in the market place, and news pictures with an Arabic commentator shown to audiences of five or eight thousand at a time'. On one occasion, when 'some Nazi prisoners were shown on the screen, a village headman rushed up and stabbed them with his dagger. It took a little while to repair the screen'.[25]

In the 1940s the Iraqi Communist Party became a significant force. This was largely due to the skilful leadership of Yusuf Salman, better known as Comrade Fahd. Fahd had been born in Baghdad in 1901 to a Christian family originally from a village near Mosul, in the north, where his father had sold pastry and cakes. When the family migrated to Basra, the young Fahd went to a church school. But at fifteen he had to abandon his education and worked as a clerk for the British forces in Basra. It is likely his political awakening came when he witnessed the rebellion of 1920. In the years that followed, he was converted to Marxism and travelled to other Arab countries, making contact with local communists. In 1935—the year of the birth of the Iraqi Communist Party—Fahd went to Moscow, where he spent two years studying at the Communist University of the Toilers of the East. On his return he rose through party ranks and in 1941 became General Secretary. During the next five years, despite a series of factional disputes, he turned the party into a well-organised movement with growing support among workers and the new urban middle class. In July 1946 it helped organise an oil workers' strike in Kirkuk, during which eight workers were killed in clashes with the police.[26]

Periods of liberalisation, when opposition parties were able to operate more freely, alternated with periods of repression (usually masterminded by Nuri). It was during one of these crackdowns, in January 1947, that Nuri had Comrade Fahd arrested. He was put on trial, accused of subverting the constitutional order, found guilty, and condemned to death. The sentence was subsequently commuted to life in prison and Fahd was sent to a jail in Kut, south of Baghdad. From here, remarkably, he continued to run the party's affairs. But in February 1949, not yet fifty, he was hanged and his body displayed in a Baghdad square.[27]

A series of events inside and outside Iraq paved the way for the monarchy's eventual demise. Popular anger was fuelled not only by social and economic grievances but by British policy in Palestine (in the run-up to the creation of Israel) and controversy over yet another agreement with Britain—the abortive Portsmouth Treaty of 1948. In January of that year, Iraqis took to the streets in a series of demonstrations which became known as the Wathbah (literally, the Leap). The Wathbah expressed a wide variety of grievances and involved students and communists—and, on one memorable occasion, a young prostitute who defied police bullets to lead a march of demonstrators over a bridge across the Tigris.

Iraqi Jews found themselves under threat. For years they had identified with different political trends—right-wing or left-wing (including the Iraqi Communist Party), pro-Zionist or anti-Zionist. But the birth of Israel in 1948 enabled their enemies to denounce them as Zionist agents, and the majority left the country.

The depth of feeling over the Palestine problem and other regional issues increasingly provoked anti-American as well as anti-British feeling, as David Newsom discovered when he arrived in Baghdad, with his wife Jean, on Christmas Eve, 1951. They found that Iraq was still in many respects a 'British domain'. Newsom was a young American diplomat working for the United States Information Agency. In a memoir, he recalls how hard it was to influence Iraqi public opinion, inflamed by the Palestine issue and anti-colonial sentiment, and largely indifferent to America's obsession with the Cold War. In June 1953, during riots in East Berlin, Newsom distributed photos to newspaper editors showing 'courageous young Germans standing in front of Soviet tanks'. None were published, and when he asked why he was told the Iraqi government had forbidden their use on the grounds that they might encourage resistance to authority.

At one point Newsom's office was burned down by an angry crowd. What began, he relates, as a demonstration by students calling for the removal of their dean was taken over by two pro-communist organisations, whose placards proclaimed 'Down with the Imperialists', 'Stalin', and 'Peace'.

> [The protestors] smashed through the steel doors and scaled the second-floor balcony. Kerosene was poured on stocks of paper and flames did the rest. Six thousand books in the library were ... set on fire ... every bit of furniture, stocks of pamphlets, files were thrown on a bonfire in the street.[28]

In May 1953 Ghazi's son, Faisal II, came of age and ascended the throne. But to all intents and purposes Nuri and Abdul-Ilah continued to run the show. Nuri's policies—repression at home and a pro-Western foreign policy abroad—were deeply unpopular. By now, when oil wealth should have begun lifting the mass of the people from poverty, disease, and illiteracy, it remained largely in the hands of a corrupt political and landowning élite. There were, to be sure, high-profile development projects—in particular, dams to harness the Tigris and the Euphrates and prevent flooding—which had a beneficial impact on Iraqi lives. But on the whole oil wealth did little to narrow the gap between rich and poor. Moreover Nuri, a paternalist to the last, did not disguise his disregard for public opinion. 'Give this man a nut, that man a banana,' he famously declared to a British diplomat, explaining his secret for governing Iraq.[29]

Once Nasser had become the champion of Arab nationalism, the days of 'the pasha and the palace'—Nuri and the monarchy—were numbered. The Suez crisis of 1956 marked the beginning of the end of British hegemony in the Middle East. 'Everyone loved Abdul-Nasser,' recalls Lamia Gailani, 'and everyone hated Nuri and the British.'[30]

Arriving in Baghdad in 1957 as Oriental Counsellor at the British embassy, Sam Falle quickly saw how precarious the situation was. The reign of the 'old gang' had gone on too long. Falle, an Arabic speaker, cultivated leading opposition figures, including Kamel Chadirchi and Muhammad Hadid, who left him in no doubt about how much the 68-year-old Nuri was feared and hated. As for Abdul-Ilah, Falle thought him a nice man but, politically speaking, 'an unqualified disaster'.

Falle had a strained relationship with the British ambassador of the day, Sir Michael Wright, but was nevertheless given free rein to travel around the country sounding out opinion. He started by making a twelve-day visit by Land Rover to the north; then made a similar visit to the south. His findings were stark. Local officials told him of 'considerable unemployment, widespread poverty, and even hunger'. Grievances were fanned by Nasser's 'all-pervasive' propaganda. All in all, there was the potential for 'serious unrest'.[31]

His warnings were not heeded. As late as April 1958, Sir Michael was assuring London that 'it is quite certain that, today, a revolutionary situation does not exist'. Three months later army officers imbued with Nasser's pan-Arabism, and with a burning hatred of the British and the monarchy, seized power.

When Lamia Gailani realised, that summer night in July 1958, that a revolution was under way, she rushed down to the street in her night-dress. For many Iraqis, it was a moment of exultation and unity: a coming-of-age. For Britain, it was something more sombre. The young king, the regent, and other members of the royal family were shot dead and Nuri was killed by an angry crowd and his body torn limb from limb. The edifice so painstakingly put together by Cox, Bell, and Wilson after the First World War came crashing down, and with it the dream of an Arab renaissance, nurtured by Britain, on the banks of the Tigris and the Euphrates.

9

THE BATTLE OF ALGIERS

In the early evening of 30 September 1956, a young Algerian woman, Zohra Drif, put on a summer dress and set off with a beach bag containing a small bomb. She was twenty-two, and a law student at the University of Algiers. After passing through a checkpoint into one of the European quarters of the city, she walked into a popular café called the Milk Bar. It was Sunday and the café was filled with mothers and children, many of whom had just come from the beach. She placed the bag under a table and left. A few minutes later the bomb went off, shattering the glass of the café, killing three people and injuring dozens more, several of them children. The Milk Bar bombing heralded the start of the battle of Algiers.[1]

The French occupation of Algeria lasted for 132 years. It began in 1830, when a French fleet of 635 ships, together with an expeditionary force of 37,000 men, sailed from Toulon and captured Algiers from its Ottoman governor. The commanders of the force had no plan to invade and occupy the country. They wanted a military victory which would help prop up the weak Bourbon monarchy. Instead, they stumbled into the fateful project of *l'Algérie française* which was to provoke one of the bloodiest and most sustained independence struggles of the end of empire.

Algeria is a vast territory, four times the size of France and the second largest country in Africa (after Sudan). Its coastal strip, where the population is concentrated, is fertile but the hinterland is an immense desert of sand and rock. In 1830 the country had a population of some three million. The French were the latest in a long line of invaders, following the Phoenicians, the Romans, the Vandals, the Byzantines, the Arabs, and the Ottoman Turks, who had annexed it in the sixteenth century and ruled it for three hundred years. The indigenous population, the Berbers, had resisted every wave of invaders. It took the Arabs over a century to conquer them. But under Arab rule they had been converted to Islam and gradually Arabised, though many retained their own Berber languages and culture.

The first significant opposition to French rule occurred in 1832, in the form of a fifteen-year rebellion led by a charismatic young warrior and Sufi scholar, Emir Abdul-Qader. The tribes of western Algeria flocked to join him, and he set up a state which at its height controlled two-thirds of the country. He created a regular army and an administration which was more modern than anything the Ottomans had established. But Abdul-Qader met his match in General Thomas Robert Bugeaud, the bluff soldier who became commander-in-chief and governor-general in 1840. Bugeaud built up the strength of his forces to over 100,000 men, and then with single-minded ruthlessness set about destroying his enemy.[2] One account of French operations in Kabylia, the eastern mountainous region which is Algeria's Berber heartland, recorded:

> ... about 18,000 trees had been cut down; houses had been burnt; women, children, and old men had been killed. The unfortunate women particularly excited cupidity by the habit of wearing silver ear-rings, leg-rings, and arm-rings ... To get them off, our soldiers used to cut off their limbs and leave them alive in this mutilated condition.[3]

Villages were razed and crops destroyed. When a thousand men of one tribe (the Ouled Riah) took refuge in caves, they were smoked out and asphyxiated.[4] Abdul-Qader finally surrendered in December 1847 and went into exile in Paris and then Damascus, where he lived on a French government pension and played an honourable part in rescuing thousands of Christians during the disorders of 1860. He died there in 1883 at the age of seventy-five.

By the time Bugeaud left in 1847, Algeria had a European settler population of 100,000. Less than half were French. The rest were from

Spain, Italy, Malta, and other parts of Europe. As colonisation got under way, its most salient features were the expropriation of Muslim land and the subordination of the Muslim majority to the interests of the settler minority. A policy of assimilation was adopted, but its meaning was ambiguous. Presented in France as a way of drawing the Muslims into French civilisation, its object was in fact, in the words of one official, 'the breakdown and dissolution of the Arab nation'.[5]

Algeria was an overwhelmingly rural society. Its social structure was both tribal and Islamic. Sufi orders and Sufi holy men (*marabouts*) were influential. The *fellahin* (peasants) lived in poverty, suffering periodic famine, drought, and disease (including malaria and cholera). There was economic progress in some sectors, as the French began to build roads and railways and introduce new crops. But the peasants were vulnerable to fluctuations in the price of their crops, and many fell into the clutches of moneylenders.

In the first four decades of the occupation, the country was under military rule. Tension built up between soldiers and settlers. Many rural areas were administered by *bureaux arabes*, run by Arabic-speaking army officers whom the settlers regarded as far too sympathetic to the Muslims. Algeria was formally annexed in 1848. It was a fateful step, creating an *Algérie française* regarded not as a colony but as an integral part of France. This was a fiction, but one to which the settlers clung tenaciously. They came into conflict with Napoleon III, nephew of Napoleon Bonaparte, who visited the country and told them they had a special responsibility towards the native population—one moreover which they were failing to fulfil. They hated him—and rejoiced in his defeat in 1870 in the Franco-Prussian war. By this time they had got their way and military rule had been replaced by a civilian régime.

The following year, to their astonishment, an insurrection flared up and spread across the country. The Muslims realised that civilian rule would mean settler rule, the further loss of their lands, and the further suppression of their rights. The revolt began in the Constantinois region east of Algiers, and was led by a Muslim notable, Muhammad al-Mokrani. The Berbers of Kabylia joined the fight, and before long the rebellion had the support of some 800,000 people. It lasted seven months. Mokrani was killed in the fighting. In the aftermath, the rebels were required to pay ruinously large fines, thousands were sentenced

to death, and over a million acres of land were confiscated. An anony-
mous Kabyle poet wrote of the bitterness left by the French in the
wake of the revolt:

> *They have sowed hatred in the villages.*
> *We store it under the ground where it remains,*
> *The abundant yield of a harvested field.*

There were other, smaller revolts against French rule, but this was
the last great uprising prior to the war of independence.[6]

The settlers acquired a degree of influence which governments in Paris
were loath to challenge. Proposals for reform which the settlers and their
supporters opposed were invariably blocked. There were certainly
Frenchmen who were not blind to what was going on. One was a former
prime minister, Jules Ferry, who in 1891 wrote a sharply critical report
on the Algerian situation. But every effort at serious reform—over land,
over political rights, over education—was rebuffed. During a fifty-year
period between 1871 and 1919, the European settlers acquired 215
million acres of land.[7] The country's main crop, which had been wheat,
became the vine. Large estates produced wine mainly for export to
France, and this proved highly profitable. Vineyards became the country's
main source of revenue, at the expense of food crops and livestock. As
the population grew, food production declined.

But, despite their image as pioneering farmers, the bulk of the *colons*
were urban rather than rural. By 1926, when the settler population had
reached 833,000, over 70 per cent of them were town-dwellers. From
1889 naturalisation had become automatic, so that European immigrants
were deemed to be part of a single 'French' community. But the culture
and temperament of the *colons* set them apart from mainland France. The
journalist Edward Behr, who came to know Algeria well, found the
European settler 'envious and resentful of the French of metropolitan
France, afraid ... of being humiliated or swindled by his quick-thinking
fellow countrymen from across the Mediterranean'. The settlers, he
wrote, were emotional, quick to anger, and displayed 'a worship of things
physical—the sun and sea, physical strength and beauty'.[8]

The colonisers did more than take the land. They dismantled the system of land ownership, destroyed the power of the tribes and the tribal

leaders, abolished the traditional Islamic legal system, and ended the charitable role of the *habous* (religious endowments). The result, writes the historian Benjamin Stora, was that 'a whole set of vital economic safety nets disappeared, leaving the rural population totally dependent on moneylenders and credit merchants during times of scarcity'.[9]

The peasants were left with few options. They could go to work on the *colons*' estates. They could migrate to the *bidonvilles* (shantytowns) that sprang up in the main cities (Oran in the west, Algiers in the centre, Constantine in the east). Or they could cross the Mediterranean and seek work in France, with all the cultural dislocation this entailed. Faced with destitution and often starvation, tens of thousands abandoned their land and villages.

The main towns were home to a small Jewish community, with roots going back millennia. In 1830 there were about 25,000 Algerian Jews, most of them poor. In 1870, as a result of the so-called Crémieux decree, all of them were given French citizenship. One effect of this was to bring the Jews into European society, setting them apart from the Muslims. Another was bitter resentment among the settlers which found expression in the 1890s in a wave of violent anti-Semitism.[10]

The First World War had a dramatic impact on both settlers and Muslims. The settlers who fought in the French army acquired a new sense of solidarity with one another, and were able to declare proudly that 22,000 of them had died for France. At the same time, 25,000 of the Algerian Muslims conscripted into the French army also fought and died, and another 100,000 were recruited to work in mainland France in munitions factories or in digging trenches. They came into contact with the French in new ways, and gained an initiation into working-class politics. For them, in Stora's words, the war marked a loss of innocence.[11]

It was in Paris rather than Algiers that the first nationalist organisation was founded in 1926. This was the Étoile Nord-Africaine (North African Star), which drew support from Algerian workers in France. It was created with the support of the French Communist Party, but in the 1930s adopted a nationalist orientation under the leadership of Messali Hadj. Born in 1898, the son of a shoemaker in Tlemcen in western Algeria, Messali was largely self-taught. He served as a soldier in France during the First World War, afterwards settling in Paris, where he became a factory worker and married a French woman, the daughter of a miner. His movement faced systematic opposition from the French authorities, and Messali found himself constantly in and out of jail. He was to become one of the leading pioneers of the independence struggle—and a bitter rival of the men who were eventually to win that struggle.

Meanwhile in Algeria itself two different currents fed the nationalist stream. One was the Islamic reformism of a group of *ulema* (scholars of Islam) led by Sheikh Abdul-Hamid Ben Badis, whose Association of Algerian Ulema was founded in 1931. The reformists, influenced by the ideas of the Egyptian scholar Muhammad Abduh, sought to combat the influence of the Sufi orders, which they considered un-Islamic. A central part of their work was the setting-up of so-called 'free schools'—independent *madrasas* which taught modern subjects in Arabic. Their motto was simple and appealing: 'Islam is our religion, Algeria is our country, Arabic is our language'.

The other trend became known as the Jeune Algérien (Young Algerian) movement. The priorities of the colonial education system were such that only one in ten Muslim children went to school; in some rural areas the figure was one in fifty.[12] But the system was geared to produce a small cadre of *évolués*, French-educated Muslims (deemed to have 'evolved' from a traditional to a modern culture) who worked as teachers or junior state officials. It was among this small élite that the movement built up a following in the early years of the twentieth century. By the 1930s its best-known leader was Ferhat Abbas, who was born in 1899 near the city of Constantine into a middle-class French-speaking family. He studied chemistry at the University of Algiers and became active in student politics. After graduating, he ran a pharmacy. 'Jovial, approachable, fluent in French and married to a French woman', Abbas with 'his trade-mark double-breasted suits exuded the air of a well-heeled provincial bourgeois'.[13] He became the leading assimilationist, setting out his position in a book called *Le Jeune Algérien*, published in 1931:

> If I had discovered the Algerian nation [he wrote], I would be a nationalist … Men who die for a patriotic ideal are honoured and respected … But I would not die for an Algerian fatherland because such a fatherland does

not exist. I cannot find it. I questioned history. I questioned the living and the dead. I searched through the cemeteries: nobody could speak to me of it. You cannot build on air.[14]

Abbas argued that the Muslims should campaign for equal rights within a French Algeria. It was a position which left him caught uneasily between the nationalists of the Étoile Nord-Africain—who opposed assimilation and wanted complete independence—and the French settlers and their supporters, who had not the slightest intention of granting the Muslims equal rights.

In June 1939 a young journalist wrote a series of newspaper articles about a famine in Kabylia.

I saw nearly 500 impoverished peasants patiently waiting their turn to receive ... wheat ... I was told that the indigents I saw had to make their 10 kilos last the entire month, supplementing their meager grain supply with roots and the stems of thistle.[15]

He saw 'children in rags fighting with dogs over some garbage', and heard that, the previous winter, 'four elderly women who had gone to collect grain handouts froze to death in the snow on their way home to their remote *douar* (village)'. Famine was not the only cause of misery. Workers were paid a pittance for a twelve-hour day: a form of slavery.

The journalist was the 26-year-old Albert Camus, who was to become (in Western eyes) Algeria's most famous son. He was born in 1913 into a *colon* family in Mondovi, a town near the border with Tunisia. His father Lucien, whose grandparents had come there from Bordeaux, had died in the battle of the Marne, in the opening weeks of the First World War. His mother, Catherine, who was of Spanish descent, was illiterate, partly deaf, and barely spoke. When he was still a boy, the family—Albert, his mother, his brother, their uncle, and their grandmother—moved to a tiny three-room apartment without electricity or running water in Belcourt, a mixed working-class district of Algiers. Camus described his early life in his last, unfinished novel, *Le Premier Homme* (The First Man), published more than thirty years after his death.

A teacher at his primary school saw young Albert's ability and helped him get a scholarship to a secondary school. He loved swimming and football, but at the age of seventeen was diagnosed with tuberculosis, from which he was to suffer all his life. He studied philosophy at the University of Algiers, graduating in 1936, and got a job as a journalist with a liberal newspaper, *Alger Républicain*. His articles on the famine upset the authorities. The paper was eventually shut down and Camus blacklisted. In March 1940, unable to get work, he set off for France in the early months of the Second World War.[16]

The war was a turning-point for France and its north African empire. The fall of France to the Germans in 1940 was a profound shock, leading to a struggle between the Vichy French and their opponents, the Free French under Charles de Gaulle. The Algerian settlers were solidly behind the Vichy leader, Marshal Pétain, and named streets and boulevards after him. For three years, Algiers was governed by a reactionary and openly anti-Semitic administration. The Crémieux decree was repealed, and Jews were expelled from the civil service and from the lycées. But a Gaullist coup in Algiers, followed by the American landings in Algeria and Morocco in 1942, changed the balance of power. De Gaulle chose Algiers as the site of his provisional government, and installed General Georges Catroux as governor-general. The Crémieux decree was reinstated. Ferhat Abbas saw the Americans as a potential ally against the French. In 1943, in response to de Gaulle's announcement of a programme of limited reforms, Abbas and Messali issued a manifesto demanding a new status for the country. Catroux had Abbas arrested. On his release in 1944, he and Messali created a new movement, the Amis du Manifeste et de la Liberté (Friends of the Manifesto and Liberty). The AML soon had 100,000 supporters. But the two leading figures wanted fundamentally different things: Abbas's aim was federation between France and a Muslim Algeria; Messali, like a growing number of Algerian nationalists, wanted independence. In 1945 the latter was deported to Brazzaville, in what was then the French Congo.

On 8 May 1945, the day the armistice was signed ending the war, a wave of violence broke out in the eastern town of Sétif which heralded a new phase in the struggle for independence. A march by Muslims in the town led to clashes, and the clashes led to a wider uprising in which some 50,000 Muslims took part. In three days of unrest, over a hundred Europeans were killed, others were wounded and mutilated, and women were raped. In the reprisals that followed, carried out by the army and by bands of settlers, some 15,000 Muslims were killed.[17] Thousands were arrested. The AML was dissolved. For many Muslims, this was the point of no return. Moderation had failed. A pattern of rebellion and reprisal was established which lasted until the French withdrawal in 1962.

Abbas made one more effort to reach a peaceful accommodation with the French, setting up the Union Démocratique du Manifeste Algérien, which called for the existence of an Algerian republic within the French Commonwealth (the Union Française, created in 1946). 'It is your last chance,' he warned the colonial power. 'We are the last barrier to secession.' The warning was not heeded. When Messali was freed, he too formed a new organisation, the Mouvement pour le Triomphe des Libertés Démocratiques. But in a political arena where the dice were loaded against them, and where elections were rigged, these groups had no prospect of success. In the words of the French historian Charles-Robert Ageron, 'Muslim Algeria saw every legal route to fundamental reform closed off.'[18] In 1952 Messali was exiled to France. His movement ultimately failed, but its legacy was significant. From its ranks the future leaders of the independence movement emerged.

On 1 November 1954, All Saints' Day, dozens of co-ordinated attacks in the Aurès mountains (in the southern Constantinois) and other parts of the country proclaimed the birth of the Front de Libération Nationale (FLN). The attacks mainly targeted French soldiers, but in one incident a young French schoolteacher and his wife were taken off a bus and shot. (The teacher bled to death, but his wife survived.) The French authorities were caught unawares. Although the overall toll from the attacks was not high—nine dead and four wounded—their synchronised nature was alarming. Moreover the 50,000 soldiers in the country were scarcely adequate to deal with a nationwide insurgency.

The nine 'historic' leaders of the FLN, as they became known, were young men in their twenties and thirties who had joined Messali Hadj's movement, but had grown impatient with the methods of the older generation of nationalists. For them, nothing could dislodge the French except armed struggle. Three of the nine had served in the French army.

171

These were men who had gone to French primary (and in some cases secondary) schools. But they were not university graduates like Ferhat Abbas. Their world was rural Algeria. In this respect, the Algerian revolution was unlike those elsewhere in the Arab world—in Syria and Lebanon, for example, where, as we have seen, nationalist resistance to the French was for the most part led by middle-class professionals.

Prominent among the nine FLN leaders was Ahmed Ben Bella. A farmer's son from Marnia, a small town close to the Moroccan border, Ben Bella was by his own account born on 25 December 1918. He studied at a French school in Tlemcen, where he first encountered discrimination. His great passion was football and he played centre-half in a local team. The teams were segregated; once a year the *colons* played the Algerians, and invariably won. Although inferior in technique, 'they were heavier and more athletic than us,' Ben Bella recalled. 'Let's face it, they were better fed.'[19]

In 1937 he entered the French army, and fought with distinction in the Second World War. De Gaulle himself pinned a medal on his chest for his role in the battle of Monte Cassino, in Italy, in 1944. 'Little did the great statesman know,' Ben Bella told his French biographer, 'that standing in front of him was the man who, eighteen years later, was to become president of the independent Republic of Algeria.'

When he returned home to Marnia the following year, Ben Bella was shocked to see the effects of wartime rationing:

Great numbers of penniless *fellaheen* had drifted into the towns from the fields, hoping for crusts of bread, a few dates, or a handful of semolina. When they found that there was nowhere to sleep in Marnia, they camped out in caves along the banks of the river, in a state of indescribable destitution.

He worked as a local councillor, but the authorities branded him a political troublemaker and apparently sent a gang to evict him from his father's land. After a shoot-out, he fled to Algiers in 1947 and joined the underground movement that was to become the FLN. After an attack on a post office in Oran, designed to raise funds for the movement, he was caught and imprisoned, but managed to escape, eventually reaching Cairo, where he became the external leader of the FLN.[20]

From the start, the leadership projected an image of a single, unified nation at war. The French had divided and ruled; the Algerians must unite and win. But this insistence on unity, however understandable, masked the very real differences between the internal leadership (under a Kabyle, Abbane Ramdane) and the external leadership (under Ben Bella in Cairo); between the more religious and the more secular; and between Arabs and Berbers. French efforts to drive a wedge between Arabs and Berbers had failed. The Berbers of Kabylia were to produce some of the FLN's most effective leaders, some of its toughest fighters—and some of Algeria's finest novelists. Kabyles such as Mouloud Mammeri and Mouloud Feraoun, writing in French, chronicled the impact on ordinary Algerians of more than a century of French rule. It is not the least of the ironies of the Algerian struggle that in the 1950s, even as the war of independence was getting under way, the best of these novels were being acclaimed by the critics in Paris.

Mouloud Mammeri's classic novel *Le Sommeil du Juste* (The Sleep of the Just), published in French in 1955, is set in Kabylia in 1940. One of its main themes is cultural dislocation. An old father in the village of Ighzer grieves at the erosion of a traditional culture based on Islam, honour, and clan solidarity:

> Nothing is respected any more, and everything is equal to everything else. This war has brought back to Ighzer all our men who had emigrated to France ... They have come back with habits and ways of speaking which make my heart bleed to see and hear.

He is afraid his son will return 'blundering into everything like a blind man because you can no longer see the true light, confused as a child with no sense of proportion, and kicking everything aside because contact with the West [has] made you become like them'.[21]

Mammeri himself was born in a Kabyle village in 1917. There were, he recalled later, no roads, electricity, or telephones. But there was a school, built in 1883, which served as a 'window on the world'. From there he went on to study at a prestigious lycée in Paris.[22] In the Second World War, like Ben Bella, he served in Europe as a soldier in the French army. He knew, from his own experience, the cultural tensions among the Kabyles, and the generation gap between fathers and sons. After independence, when the new post-colonial régime sought to create a monolithic Arab and Arabic-speaking state, Mammeri became a symbol of the Berbers' pride in their distinctive culture.

It took the FLN two years, between 1954 and 1956, to establish its supremacy among the different factions of the nationalist cause. This involved a bitter feud with the supporters of Messali Hadj. The quarrel was not about policy but about power, and was conducted with the utmost ruthlessness. In one notorious incident in May 1957, the FLN massacred 374 villagers in the eastern region of Mélouza who were deemed to be Messali's supporters. Stora estimates that in the brutal conflict between the two groups—waged in France as well as Algeria—some 10,000 Algerians lost their lives.[23]

Gradually, other groups fell into line. Ferhat Abbas's movement, the Algerian communists, the reformist *ulema*—one by one, all gave their allegiance to the FLN. The movement's strengths and weaknesses were highlighted at the Soummam Congress, held in Kabylia in August 1956. It was organised by Abbane Ramdane, an intelligent and ruthless Kabyle who commanded the forces of the interior, and it took a number of important decisions. The congress restructured the movement along new lines and affirmed the primacy of the political over the military, and of the interior over the exterior. It also set out the rebels' main objective: a single democratic and socialist Algerian republic. From outside, Ben Bella fumed that the congress was unrepresentative, and tensions between the rival leaderships—and between Arabs and Berbers—were to simmer and periodically erupt throughout the war, and beyond.

In January 1955 Jacques Soustelle, a respected liberal academic loyal to de Gaulle, was appointed governor-general. Sensing that reform was in the air, the settlers took an instant dislike to him. Soustelle's instincts were indeed reformist, and he replaced the word 'assimilation' with the softer-sounding 'integration'. Working with a fellow ethnographer, the remarkable Germaine Tillion, he set up *centres sociaux*, social-welfare centres designed to improve relations between the French and the Muslims, and provide educational and material aid to deprived areas. But Soustelle's views changed abruptly with the violence that erupted in August 1955, known as the Philippeville massacres, when thousands of Muslims attacked police stations and public buildings in thirty towns and villages. The death toll was seventy-one Europeans and fifty-two Muslims. As in Sétif, the reprisals were fierce. Soustelle gave the army *carte blanche*, and thousands of

Muslims were killed. When he left the country the following year, he did so to the cheers of the settlers, who had come to see him as their champion. He was subsequently to break with de Gaulle and became an 'ultra', a hard-line supporter of *l'Algérie française*.

In January 1956 Camus, now an acclaimed writer in France and world-wide, returned to Algiers to make a doomed appeal for a truce. He tried desperately to be even-handed, condemning atrocities by both sides. He sympathised with the Muslim majority, yet was opposed to independence. He was a humanist, a man of the left, but also a *colon*, and his elderly mother was still living in Algiers. When awarded the Nobel prize for literature the following year, he told an audience at Stockholm University:

> I have said and repeated that we must give justice to the Algerian people and grant them a fully democratic régime ... I have always condemned terrorism, and I must condemn a terrorism that works blindly in the streets of Algiers and one day might strike at my mother and my family. I believe in justice, but I will defend my mother before justice.[24]

Camus was to die in a car crash in France in January 1960. The manuscript of his unfinished autobiographical novel, *Le Premier Homme*, was found in his briefcase. He was forty-six. His mother outlived him.

A socialist government came to power in France, under Guy Mollet, in January 1956. The new prime minister wanted to bring back the 79-year-old Catroux as governor-general, but the settlers had other ideas. When Mollet visited Algiers in February, they pelted him with tomatoes and cabbages. He backed down and appointed Robert Lacoste, a bluff socialist with a trade-union background whose views were far more congenial to the *colons*. The governor-general was upgraded to resident minister, with enhanced powers. But increasingly it was the generals who took the important decisions. With 400,000 soldiers at their disposal, they divided the country into three military zones and began to fortify the borders with electrified barriers. Two million Muslims were uprooted from their villages and put in 1,200 detention camps where they could more easily be controlled. Every other consideration, political or administrative, was now subordinated to the need to crush the rebellion. It was all-out war.

In the autumn of 1956, Ted Morgan arrived in Algeria, an unwilling soldier in a brutal colonial war. Born Sanche de Gramont, the son of a French diplomat, in 1932, he had grown up in Washington, DC, gone to Yale, and decided he wanted to be a journalist and an American. He got a job with a newspaper in Massachusetts, the *Worcester Telegram*, and changed his name to Ted Morgan (an anagram of de Gramont). But in 1955, when he was twenty-three, the long arm of the French republic reached out and conscripted him into the army. His vivid, bawdy memoir, *My Battle of Algiers*, is a Franco-Algerian *Catch-22*.

The young Morgan had his baptism of fire in the *bled*, the Algerian countryside. He was sent to the village of Champlain, fifty miles south of Algiers. The *colons* had fled, and the village was occupied by local Arabs and a tent city of soldiers. The officers, hardened and cynical, were French; most of the troops Senegalese. One of Morgan's tasks as an intelligence officer was to interrogate prisoners. There was one captured *fellagha* (fighter) who refused to speak.

> The *fellagha* had been strung up with his wrists tied over a horizontal beam, so that his feet didn't touch the ground ... His gaze was more defiant than fearful ...
> I asked him his name, but he did not reply ...
> 'Ask him a bit more forcefully,' Lastours [his commanding officer] said. I punched him hard in the stomach.
> '*Hakarabi. Makache*,' the man said. 'I swear I don't know.' I hit him again ... Then something happened to me. I started to lose it ... My role was to punch him, and his role was to repeat his line. This went on for about two minutes, and then he stopped repeating.
> Lastours felt his pulse and said, 'He's dead. And he didn't talk.'

Morgan asked Lastours to place him under arrest. 'Don't be ridiculous,' the officer replied. 'When you go to the *hamam* [steambath], you sweat, and in war there are losses.' In his memoir, written fifty years later, Morgan does not try to excuse his action. 'I've been my own judge and jury,' he writes, 'and I can't let myself off ... It's a form of inner disfigurement that I've had to live with.'

Lastours sent him to Algiers to rest and recover. There, as chance would have it, he was to become an eye-witness to the battle of Algiers.[25]

External events increasingly impinged on Algeria's future, despite French insistence that the conflict was a purely internal affair. (It was never officially described as a war, merely as a law-and-order operation.) In 1956 Tunisia and Morocco gained their independence, which could not fail to encourage the Algerian nationalists. Egypt's President Nasser began to supply the FLN with money and weapons. International opinion, as reflected at the United Nations, became increasingly unsympathetic to France's position. This was further eroded in October 1956 when the authorities in Algiers ordered a Moroccan airliner on its way from Rabat to Tunis to land in Oran. On board were four senior FLN leaders—Ahmed Ben Bella, Hocine Ait Ahmed, Muhammad Boudiaf, and Muhammad Khider—who were detained in France for the remainder of the war. Also on board were French journalists and the correspondent of the *New York Times*. The French congratulated themselves on capturing such big fish; but in propaganda terms it was a disaster. France's involvement in the ill-fated Suez expedition shortly afterwards contributed to its international opprobrium, and had the unintended effect of boosting Arab nationalism in the region.

Abbane Ramdane, who had taken charge of operations in the Algiers area at the end of 1955, now embarked on a calculated escalation of the war. The focus of his strategy was the Casbah, the old Arab quarter of Algiers, a forty-five-acre maze of tiny twisting alleyways home to 80,000 inhabitants. Ramdane's aim was simple and cold-blooded: to take the war to Algiers by deliberately targetting civilians in the European quarters of the city.

First, the FLN had to bring the Casbah under its control. For this purpose Ramdane recruited Saadi Yacef, who worked in his father's bakery in the quarter. Twenty-five years old, Yacef was 'dapper and voluble, with big brown eyes in a face where one could still see the mischievous child'. Yacef in turn recruited Ali Ammar, better known as Ali-la-Pointe (because he came from the seaside town of Pointe). Ali had started life as a street seller and went on to become a pimp. Tall and good-looking, with a violent streak, he knew the quarter—and its gangsters and drug dealers—intimately. A spell in jail in 1954 had politicised him, and when he escaped in 1956 he started working with Yacef.[26] They made a good team, building up a network of FLN cells in the Casbah and imposing strict morality and discipline on the area. When two FLN men were guillotined—the first time the French had officially executed their prisoners—Yacef responded with three days of reprisal killings. Among those he targetted were guards working at the notorious Barberousse prison.

In August 1956 a group of 'ultras'—*colon* extremists who enjoyed the quiet support of the security forces—bombed four houses on the rue de Thèbes, in the heart of the Casbah, killing seventy Algerians, including women and children. This spurred Yacef to retaliate. He had begun recruiting young women who spoke French and could pass for Europeans. The FLN, sensitive to the norms of a conservative society, had been ambivalent about using women in front-line roles. But Yacef knew that women had a much better chance of getting through check-points than men.

Among the recruits were Zohra Drif, Samia Lakhdari, and Djamila Bouhired. Drif was the daughter of a judge, and had attended a presti-gious lycée—one of only four Muslims among the 3,000 girls.

> In the lycée I became very interested in politics, but I never dared discuss this with the French girls because of the antagonism it produced. I concen-trated on getting my baccalauréat. But like the other Muslim girls, I was very concerned with what would happen after graduating from the lycée. Most Muslim families wanted their daughters to return home and marry, but many of my friends and I wanted to enter the university.[27]

She got her wish, and enrolled to study law at the University of Algiers.

On 30 September 1956, Yacef gave the three young women their orders. The targets were the Milk Bar, the Cafeteria, and the Air France terminal. They were not suicide bombers: the women were to place their bombs, then make their escape. With some misgivings—they had not been told women and children would be among the likely casual-ties—they set off on their mission. It was early on a Sunday evening, and the cafés were crowded. One of the bombs failed to go off, but the other two caused horrific carnage and destruction. The number of casualties was relatively small—three dead and over fifty wounded—but they included children, and several were seriously maimed. The *colons* were badly shaken. The war had previously seemed far-off; now they were no longer safe in the heart of their main city.

FLN leaders followed up by assassinating one of the 'ultras', a 74-year-old mayor, Amédée Froger. The assassin was Ali-la-Pointe.

Froger's funeral on 29 December 1956 turned ugly: Arab passers-by were shot or beaten up, and four were killed. Yacef now had 1,400 armed men in Algiers, and the police were at a loss to know how to handle the situation. In desperation, Lacoste, the resident minister, turned to General Jacques Massu, a tough veteran of the war in Indochina, and entrusted him with the task of pacifying Algiers.

Ted Morgan arrived in Algiers as French forces were preparing to crush the Casbah. At the house of the American consul, an old family friend, he was introduced to Massu—a towering figure with 'a bony face, a black mustache, a granite jaw'. Learning he had worked as a journalist, Massu offered him a job producing propaganda for the military. Morgan was sceptical about the work, but calculated that it would be more congenial than soldiering in the *bled*.[28]

What followed was a trial of strength between Massu and the FLN. The rebels called a general strike in Algiers at the end of January 1957, to coincide with a meeting at the UN where Algeria was due to be discussed. Determined to break the strike, Massu sent his paratroopers into the Casbah at night. (They had prepared by making detailed maps and conducting a census of the area.) Over 1,000 residents were arrested. 'The paras have kicked the anthill,' Morgan's boss remarked, 'and the ants are scurrying.'

But the bombs continued to go off. Morgan and his colleagues were under pressure to produce the first issue of a weekly newspaper, *Réalités Algériens*, ahead of the strike. Once it was printed, they bundled copies onto a helicopter, to be dropped over the Casbah—'but a gust of wind came up and most of them blew out to sea. I watched them fly off, the pages flapping like pelican wings'.[29]

The remorseless pressure on the Casbah—and the systematic torture of prisoners—paid off. The cells were destroyed, Ali-la-Pointe was killed, and Saadi Yacef captured (he was only released at independence). Zohra Drif was also captured and sentenced to twenty years' hard labour. But it was at best a partial victory. While both sides had crossed a new threshold of violence, the Casbah acquired an iconic status as a fortress of resistance, immortalised a decade later in Pontecorvo's film, *The Battle of Algiers*. When the use of torture, including electric-shock treatment, became known in France, it caused an outcry. What price *l'Algérie française*, if this was how it was to be defended?

As public opinion shifted, the *colons* became increasingly determined to fight it out, by whatever means. They had hitherto shown their power to influence developments in Algeria, but only indirectly developments in France. Now, in a remarkable chain of events, a group of settlers, backed by a group of army officers, succeeded in overthrowing the Fourth Republic.

To understand the role of the generals, it is necessary to recall the string of humiliations they had suffered in the previous two decades: the fall of France, the loss of Syria and Lebanon, the defeat in Indochina, the independence of Tunisia and Morocco—and now the prospect (as they saw it) of betrayal in Algeria. Casting around for scapegoats, they blamed an assortment of enemies—the Americans (out to supplant France at every turn), left-wing politicians and journalists in France (who routinely stabbed them in the back)—and international communism, which they conflated with Algerian nationalism as a monster which it was their mission to destroy.[30]

This mix of fear, anger, and paranoia came together in Algiers in May 1958 when, frustrated by the political paralysis in Paris, the settlers and their military allies rose up in revolt. Taking charge of the rebellion, the commander-in-chief of French forces in Algeria, General Raoul Salan, another veteran of the war in Indochina, led the call for de Gaulle to return to power in France. Salan and the settlers believed the 67-year-old general was the strongman who would save *l'Algérie française*. They were mistaken.

On 1 June 1958, de Gaulle became prime minister. His message to the people of Algeria was at first emollient. 'I have understood you,' he told large crowds on a visit to Algiers later that month. In October he went further, and in a speech in Constantine proposed a five-year plan of reform that would provide 100,000 new jobs over the next five years and a programme to combat illiteracy. It was a belated attempt to institute the sustained economic and social development that Algeria had so sorely lacked. He called it a 'peace of the brave'. The FLN dismissed the idea.

But de Gaulle was biding his time, and his thinking about Algeria had probably not yet crystallised. He had taken the job of prime minister on the clear understanding that a new constitution would be introduced, and endorsed in a popular vote, which would give him greatly enhanced powers. Once this had happened, at the end of the year he was elected president of the Fifth Republic. Now, with his position secure, he could begin to reveal his hand. Massu and Salan were replaced. Braving the wrath of the settlers and their allies, in a speech in September 1959 he offered the Algerians the right to determine their own future. To be sure, independence was not de Gaulle's preferred option, but he was prepared to give the country, for the first time, the choice between integration and secession. It was a turning-point in the conflict, opening up the possibility of a solution.

By now Algeria had a population of nine million Muslims and a million settlers. The French army, with 500,000 soldiers in the country, believed it had won the war. The FLN was on the ropes. Repression had taken its toll, and by sealing the borders the French had prevented the rebels from smuggling in arms and men. But as de Gaulle understood, and the settlers did not, military victory could not hide the reality of political defeat. The 'old Algeria' was indeed dead, as he proclaimed, and in a changed world, holding on to the remnants of empire by force was no longer an option.

In a last-ditch effort to stave off the inevitable, three generals seized power in Algiers at midnight on 21 April 1961. Their leader was a popular general, the white-haired Maurice Challe. Salan, who had retired from the army and settled in Franco's Spain, arrived from Madrid to join them. For a tense moment, France seemed on the edge of civil war. But the bulk of the armed forces remained loyal to de Gaulle, and after four days the putsch fizzled out. The focus of the 'ultras' now shifted to terrorism. A campaign of violence and assassination—in both France and Algeria—was waged by the Organisation de l'Armée Secrète, or OAS, founded in Madrid in early 1961 under Salan. Its active membership was relatively small, but it enjoyed considerable support in the army and among the *colons*. It plotted not only to overthrow de Gaulle but (as viewers of *The Day of the Jackal* will recall) to assassinate him.

In October 1961, while OAS gunmen were spreading terror, 30,000 Algerians took to the streets of Paris. The police (under the notorious Maurice Papon) made 12,000 arrests, and some 200 demonstrators were killed. The last months of French rule witnessed violence and chaos on an extraordinary scale. Public opinion in France was horrified by the excesses of the OAS. At the same time, in the nationalist camp, 'the leadership of the FLN imploded'.[31] With victory in sight, the battle for the spoils began, and the internal leaders—who had borne the brunt of the conflict—watched aghast as the external leaders made a determined bid to impose their control over the movement. The infighting did not deny the FLN the prize of independence, but ensured that on the morrow of liberation its ranks would be riven by personal and ideological divisions.

Among the victims of the OAS assassins was the novelist, humanist, and friend of Camus, Mouloud Feraoun, gunned down in Algiers on 15 March 1962. He was only forty-nine, and was working as an inspector for one of the *centres sociaux* set up by Soustelle and Tillion in the mid-1950s. Feraoun and a group of colleagues were holding a meeting at their office when three young OAS gunmen burst in and read out a list of names. Six people, three French and three Algerians, were taken outside and shot.[32] The violence continued to the bitter end, even as peace talks between France and the FLN got under way in Évian, on the shores of Lake Geneva. Once the die was cast, the settlers had to choose (in their own grim phrase) between 'the suitcase and the coffin'. Most fled to France. Feraoun, like thousands of other Algerians, did not live to see the proclamation of an independent Algerian republic on 3 July 1962. Lasting almost eight years, this 'savage war of peace' may well have cost half-a-million lives.[33]

10

ARABIAN ENDGAME

Even in her late eighties, Doreen Ingrams vividly remembered the moment she first arrived in Aden.

> It was the first of April 1934, in the early morning. We'd come by the P&O ship which always arrived on a Sunday morning, when a gun went off to let the people know that their mail had arrived. And we got up early to see the sun rising over that massive volcanic range of Jebel Shamsan, which gives such a dramatic backdrop to Aden.

Twenty-eight years old and newly married, she had been born in London into a conventional Edwardian family. Rebelling against an upbringing she found constricting, she became an actress and for six years toured provincial towns with a repertory company, and was much admired as Ophelia and Desdemona. Her views, like those of many young people at the time, were liberal and anti-imperialist. In 1930 she met and married Harold Ingrams, a young colonial officer who four years later was transferred to south Arabia. Despite its dramatic setting, the young Englishwoman found Aden stiflingly dull. It was laid out like a military camp. She was called *memsahib* (which she hated) and was served mulligatawny soup. It was a piece of the Raj, transplanted to southern Arabia.[1]

Aden was the first Arab territory the British acquired and virtually the last it relinquished, 128 years later. It had been well known as a port

183

for centuries, but its importance had waxed and waned. In the thirteenth century, in Marco Polo's day, it was large and prosperous, but from the mid-seventeenth century, under the Ottomans, it had declined. In 1839 Captain Stafford Haines arrived with two warships and 700 men and captured it in the name of Queen Victoria. For the next hundred years it was run from the government of India in Bombay, rather than from London. It was in a state of 'squalid poverty', with a population of 500, but had two invaluable features—one of the finest natural harbours in the world, and a strategic location on the route to India.[2]

But as the territory grew in value, especially after the opening of the Suez Canal in 1869, it needed protecting. The British navy could defend it from invasion by sea, but more problematic was attack by land. There were three potential aggressors—the rival imperial power, France; the Ottoman empire; and the Imam, the ruler of Yemen to the north, who had a long-standing claim to southern Arabia, including Aden. When the Imam sought to activate this claim in the 1920s, Britain fought him off, using Royal Air Force planes against his troops and bombing one of his cities, Taiz. It eventually signed a treaty with him in 1934, which produced a temporary stability. But it was decided Aden needed a protective belt of territory—a *cordon sanitaire*—to serve as a buffer against attack or infiltration. As a result Britain began, gradually, to intervene in the hinterland, which it had hitherto largely ignored—wild and inaccessible country, inhabited by feuding tribes jealous of their autonomy and suspicious of outside interference. In 1937 Britain declared Aden to be a Crown Colony—in other words, British sovereign territory—which would no longer be governed from Bombay but from the Colonial Office in London. And it divided the hinterland into a western and an eastern protectorate. The challenge now was to pacify these territories, without undue cost, and make the first modest efforts at development by building roads, schools, and clinics.

To implement this 'forward policy', Harold and Doreen Ingrams journeyed into the eastern protectorate, an area of 68,000 square miles and a population of perhaps 200,000 of which officials were almost entirely ignorant. After the stultifying atmosphere of Aden, Doreen Ingrams found it a liberating experience.

Once you got into the protectorate, you had these arrays of sultans, emirs, sheikhs, and what-have-you, ruling over large or small territories, some of them very green—cultivation and palm-trees—others almost desert. But in any case they were free and independent spirits. Your spirits lifted when you went into the protectorate out of the military dullness of Aden. The protectorate was never dull for a moment.[3]

Since there were few roads, they travelled through the plateaux and valleys of the Hadhramaut on donkey and camel. They were the first Europeans to live there. The Hadhramaut had one important feature that distinguished it from the western protectorate: its trade links with the outside world. In the mid-1930s 110,000 Hadhramis lived abroad in Africa, India, and south-east Asia. Some brought their wealth home when they returned; others sent it to their families in the form of remittances.

The Ingrams' task was to gather information and persuade tribal leaders to enter into a three-year truce under which Britain would offer them protection and they would promise to keep the peace. Remarkably, they succeeded, and the truce became known as the Pax Ingrams, with some 1,200 signatures. Pacification required, however, the RAF. Villages which were unwilling to sign were bombed, usually without casualties or much damage, to make them change their minds. This method was used elsewhere in the protectorate against unruly tribes: the same imperialism on the cheap that Churchill employed in Iraq.

Aden prospered. After the Second World War, it became the world's second busiest port after New York, a stopping-off point for tourists and businessmen as well as soldiers and colonial officials. No less important, it was by now a military base with a vital strategic role for the British empire. It had excellent schools, including the prestigious Aden College, and an efficient system of justice. Its population grew and, with an influx of Asians, Arabs, Africans, and Europeans, became increasingly cosmopolitan. The British community socialised at the Union Club and organised cocktail parties and dances on the roof of the Crescent Hotel. The colony seemed to have a charmed life.

But in the 1950s—Aden's economic heyday—the political situation began to change significantly. The successful coup in Egypt in 1952, and the rise of Nasser as the champion of Arab nationalism, electrified the region—and underlined to the British that they now faced a more assertive anti-colonial mood.

The new climate became evident in Lahej, the largest, most fertile, and wealthiest state in the western protectorate, lying twenty miles north of Aden. Here the young ruler, Sultan Ali Abdul-Karim, was openly sympathetic to Nasser's revolution. In the main town, pictures of the Egyptian leader were to be seen in the shops, and before long Egyptian teachers were working in the schools and Egyptian films were being screened in the cinema.

British officials, having initially warmed to the sultan as an educated and intelligent ruler who seemed ready to work with them, now regarded him as a troublemaker. But an adventurous English woman, June Knox-Mawer, struck up a friendship with Ali Abdul-Karim. She was twenty-one and had arrived in Aden in 1952 as the wife of the new chief magistrate and as a stringer for the *Daily Express*. She soon noticed the contrast between the social conformism of expatriate life and the colour and energy of Crater, the old part of Aden where Arab and Indian traders congregated.

> Here, white-robed merchants flitted like cabbage butterflies in and out of hot sleek Cadillacs and the air was full of the smells of burning incense, coffee beans, moth-balls, roasting corn on smoky braziers—and goats, goats, goats ... Not far away someone was beating a drum. There was the busy insect whir of sewing machines outside the tailors' shops, clank and rumble of trucks and camel carts, an Indian song and an Arabic voice throbbing and mingling, magnified by fifty different radios.[4]

The Knox-Mawers drove out of Aden one Saturday morning, crossing the frontier (a ten-foot wooden bar) between the colony and the protectorate, to visit Lahej and its ruler. Sultan Ali was thirty-four, with a face like 'a polished wood-carving' and a schoolboy grin. He was an 'unwilling sultan', he told them, explaining that he had become ruler only after his half-brother, Fadhl, had lost his mind. (The British had in fact removed Fadhl in 1952 and put Ali in his place.) Cotton production had made Lahej prosperous, but politically the sultan felt uneasy: 'I am walking a tightrope between my people and yours.' He was, paradoxically, a dynastic ruler and a staunch republican. 'Quite soon,' he told June Knox-Mawer, 'there will be no such thing as a Sultan here. We shall all be swept away and my comment would be—a very good thing too.'[5]

In 1954, British Petroleum opened a big new refinery in Aden, after its expulsion from Abadan, at a cost of £45 million. The colony became a magnet for migrant labour, especially from Yemen. By the mid-1950s there were 50,000 Yemeni workers in Aden, the largest group in a population of 138,000.[6] Many of them lived in crowded shantytowns, and they had a particular grievance—they were disenfranchised. British officials insisted that voting for the Legislative Council, a body set up in 1946, should be restricted to those born in the colony and British subjects long resident there. But this produced an anomaly: Indians, Pakistanis, Greeks, and Britons who had settled there could vote, but native Yemenis could not. (The notion of whether south Arabians shared a common identity with the Yemenis of the north was contested. Such an identity was indeed to evolve, but in the 1950s the British had an interest in denying it, while Nasser had an interest in promoting it, under the banner of a common Arab identity.)

For years British officials had had no clear plan for the political future of south Arabia. They had proposed bringing the states of the protectorate together in a federation, but the local rulers—jealous of their autonomy—had rejected the idea. The main advocate, and eventual architect, of federation was Kennedy Trevaskis. After colonial experience in Northern Rhodesia and Eritrea, Trevaskis had arrived as a political officer in the protectorate in 1951. Nothing had prepared him for the area's social anarchy and wild beauty: 'a land of mountains and plateaux, where complex labyrinths of ravines and gorges stand out against the Alpine panorama like veins in the human body'.[7] He became the resident adviser to the sheikhs and emirs of the western protectorate, whom he came to know and identify with. Reflecting on their political future, as traditional rulers in an age of rising nationalism, he concluded that Britain had a duty, in its own interests as well as theirs, to coax them into a union.

Known affectionately to his colleagues as 'Uncle Ken', Trevaskis was single-minded—his critics would say stubborn and domineering—and once he had reached this conclusion, he did his utmost to persuade his boss, the governor of Aden, William Luce, and officials in London to adopt it. But the solution he had in mind—an independent federal south Arabia, run by Britain's friends with Britain's help—was not something Whitehall was ready to endorse. The issue was highlighted when a senior British official, Lord Lloyd, came out from London in May 1956, and made it clear that a degree of self-government was the most Britain would offer. Independence was not on the cards. Local officials, as well as local rulers including Sultan Ali, were shocked.

By now, British officials were becoming increasingly suspicious of the ruler of Lahej, and of his close association with Muhammad Ali Jifri, leader of a nationalist group called the South Arabian League, founded in 1951. June Knox-Mawer knew them both. She thought Jifri 'extremely intelligent ... with the look of a naughty boy dressed up as an angel for the school play'. In official eyes, however, both men were dangerous. Sultan Ali was accused of being a friend of the Imam of Yemen, a gun-runner, even a crypto-communist. (The first of these charges had some truth, the third had none.) When she asked him if he was anti-British, he replied, 'I am not anti-British, I am merely pro-Arab.' She liked his charm and intelligence and his way with words: he described Louis Armstrong as having 'the voice of an old slave grumbling to himself'.

When Knox-Mawer met the two of them again, Jifri had been exiled from the colony and taken refuge in Lahej. She thought he had become plumper and more fanatical. 'Half-way through a sentence, he suddenly remembered something and sprang to his feet to turn on the radio.' What followed revealed the gulf between Knox-Mawer and her Arab friends.

> The voice that came through was that of Colonel Nasser speaking at Alexandria on the anniversary of the Egyptian seizure of the Suez Canal. The roars from the massed crowds of his audience, the ranting torrent of guttural-sounding language had an uncanny flavour of the pre-Munich broadcasts from Berlin ... Everyone in the room was listening with the closest attention. The atmosphere was startlingly transformed ... I felt like someone who sees the ice begin to crack under his feet in all directions.[8]

In April 1958 Luce decided to act against Sultan Ali and his nationalist associates. He gave orders for the arrest of Jifri—who, however, managed to escape to Yemen—and put pressure on Ali to abdicate. When the sultan joined other rulers on a visit to London, Luce tried to make sure he would not return. In the end Ali chose exile in Cairo, where he made common cause with Nasser, and Luce installed a more pliant ruler in his place. 'The process of ousting Ali,' writes a British

historian, 'was accompanied by a degree of intrigue involving all par-
ties, remarkable even by the exacting standards of south-west Arabia.'[9]
Their failure to engage with intelligent nationalists such as Ali Abdul-
Karim was something British officials were later to regret.

Luce was at first cool to the idea of federation, but Trevaskis swung
him round. In March 1958 the governor of Aden presented Colonial
Office officials with a plan that startled them. It called for the setting-
up of a federation, combined with a ten-year strategy for 'a gradual
disengagement from our position in south-west Arabia'. In other
words, a federation would be created and groomed for independence
by 1968. Luce was a respected figure in Whitehall, but this was considered too radical. Senior officials, both civilian and military, wanted
Britain to hold on to Aden and its military base indefinitely, and they
feared talk of independence would put the base in jeopardy. The plan
was significantly watered down.[10]

The other rulers now had a stark choice: to follow Ali's example,
which held little appeal, or stick with the British and set up a federation. Regional events, above all the Suez crisis of 1956 and the Iraqi
revolution of 1958, forced their hand. In February 1959 the Federation
of the Arab Emirates of the South came into being. The federation
would be heavily dependent on British help, and the governor would
retain considerable powers, especially in defence and security. It did
not embrace the whole of the protectorate, but six (and eventually
twelve) of the western states. The states of the east, feeling safer and
cherishing the vain hope that oil would be found on their territory,
stayed out. Britain blessed the union with £5 million of aid for development and the creation of a federal army.

Godfrey Meynell, a young political officer in his mid-twenties, arrived
in Aden by cargo ship in January 1959. The first thing that struck him
was the bright light: 'the harbour full of ships, the blue sparkling sea,
the white buildings of Steamer Point and the brown, two-thousand-
foot bulk of Jebel Shamsan behind'. He was impressed by the remarkable development of a colony which Britain 'had built up from nothing'. 'The achievement in Aden was one of the greatest advertisements
for imperialism.'

Meynell had been educated at Eton and Cambridge, and then taken
an office job which he found dull. He applied to the Colonial Office,

which offered him a choice between Nyasaland (now Malawi) and south Arabia. He chose south Arabia, and began work as a political officer in the protectorate just as the federation was coming into being. 'The political job,' he wrote in an unpublished memoir, 'was to increase the pull of prosperity and security, while the Federation was built up with British support.'

Among his mentors was Trevaskis, whom he greatly admired: 'a massive, subtle man of great charm … unflappable … formidable in argument'. 'A convinced imperialist … his politics were pretty far right, and he was highly sceptical about the wisdom of a too hasty development of democratic institutions or a political middle class.'[11]

Meynell was to work in the protectorate for the next eight years.

A significant development of the mid-1950s was the emergence of the Aden Trades Union Congress. This was led by Abdullah al-Asnag, a young nationalist, born in Crater in 1934 and educated at the prestigious Aden College, who worked as the chief reservations clerk for the local airline, Aden Airways. Al-Asnag was intelligent, articulate, and a good organiser. The aims of the ATUC, which got help from its British counterpart, were as much political as economic. It succeeded in mobilising the colony's Yemeni workers behind the call for a single state, uniting Yemen and south Arabia. At the same time it lobbied for better wages and living conditions, which the more ruthless employers resisted. The movement showed its muscle in early 1956 with a series of strikes at the port and the oil refinery.[12] In 1959 alone, there were eighty-four strikes in the colony. Luce, seeing the ATUC as a political threat, wanted to ban it, but the Colonial Office vetoed the idea. However, he did outlaw strikes and have labour leaders arrested. In 1961 the movement set up a political arm, the People's Socialist Party.

British officials now had to contend with threats from within and from without. To counter the influence of the Yemeni ruler, Imam Ahmad, they embarked on what was known locally as *keeni-meeni*—a campaign of subversion and intrigue. Since the Imam was seeking to interfere in south Arabia, Luce and Trevaskis sought to weaken his hold on Yemen. This involved arming Yemeni dissidents, cross-border raids, and the use of the RAF. Luce even contemplated organising a coup in Yemen to replace the Imam with his brother. How far this idea was taken is not clear, but in any case it did not succeed.[13]

Meanwhile, there was the question of whether Aden should join the federation. The federal rulers felt it should. (Captain Haines had, after all, seized the territory from the then sultan of Lahej, and they felt entitled to get it back.) But many Adenis were aghast. They regarded themselves as far more advanced than the tribesmen of the hinterland, and saw no reason to merge with them. They also disliked the proposed terms, which gave the federal rulers a dominant role. Al-Asnag led the opposition to the plan in Aden, and in the run-up to the merger the colony experienced considerable unrest. But in the end the British pushed it through. The merger—many called it a shotgun wedding— took place in September 1962.

The following day, the Imam was overthrown in a revolution backed by Egypt. The Yemen Arab Republic was born. The revolution changed everything. It triggered a Yemeni civil war in which Nasser supported the revolutionaries and Saudi Arabia (and British mercenaries) backed the monarchists. And it had a dramatic impact on the future of south Arabia. As the historian Spencer Mawby puts it, the Yemeni revolution 'brought radical Arab nationalism to Britain's Arabian doorstep'. British officials now had three enemies to contend with: 'the urban radicals of Aden, the insurgents in the federation, and the Republican government north of the frontier'.[14]

In the protectorate, where there was now growing violence, much of Godfrey Meynell's time was spent trying to win hearts and minds. In some Arab homes he saw a picture of Nasser hanging side by side with one of the British Queen. People were hedging their bets. Meynell did his bit in the campaign of *keeni-meeni*, handing out rifles and ammunition to tribesmen. 'I offer no defence of these arms distributions,' he wrote later. 'If we wanted colonialism on the cheap, however, they seemed indispensable.'

Meynell's account of his time in south Arabia reflects the idealism of a young official. He enjoyed nothing better than digging wells and handing out pumps to alleviate the chronic water shortage. A meal with a notable meant 'scalding hot, fatty goat soup with a squeeze of lime'. He ate (baked) locusts, a local delicacy, and wild honey. The mountains had a stunning beauty—though travelling on the road from Aden to Lodar, where he worked in the mid-1960s, was hair-raising as it had fifty-seven bends.

His account is shot through with self-deprecating humour. He once found himself in the middle of an ambush: "'Who are you?' asked some local. "A *dhabit siyasi* (political officer)," I replied. "*Siyasat-akfashalat* (Your politics have failed)," he replied succinctly. I could only agree.'[15]

Meynell believed in the federation, and was convinced Nasser had nothing to offer the people of Arabia. But he sometimes had doubts about the methods he was using. 'Pretending to be a Political Officer calming things down,' he wrote, 'while in fact giving the bulk of one's time to getting them blown up, is a mistake.'

In 1963 an urban insurrection began in Aden which continued, with greater or lesser intensity, until the British withdrawal in 1967. A grenade was thrown at Trevaskis, who was now High Commissioner (as Aden's governor had been restyled), and he was lucky to survive unharmed. He declared a state of emergency: scores were arrested and hundreds of Yemenis deported. On the political front, Trevaskis was still pressing for eventual independence. In his dispatches to London he was candid about what he had in mind: 'a nominally independent Federation ... dependent on us ... something akin to Cromer's Egypt'. Britain would retain the base.[16] Officials in Whitehall, not without misgivings, eventually came round to his way of thinking, and at a conference in London in 1964 offered south Arabia independence by 1968.

With elections for the Legislative Council looming, Trevaskis resorted to 'a substantial dose of *keeni-meeni*' to undermine Abdullah al-Asnag's People's Socialist Party. He was authorised to spend £15,000 on encouraging the nationalists to 'slit each other's throats'.[17]

Doreen Ingrams returned to south Arabia in 1963, almost twenty years after she'd left, and was glad to see old friends. But as she visited the new federal ministers, each with their British adviser, she thought officials were living in a 'dream world'. She was also startled by the dramatic growth of the British community, with the proliferation of soldiers, officials, engineers, technicians, doctors, and teachers engaged in trying to make the federation work.[18]

Violence escalated in the western protectorate. In October 1963 an insurgency began in Radfan, an area of jagged 7,000-foot mountain peaks which provided ideal terrain for guerrilla warfare. The revolt was local in origin but quickly taken over by the National Liberation Front, under the leadership of Qahtan al-Shabi. Born in Lahej in 1920, al-Shabi had been educated in Aden and had worked for the British as an agricultural offi-cer.[19] The NLF, supported by Yemen and Egypt, had emerged in the early 1960s as a nationalist coalition of very diverse elements:

> tribal leaders who supported the [Yemen Arab] Republic, army officers who had been serving as mercenaries in Saudi Arabia and the Gulf, work-ers from Aden and the Gulf, intellectuals from the hinterland who had been studying in Aden, as well as militants who had rushed to the North in October and November [1962] to participate in the first battles for the defence of the Republic.[20]

From these beginnings, it evolved into a ruthless and highly organ-ised Marxist-Leninist revolutionary movement. Relying on a cell-based structure, it succeeded in doing what the urban-based nationalists had failed to do: it captured the countryside. One of the movement's lead-ers, Saleh Musleh Qassem, later explained how its tightly-knit struc-ture worked:

> The internal party cells were made up of three to five members and there were periodic secret meetings, mostly at night. That was the time when the armed commandos would tour the villages and meet with each of the organisation's secret cells separately. During such meetings they would clarify the latest developments, gather information, assign tasks, and dis-tribute pamphlets ... No cell knew of the others except in extraordinary circumstances related to security.[21]

The NLF set out to transcend tribal loyalties and unite feuding tribes in a national struggle: no easy task given the character of Arabian soci-ety. It recruited women as well as men. One famous woman fighter, Da'rah, fought in men's clothing. When wounded and captured, she killed five guards and escaped.[22]

In April 1964 Nasser flew to Yemen to give his personal blessing to the struggle against British colonialism in south Arabia. Soon he had 70,000 Egyptian troops in Yemen, who were to become bogged down in an entanglement for which they and their country paid a high price.

The RAF bombed Radfan and other dissident areas throughout 1964. But although British forces had far superior firepower, they were up against a determined and resourceful enemy, and had precious little good intelligence. The NLF tied down British and federal troops in Radfan for nine months before withdrawing. In the aftermath British officials embarked on a belated attempt at economic development: 'More effort went into development [in the western protectorate] during the last decade of British rule than had occurred in the century after Haines's arrival.'[23] The eastern protectorate, in contrast, was more developed, and for the time being outside the field of battle.

A Labour government came to power in Britain in October 1964. Harold Wilson and his defence minister Denis Healey entered office with the intention of retaining a British role 'east of Suez'. But they changed their minds after concluding that Britain's position in south Arabia was both politically and economically untenable. The decision to withdraw was taken in mid-1965 but not made public until early 1966.

In the meantime the new Colonial Secretary, Anthony Greenwood, replaced Trevaskis with Sir Richard Turnbull, and set about trying to woo Abdullah al-Asnag, whom he regarded as a potential leader of south Arabia. Meynell and his colleagues were dismayed at the sacking of 'Uncle Ken' and quietly lobbied, with their friends in London, to subvert the emerging Labour policy.[24]

Greenwood thought he could strike a deal. His aim was to set up a government that combined the Aden nationalists and the more capable of the rulers—and that would let Britain retain the base. But the rise of the NLF put paid to the idea. In May 1965 Nasser brought the rival Arabian factions together in an umbrella group under al-Asnag, who had left Aden for Cairo. This became known as the Front for the Liberation of Occupied South Yemen—or, more memorably, Flosy. There were now two main contenders for power—Flosy, which accepted Egyptian tutelage, and the NLF, which rejected it. In a bid to weaken the NLF, Nasser put its leader, Qahtan al-Shabi, under virtual house arrest in Cairo. But this only had the effect of bringing a more militant NLF leadership to the fore.

The collapse of order in Aden led to the imposition of direct rule in September 1965. Turnbull was by now a prime target for assassination. Shut up in Government House amid tight security, he 'kept a home-made catapult beside his papers, venting his spleen on crows attempting to raid flower beds on his terrace'.[25] His relations with the Labour government became increasingly strained, and he did not hide his hostility to its new policy. In November 1965 he pointedly reminded ministers that the federation 'was an artificial creation brought into being essentially in order to buttress the Aden base; it was economically unviable, socially underdeveloped, politically unstable'. Britain bore complete responsibility for creating it: was it now going to abandon the rulers it had coaxed into a makeshift union?[26]

His appeals were to no avail. In the same month, the British government took the fateful decision not only to abandon the base but also to revoke all defence commitments to south Arabia. In 1966 it made this decision public. Lord Beswick, a junior Foreign Office minister, flew out to Aden to break the news. There were stormy meetings with the federal rulers and with the political officers. Godfrey Meynell listened to the minister with mounting indignation. 'He said we must persuade the rulers to stick together. I said, "What's the point of sticking together in a sinking ship? It makes more sense to swim for the shore." "Don't you shake your head at me," the poor fellow replied.'[27]

In August 1966 George Brown became Foreign Secretary, and decided that the key to a solution lay with Nasser. He replaced Turnbull with Sir Humphrey Trevelyan, an experienced diplomat who knew the Egyptian leader well. Trevelyan arrived in Aden in May 1967, charged with finding Brown an exit strategy.

British intelligence thought that, in the looming power struggle, Flosy would win, thereby giving victory to Nasser. In a bid to prevent this, secret talks were held with nationalists the British had previously shunned. These included Muhammad Ali Jifri and the ex-sultan, Ali Abdul-Karim. There were also overtures to al-Asnag. But it was all too little, too late. By now the more moderate nationalists who might have been inclined to work with the British were either too disillusioned or too scared to do so.

As the Arabian endgame approached, British policy began to smack of desperation. Brutal measures, including torture and disorientation techniques, were used against detainees. Unemployed Yemenis were rounded up and deported from Aden, even when there was no evidence of their involvement in violence.[28]

Two developments precipitated the end. The first was Nasser's humiliating defeat by Israel in the June War of 1967. This forced him to withdraw his forces from Yemen and his support from Flosy. The second was the mutiny which broke out in the federal army and police, which had been infiltrated by the NLF.

THE POISONED WELL

The last days in Aden were violent and chaotic. After nationalists captured Crater, killing twenty-two British soldiers, it was recaptured, to the accompaniment of drums and bagpipes, by a force of Highlanders led by Colonel Colin Mitchell, better known in the British media as 'Mad Mitch'. Out to avenge their dead comrades, the 'Jocks' tended to shoot first and ask questions later. In the end, Britain connived at the NLF's takeover. It had shown itself to be tougher and better organised than Flosy—and, although Marxist, in British eyes it was at least not Nasser's protégé. In November 1967 negotiations took place between Britain and the NLF in Geneva. By the end of the month, the British had withdrawn and the NLF, under Qahtan al-Shabi, had taken over. As the last British soldiers left Aden, a military band played 'Fings ain't what they used to be'. It seemed apt.

Forty-five years later, at his home in Derbyshire, Godfrey Meynell was still angry. 'I thought it was a tremendous betrayal of our friends,' he said in an interview. 'The Labour government had decided to ditch the whole thing—and pitched [the people of south Arabia] into the most dreadful communist régime.'

Feeling he had no useful role left, Meynell had resigned. He spent the rest of his working life in a civil-service job back in Britain— 'twenty-six grey years', he calls them. His happiest time was in Arabia.[29]

The verdict of most historians is that the British withdrawal was inevitable but in two respects badly executed. First, for the federation to succeed, it should have been created much earlier, not cobbled together under the pressure of events. Second, when the federation was created, not enough was done to ensure its defence. 'The greatest error of the Wilson government,' writes Spencer Mawby, 'was its decision not to offer a defence treaty to the federation or to any successor government.'[30]

The withdrawal was an imperial humiliation. The British had not simply retreated under fire. They had handed power to the first Marxist régime in the Arab world, which established the People's Democratic Republic of Yemen and became an ally of the Soviet Union.

In south Arabia, as in Palestine, the end was bitter.

EPILOGUE

THE POISONED WELL

By 1967, with the retreat from Aden, the British Raj in the Middle East was virtually over. The French had already left the Levant and north Africa. For a while Britain retained its role as protector of the oil-rich sheikhdoms of the Gulf, by mutual agreement with their rulers. Indeed so worried were they by the threat from their bigger neighbours that, when Britain announced it would leave in 1971, they offered to pay it to stay.[1] But this was no longer feasible. The world had changed, and Britain with it. Under the circumstances, it was remarkable that the federation put together to bind seven of the sheikhdoms together—the United Arab Emirates—survived the British departure. Lessons had been learned from federation-making in south Arabia: having bungled their exit in 1967, officials were determined to get it right in 1971.

What was the legacy of colonial rule in the Middle East? In the broad span of history the period of Europe's hegemony was brief—a mere three decades in Palestine, four in Iraq, seven in Egypt—yet it marked a profound rupture in the region's history, ending one era and ushering in another. After 1914 Middle Easterners found their world turned upside down. The sweep of Western armies through the region, defeating the Turks and putting an end to four centuries of Ottoman rule, was first and foremost an expression of Western power—an early-twentieth-century example of 'shock and awe'. As many saw it, the Christian West had destroyed the greatest Muslim empire of its day.

What followed was a direct consequence of this display of power, as Britain and France, anxious to fill the vacuum left by the Ottoman collapse, set about drawing borders, creating new administrations, and establishing law and order in the territories they had conquered. As we have seen, much of this was improvised rather than planned. But it can scarcely have seemed that way to the newly-conquered peoples of the region. For them, the implications of the new Western-dominated order were as much cultural and social as political and economic. They became willy-nilly citizens of nation-states, a novel concept, and the European powers not only controlled these states, building armies and bureaucracies and suppressing dissent, but tied them into imperial networks of commerce, finance, and industry.

There was no single uniform legacy of empire. The consequences of colonial rule varied considerably, depending on its duration and intensity and on local conditions. Two extreme cases prove the point. At independence Algeria was left, to a greater extent than any other Arab state, ravaged and impoverished. The war of independence had been so long and brutal that the task of recovery was especially arduous—and the legacy of bitterness towards the former colonial power correspondingly deep and long-lasting. That legacy, albeit mitigated to some extent by economic ties and the influence of French language and culture, persists stubbornly to this day.

A second case is that of the Palestinians, who at the end of colonial rule were left stateless, living either as a minority under Israeli rule or in exile in neighbouring states or beyond. For them, the sense of betrayal by Britain, and of a legacy of dispossession, has been passed from one generation to the next, and kept alive in poetry and fiction.

> *Soft rain in a distant autumn*
> *& the sparrows are blue ... blue*
> *& the earth is a festival.*
> *Don't tell me I'm a cloud in the airport*
> *because I want nothing*
> *from my country which fell out of the train window*
> *but my mother's handkerchief*
> *& reasons for a new death.*[2]

Of all the problems bequeathed from the colonial era, the Palestine issue has proved the most enduring and the most toxic. By sponsoring

Zionist settlement in Palestine and then failing to resolve the conflict between Arab and Jew which this provoked, Britain bears a direct and inescapable responsibility for creating the Palestine problem—which, despite claims to the contrary, remains one of the principal root causes of the region's malaise.

In Palestine and Algeria, it may be said, colonialism is a raw wound.

Elsewhere persistent problems have their origins in the post-war division of the region: the plight of another stateless nation, the Kurds; the creation of Lebanon as a Christian-dominated state, which inevitably alienated the country's Muslims and led eventually to a fifteen-year civil war; the resentment felt towards groups whom the colonial powers had favoured (Maronite Christians in Lebanon, Kabyles in Algeria, a Sunni élite in Iraq).

The character of each country was shaped indelibly, and in a variety of ways, by the manner in which statehood was achieved. Why do so many Turks cling to an embattled nationalism? Why is the process of national unification in Saudi Arabia still incomplete? Why is Jordan weak and dependent? Why do Iranians so often detect the hidden hand of Britain in their affairs? In each case the answer, or part of the answer, lies in the circumstances of their birth as modern states.

In addition to the difficulties posed by artificial borders, aggrieved minorities, and the lack of social cohesion, the nationalists who took power faced a broader political challenge: what kind of state were they trying to build? They had inherited the colonial state, with its infrastructure and institutions, but in ideological terms their priority was to create its antithesis. The post-colonial state was to be based on social justice, the redistribution of wealth, and the rebirth of a language and identity which had been suppressed or marginalised. Above all, the new states were to be proudly independent, not abjectly dependent on the West. These at least were the ideals.

To take the political legacy first, the nationalists tended to mistrust democracy, or at least Western-style democracy. The attempt to implant parliamentary democracy in British-ruled Egypt and Iraq in the 1920s and 1930s had failed dismally. Shrewd politicians—such as Nuri al-Said in Iraq and Ismail Sidqi in Egypt—had subverted these multi-party systems for their own ends. Too many political parties had been artificial; too many parliamentarians had been corrupt. Moreover the British were not above manipulating these pseudo-democracies—in Iran no less than the Arab countries—in order to promote their interests, thereby undermining the very principles they claimed to profess. In short, multi-party democracy had been discredited. Now, in the post-colonial era, it was seen as inherently divisive, and thus inimical to the challenges of nation-building, which required the unity (and in effect the obedience) of the people in supporting the leaders who had won the independence struggle. In the republics these were often military men, and the armed forces became the arbiter of political power.

In the monarchies of the Gulf, where British influence on internal affairs had been less intrusive, state-building took a different form. With regard to their domestic policies, the colonial power had by and large left the rulers to their own devices. At independence the foundations of these new states were family rule and oil wealth. The ruling dynasties were those with whom the British had signed treaties of protection which had preserved them 'as in aspic'.[3] While they too faced challenges of nation-building and modernisation, their populations were small and petrodollars created the comforting illusion that they were cushioned from the harsher realities evident elsewhere in the region.

Second, the new states sought to take ownership of the economy. There was a deep mistrust of both the private sector and foreign investment, and a conviction that the state must be the engine of economic development. In the new republics such as Egypt, old landowning élites were displaced and dispossessed (though land reform was patchy and incomplete). Since the colonialists had promoted agriculture at the expense of industry, ambitious programmes of industrialisation were undertaken. The 'statist' model was adopted not only in relatively advanced countries such as Turkey and Egypt, but also in the socially less developed states of Arabia. Here the aim was to take over oil companies formerly run by international consortia, and use oil wealth to create cradle-to-grave welfare states. In rich countries and poor, the centralising, paternalistic state was (and to a remarkable extent has remained) the order of the day.

A third legacy was cultural. Even when colonial powers had professed a 'civilising mission', they had educated only a small collaborative élite who were useful to them as teachers or junior functionaries.

The mass of the population remained illiterate. In Algeria there was a double challenge: to increase literacy while at the same time reviving the Arabic language. Underlying such educational challenges was the sensitive issue of identity. Despite the deceptive certainties of national-ist rhetoric, it was not self-evident who an Algerian or an Iraqi or a Lebanese actually was. The issue was complicated by the fact that there were two sorts of nationalism: the Arab nationalism promoted by Nasser and other republican leaders, which favoured the unity of all Arabs from the Atlantic to the Gulf, and a narrower, country-specific nationalism which gained in strength as, one after another, practical attempts to achieve Arab unification failed. But even this narrower nationalism faced the obvious challenge that these were not nations but nations-in-the-making, and the making was slow work.

Aggravating these internal issues was a set of external challenges of the most exacting kind. The historian L. Carl Brown has argued that, in its relations with the West, the Middle East is unique among the regions of the world:

> For roughly the last two centuries the Middle East has been more consis-tently and more thoroughly ensnarled in great power politics than any other part of the non-Western world ... Other parts of the world have been at one time or another more severely buffeted by an imperial power, but no area has remained so unremittingly caught up in multilateral great power politics.[4]

Brown traces the origins of this phenomenon to the period between 1798 and 1918 'during which the European powers slowly picked the Ottoman empire to pieces'. This set up a pattern of intense and often destructive interaction between local and foreign actors that has per-sisted to the present day. Even if the context has changed, he argues, the game has remained essentially the same. A set of issues in which outside powers have strong interests—oil, the Arab-Israeli conflict, the Cold War, and more recently the battle against Islamic radicalism—have locked the region into a 'bitter embrace between the Middle East and the West'.[5]

It is against this backdrop that the region has struggled to modernise and develop and achieve some meaningful independence. In material terms, there has certainly been significant and far-reaching change in the decades following European rule. As Roger Owen points out, most people in the post-colonial Middle East are undoubtedly healthier and better educated than their parents and grandparents were. 'In the Arab states, for example, infant mortality rates were cut in half between 1965 and 1991, while a child born in 1991 could expect to live thirteen years longer than his or her parents.' Cities now offer a much higher standard of living, and as a result of modern communications few outlying areas are cut off, as they once were, from the metropolis and the wider world.[6]

But in other respects the promises of independence have not been fulfilled. In the name of the politics of unity, the new states suppressed dissent and treated minorities (Kurds, Copts, Kabyles) with suspicion. In the name of reclaiming the national wealth, they created top-heavy, inefficient state-dominated economies. The new dawn of freedom did not materialise. Political systems ossified. Human rights were abused. The struggle against internal and external enemies—including the all-important conflict with Israel—was used as a pretext to justify authoritarian rule. Women protested that they had played a new and more fulfilling role during the struggle for independence, only to be pushed back to the margins. Meanwhile populations grew rapidly, creating pressures which even the wealthier régimes were unable to cope with.

Such failures have brought about what may be called the crisis of the state. At its heart is the absence of legitimacy. Republican rulers have discovered that strong states may be brittle. As for the rulers of the oil-rich states of north Africa and the Gulf, they have found that petrodollars can buy time, and material benefits, but not in any durable sense legitimacy. And if these rulers, whether republican or monarchical, resort to what the French scholar Maxime Rodinson ironically called 'Muslim gesticulation'—symbolic acts of piety—they run the risk of being charged with hypocrisy, and of being outflanked by Islamist groups in a holier-than-thou contest they cannot be sure of winning.[7]

As to such basic sources of legitimacy as good governance and political representation, most rulers have been unwilling or unable to embrace them. Good governance would require an end to corruption and crony capitalism. Political representation would imply that the majority decide who governs them. For most ruling élites, the risks of either course are simply too high. They have for the most part contented themselves with political window-dressing.

The legitimacy deficit has made these rulers vulnerable to challenges of various kinds. One of the strongest has been that from the Islamic revival which got under way in the 1970s, exemplified by mainstream movements such as the Muslim Brotherhood in Egypt. Although its origins lie in the colonial era—as one among several possible responses to Western imperialism—Islamism gathered strength from the idea that the nationalist leaders had lost their way because they had lost their identity. They had become secular, aping the West in their attitudes and lifestyles. Islam, authentic and authoritative, was the solution. These movements have been aptly described as Islamo-nationalist.

A very different kind of response to the crisis of the state was exemplified in the Arab Spring. The uprisings of 2011, in which four dictators (in Tunisia, Egypt, Libya, and Yemen) were toppled in short order, represented a collective rejection of decades of autocracy, corruption, and failure. The driving-force behind them was not religious, or indeed ideological in any conventional sense, but something more novel and of potentially far-reaching significance: an appeal for the application of universal principles of citizenship and human rights. Because it touched on widely-held grievances, this idea—popularised by the social media and satellite television—generated a remarkable degree of grass-roots Arab solidarity. The immediate impact of the uprisings was felt in half a dozen states, but every Arab régime was shaken by them. The Arab Spring was in some respects a replay of the struggle for independence. On both occasions, an initial burst of euphoria and popular empowerment was followed by the grim realisation that freedom was illusory—and that the business of decolonisation was in important respects unfinished.

At the time of writing (2016), both trends, the Islamo-nationalist and the universalist, have failed. The states of the region have proved strong enough to crush both, at least for the time being. Less clear is whether they will be able to defeat the latest challenge to confront them. Now the danger is coming not from wired-up young demonstrators in Tahrir Square, or from mainstream political Islam, but from a movement of violent jihadist internationalism, set on destroying régimes, eradicating frontiers, and reviving a borderless caliphate.

Is the turbulent, intolerant, strife-torn Middle East we see on our television and computer screens still recognisably the Middle East the colonialists left behind? At first sight, far from it. Indeed it has become fashionable to say that the Sykes-Picot agreement—an outline of the post-Ottoman partition drawn up secretly by Britain and France in 1916—has been torn up, leaving a scarred landscape of failed and failing states. This, I think, is to miss the point. It is not the 'lines in the sand'—the borders inherited from the colonial era—that are at the heart of the problems of the Middle East, but what goes on within them. Islamism, the Arab Spring, and global jihadism are the products, not of artificial borders, but of the long-simmering crisis of the state. In any case, the most striking thing about those lines in the sand is not how ephemeral they have proved to be, but how durable. All the region's governments (in Iran and Turkey no less than the Arab states) have a strong vested interest in preserving them. It is not self-evident that the new jihadists—or insurgent minorities such as the Kurds—will succeed in permanently redrawing the map.

If Western powers are at fault, it is not primarily for the way they drew the borders of the Middle East after the First World War, but because their interaction with the region—that 'bitter embrace' described by Brown—has often served to accentuate the crisis of the state, rather than helping to resolve or mitigate it. The demise of colonial rule did not end the West's multi-dimensional involvement in the region; nor did it produce genuinely independent states. The post-colonial West has been deeply complicit in Middle East autocracy. It has propped up dictators who served its interests or, reversing itself, has intervened to topple them (Saddam Hussein, Qaddafi), leaving chaos in its wake. It is as if the region, with its wealth and wars and strategic location, serves as a standing invitation to outside meddling of the most ignorant kind. Of all the features that link the colonial and post-colonial eras, this is the most striking.

Anti-Western sentiment has been a constant feature of the modern Middle East, and one that is too often discounted or misunderstood. Like their colonial predecessors, Western officials have sometimes chosen to dismiss such hostility as something artificial, whipped up by a few malcontents. A little history ought to dispel this delusion. Regardless of their ideological differences, Khomeini and Mossadeq, Nasser and Bin Laden all believed that the big burning issue was standing up to the West: it was on this issue that they would sink or swim.

Anti-Western grievances have, to be sure, been exaggerated and manipulated. But hostility to Western power and influence is not baseless, but rooted in a shared historical experience.

The post-colonial rulers and élites of the Middle East have played their part in the region's disarray: the crisis of the state is, first and foremost, of their making. What's more, Middle Easterners, whether in government or in opposition, have often invited outside intervention, either to win power (Iraq, 2003) or to regain it (Kuwait, 1990)—though they have generally paid a political price for doing so. The notion that they are passive victims of Western conspiracies is both self-serving and facile.

Nevertheless it requires wilful blindness to deny that the West is deeply implicated in the region's failures. With its reckless and ill-planned interventions, its indulgence of autocratic rulers, its double-talk about democracy and human rights, it has contributed in no small measure to the instability of the region, and to the poisoning of relations between the Middle East and the West. Western policies and objectives may have evolved in complexity since colonial times—no one in the 1950s could have foreseen the internet or Al-Qaeda—but their effect on the region has been essentially the same: to lock it into a web of interests which the West feels a constant need to protect, either through proxies or through direct intervention. In Iraq in 2003 as in Egypt in 1882, the itch to intervene has persisted. The shadow of Curzon and Cromer hovered over Bush and Blair as they attacked and occupied Iraq, even if they were oblivious to it.

NOTES

1. OUT OF THE ASHES

1. Halidé Edib, *The Turkish Ordeal*, New York: The Century Company, 1928, pp. 30–33. (She gives the date of the meeting as 6 June, a mistake corrected by later historians.)
2. Caroline Finkel, *Osman's Dream: The Story of the Ottoman Empire, 1300–1923*, London: John Murray, 2005; Bernard Lewis, *The Emergence of Modern Turkey*, Oxford: Oxford University Press, 1961.
3. Lewis, *The Emergence of Modern Turkey*, p. 23.
4. Albert Hourani, *The Ottoman Background to the Modern Middle East*, Harlow: Longman, 1970, p. 16.
5. Quoted in Finkel, *Osman's Dream*, p. 459.
6. Sir Charles Eliot, *Turkey in Europe*, London: Edward Arnold, 1900; 2nd edition, 1908, p. 59.
7. Halidé Edib, *Memoirs*, New York: The Century Company, 1926. Quotations are from a recent reprint, *House with Wisteria: Memoirs of Turkey Old and New*, New Brunswick: Transaction Publishers, 2009, pp. 81–82.
8. Eliot, *Turkey in Europe*, pp. 138–139.
9. Aubrey Herbert, quoted in Lord Kinross, *Atatürk: The Rebirth of a Nation*, London: Weidenfeld & Nicolson, 1964, p. 29.
10. Quoted in Mark Mazower, *Salonica: City of Ghosts*, London: HarperCollins, 2004; paperback edition, 2005, p. 275.
11. Andrew Mango, *Atatürk*, London: John Murray, 1999, p. 85.
12. Mazower, *Salonica*, p. 228.
13. Mango, *Atatürk*, pp. 26–28.
14. Edib, *House with Wisteria*, p. 225.
15. Lewis, *The Emergence of Modern Turkey*, p. 226.
16. Edib, *House with Wisteria*, pp. 253–254, 292.
17. Eugene Rogan, *The Fall of the Ottomans: The Great War in the Middle East, 1914–1920*, London: Allen Lane, 2015, p. 214.

18. Kinross, *Atatürk*, pp. 105–106.

19. Eric Zürcher estimates that by the end of the war of independence the death toll was 2.5 million Turks, 600,000–800,000 Armenians, and 300,000 Greeks—which suggests a total of about 3.5 million. Eric J. Zürcher, *Turkey: A Modern History*, London: I.B. Tauris, 1993, p. 171. (On mass migrations, see note 31, below.)

20. Quoted in Nicole and Hugh Pope, *Turkey Unveiled: Atatürk and After*, London: John Murray, 1997, p. 40.

21. Eliot, *Turkey in Europe*, p. 408.

22. Nicole and Hugh Pope, *Turkey Unveiled*, pp. 42–43.

23. Zürcher, *Turkey*, pp. 120–121.

24. Further biographical details can be found in Mango, *Atatürk*, pp. 542, 549, 552.

25. Edib, *The Turkish Ordeal*, p. 73.

26. Edib, pp. 74, 81.

27. Edib, p. 185.

28. G. Ward Price, *Extra Special Correspondent*, London: Harrap, 1957, p. 128. See also Giles Milton, *Paradise Lost: Smyrna 1922*, London: Sceptre, 2009.

29. Quoted in Kinross, *Atatürk*, p. 343.

30. Lewis, *The Emergence of Modern Turkey*, p. 258.

31. Some 400,000 Muslims were forced to move from Greece to Turkey, and at least 1.2 million Orthodox Christians to move from Turkey to Greece. Their story is told in Bruce Clark, *Twice a Stranger: How Mass Expulsion Forged Modern Greece and Turkey*, London: Granta, 2006.

32. Hourani, *The Ottoman Background*, p. 2.

2. SWORD OF ARABIA

1. The author's interview with Sir Philip Adams; London, 1990.

2. Mohammed Almana, *Arabia Unified: A Portrait of Ibn Saud*, London: Hutchinson Benham, 1980, p. 33.

3. Almana, *Arabia Unified*, pp. 34–37.

4. Robert Lacey, *The Kingdom*, London: Hutchinson, 1981, p. 68.

5. Daniel van der Meulen, *The Wells of Ibn Sa'ud*, London: John Murray, 1957, p. 63.

6. Lacey, *The Kingdom*, pp. 145–146.

7. Almana, *Arabia Unified*, p. 83; Lacey, *The Kingdom*, pp. 142–143.

8. Michael Field, *The Merchants: The Big Business Families of Saudi Arabia and the Gulf*, London: John Murray, 1984; Woodstock, New York: The Overlook Press, 1985, p. 195.

9. Lacey, *The Kingdom*, p. 126.

10. Quoted in Field, *The Merchants*, p. 195.

11. Lacey, *The Kingdom*, p. 162.

12. Madawi al-Rasheed, *Politics in an Arabian Oasis:The Rashidi Tribal Dynasty*, London: I.B. Tauris, 1991, pp. 244–249.

13. Lacey, *The Kingdom*, p. 189.

14. Ibid., pp. 194–195.

15. Daniel van der Meulen, 'Memories of Old Jiddah', *Aramco World*, March–April 1967.

16. Van der Meulen, *The Wells of Ibn Sa'ud*, p. 10.

17. Van der Meulen, *Aramco World*.

18. Reader Bullard, *Two Kings in Arabia*, ed. E. C. Hodgkin, Reading: Ithaca Press, 1993.

19. Laurence Grafftey-Smith, *Bright Levant*, London: John Murray, 1970.

20. Elizabeth Monroe, *Philby of Arabia*, London: Faber, 1973.

21. Lacey, *The Kingdom*, p. 197.

22. Almana, *Arabia Unified*, p. 194.

23. Grafftey-Smith, *Bright Levant*, p. 267.

24. Almana, *Arabia Unified*, pp. 88–89.

25. Almana, *Arabia Unified*, p. 226; Monroe, *Philby of Arabia*, pp. 203–205. For the discovery of Saudi oil, see Daniel Yergin, *The Prize:The Epic Quest for Oil, Money, and Power*, London: Simon & Schuster, 1991.

26. Thomas W. Lippman, *Inside the Mirage: America's Fragile Partnership with Saudi Arabia*, Boulder, CO: Westview Press, 2004, Chapter 1.

27. Bullard, *Two Kings*, pp. 218, 224.

28. BBC Sound Archive, 30 November 1937.

29. Thomas W. Lippman, *Arabian Knight: Colonel Bill Eddy USMC and the Rise of American Power in the Middle East*, Vista, California: Selwa Press, 2008.

30. Lippman, *Arabian Knight*, p. 133.

31. Ibid., p. 140.

32. Ibid., p. 153. For Anglo-American tensions, see Aaron David Miller, *Saudi Arabian Oil and American Foreign Policy, 1939–1949*, Chapel Hill: University of North Carolina Press, 1980, especially Chapters 4 and 5.

33. Lippman, *Inside the Mirage*, p. 34.

34. Ibid., p. 17.

35. Robert Vitalis, *America's Kingdom: Mythmaking on the Saudi Oil Frontier*, Stanford: Stanford University Press, 2007, pp. 92–95.

3. THE STRUGGLE FOR THE LEVANT

1. Quoted in Wm. Roger Louis, *The British Empire in the Middle East, 1945–1951*, Oxford: Oxford University Press, 1984, p. 170.

2. Patrick Seale, *The Struggle for Arab Independence: Riad al-Solh and the Makers of the Modern Middle East*, Cambridge: Cambridge University Press, 2010, p. 29.

3. Wadad Makdisi Cortas, *A World I Loved*, New York: Nation Books, 2009, p. 9. (Wadad was the mother-in-law of the Palestinian scholar Edward Said.)

4. A. H. Hourani, *Syria and Lebanon*, Oxford: Oxford University Press, 1946, p. 49.

5. Wadad Makdisi Cortas, *A World I Loved*, p. 12.

6. Ali A. Allawi, *King Faisal I of Iraq*, New Haven and London: Yale University Press, 2014, pp. 290–291.

7. Hourani, *Syria and Lebanon*, p. 57.

8. Michael Provence, *The Great Syrian Revolt and the Rise of Arab Nationalism*, Austin: University of Texas Press, 2005, p. 51.

9. Bennett J. Doty, *The Legion of the Damned*, London: Jonathan Cape, 1928, p. 68.

10. Ibid., pp. 51–52.

11. Ibid., p. 95.

12. Ibid., pp. 110–122.

13. Quoted in Provence, *The Great Syrian Revolt*, pp. 81–82.

14. Philip S. Khoury, *Syria and the French Mandate*, Princeton: Princeton University Press, 1987, pp. 141–145.

15. Provence, *The Great Syrian Revolt*, pp. 95–98.

16. Alice Poulleau, *À Damas sous les bombes*, Yvestot: Bretteville Frères, 1926. The translation is from Daniel Neep, *Occupying Syria under the French Mandate*, Cambridge: Cambridge University Press, 2012, p. 53.

17. Khoury, *Syria and the French Mandate*, p. 196.

18. Ibid., p. 237.

19. Doty is said to have gone to Spain in the 1930s to fight Franco; his family never heard from him again.

20. Khoury, *Syria and the French Mandate*, pp. 245ff.

21. Seale, *The Struggle for Arab Independence*, p. 226.

22. Seale, pp. 80ff; 228–234.

23. Sami Moubayed, *The George Washington of Syria: The Rise and Fall of Shukri al-Quwatli*, Beirut: Dar al-Zakira, n.d. [c. 2005], p. 94.

24. Wadad Makdisi Cortas, *A World I Loved*, p. 46.

25. Ibid., pp. 78–80.

26. For the background, see Jennifer M. Dueck, *The Claims of Culture at Empire's End: Syria and Lebanon under French Rule*, Oxford: Oxford University Press, 2010.

27. Moubayed, *The George Washington of Syria*, p. 118.

28. Seale, *The Struggle for Arab Independence*, p. 324.

29. Moubayed, pp. 119–121.

30. Seale, pp. 346–347.

31. Ibid., p. 352.

32. Wilfred Thesiger, *Desert, Marsh and Mountain*, London: Collins, 1979, p. 31.

33. Sherifa Zuhur, *Asmahan's Secrets*, Austin: Center for Middle Eastern Studies, University of Texas, 2000, p. 38.

34. Sir Gawain Bell, *Shadows on the Sand*, London: Hurst, 1983, p. 131.

35. Stephen Hastings, *The Drums of Memory: An Autobiography*, London: Leo Cooper, 1984; paperback edition, 2001, p. 81.

36. James Barr, *A Line in the Sand: Britain, France and the Struggle that Shaped the Middle East*, London: Simon & Schuster, 2011; paperback edn, 2012, p. 221.

37. Max Egremont, *Under Two Flags: The Life of Major-General Sir Edward Spears*, London: Weidenfeld & Nicolson, 1997, p. xii.

38. Sir Edward Spears, *Fulfilment of a Mission*, London: Leo Cooper, 1977, p. 171.

39. Ibid., p. 172.

40. It is likely that Amal was born in 1912. On this, and the conspiracy theories that swirled round her death, see Sherifa Zuhur, *Asmahan's Secrets*.

41. Seale, *The Struggle*, pp. 505ff.

42. Spears, *Fulfilment of a Mission*, p. 224.

43. Seale, pp. 522–545.

44. Ibid., p. 575.

4. LOVERS OF ZION

1. Edward Keith-Roach, *Pasha of Jerusalem: Memoirs of a District Commissioner under the British Mandate*, London: Radcliffe Press, 1994, pp. 60–62. The description of Keith-Roach is from the diaries of Flora Moody, November 1921; Moody Papers, Rhodes House, Oxford.

2. Fadwa Tuqan, *A Mountainous Journey: An Autobiography*, tr. Olive Kenny, London: Women's Press, 1990, especially pp. 16ff.

3. Tom Segev, *One Palestine, Complete: Jews and Arabs under the British Mandate*, tr. Haim Watzman, New York: Henry Holt, 2000; paperback edition, 2001, pp. 86ff.

4. Noah Lucas, *The Modern History of Israel*, London: Weidenfeld & Nicolson, 1974, p. 83.

5. Keith-Roach, *Pasha of Jerusalem*, p. 96. For the career of Hajj Amin, see Philip Mattar, *The Mufti of Jerusalem: Al-Hajj Amin al-Husayni and the Palestinian National Movement*, New York: Columbia University Press, 1988.

6. Anbara Salam Khalidi, *Memoirs of an Early Arab Feminist*, tr. Tarif Khalidi, London: Pluto Press, 2013, p. 131.

7. Stewart Perowne, Perowne Papers, Middle East Centre Archive, Oxford.

8. Stewart Perowne, *The One Remains*, London: Hodder & Stoughton, 1954,

p. 27; letter of 18 June 1929, Perowne Papers, Middle East Centre Archive, Oxford.

9. Jabra Ibrahim Jabra, *The First Well: A Bethlehem Boyhood*, tr. Issa J. Boullata, University of Arkansas Press, 1995; paperback reprint, London: Hesperus Press, 2012, p. 214.

10. Sadiq Ibrahim Odeh, 'The Arab College in Jerusalem, 1918–1948: Recollections', *Jerusalem Quarterly*, Summer 2000, pp. 48–58. See also Rochelle Davis, 'Commemorating Education: Recollections of the Arab College in Jerusalem, 1918–1948', *Comparative Studies of South Asia, Africa and the Middle East*, 2003, 1 & 2. For a critique of the mandate authority's educational policy, see Naomi Shepherd, *Ploughing Sand: British Rule in Palestine*, London: John Murray, 1999.

11. Perowne, letter of 23 August 1929, Perowne Papers, Middle East Centre Archive, Oxford.

12. For a detailed and graphic account of the Hebron massacre, and the role of Cafferata, see Segev, *One Palestine*, Chapter 14.

13. Tuqan, *A Mountainous Journey*, pp. 51, 71, 78.

14. Shabtai Teveth, *Ben-Gurion and the Palestinian Arabs*, Oxford: Oxford University Press, 1985, p. 132.

15. Segev, *One Palestine*, pp. 359–363.

16. Issa J. Boullata, 'My First School and Childhood Home', *Jerusalem Quarterly*, Spring 2009, pp. 27–44. This and other essays are brought together in Issa J. Boullata, *The Bells of Memory: A Palestinian Boyhood in Jerusalem*, Quebec: Linda Leith Publishing, 2014.

17. Ibrahim Abu-Lughod, *Resistance, Exile, and Return*, Birzeit: Birzeit University, 2003, http://ialiis.birzeit.edu/fmru/userfiles/Ibrahim-abu-lughod-resistance-exile.pdf. See also Lila Abu-Lughod, 'My Father's Return to Palestine', *Jerusalem Quarterly*, Winter 2001, pp. 5–10.

18. Tuqan, *A Mountainous Journey*, pp. 82ff.

19. Ilan Pappé, *The Rise and Fall of a Palestinian Dynasty: The Husaynis 1700–1948*, London: Saqi, 2010, p. 261.

20. Segev, *One Palestine*, p. 370.

21. Keith-Roach, *Pasha of Jerusalem*, p. 198.

22. Boullata, 'My First School'.

23. Tuqan, *A Mountainous Journey*, pp. 86ff.

24. Bell, *Shadows on the Sand*, p. 97.

25. Jabra Ibrahim Jabra, *The First Well*, p. 48.

26. Elizabeth Monroe, 'The Origins of the Palestine Problem', in Peter Mansfield (ed.), *The Middle East: A Political and Economic Survey*, Oxford: Oxford University Press, 1973, p. 61.

27. Monica Wilson (née Monica Dehn), unpublished letters from Palestine, 1944–48, Middle East Centre Archive, Oxford. I am indebted to Monica

for allowing me to quote from the letters, and to Zina Rohan, who first alerted me to their existence.

28. For the origins of Sharq al-Adna, see John Connell, *The House by Herod's Gate*, London: Sampson, Low, Marston, 1947.

29. Dehn, letter of 28 March 1945.

30. Dehn, letters of 7 and 18 July 1945. Whether her boss at the radio station, Teddy Hodgkin—later, as E. C. Hodgkin, foreign editor of *The Times*—was aware of her extra-mural activities one can only wonder.

31. Richard Stubbs, *Palestine Story: A Personal Account of the Last Three Years of British Rule in Palestine*; privately printed, Brettenham, Suffolk: Thurston, 1995. See also Stubbs' obituary, *Guardian*, 2 January 1997, written by his friend Grahame Isard, to whom I'm grateful for further information about Stubbs.

32. Dehn, letter of 5 May 1946.

33. Dehn, letter of 29 June 1946.

34. From an unpublished manuscript by Barbara Board, covering her work in Palestine in 1945–46; I am grateful to her daughter, Jacqueline Karp, who is editing the manuscript, for permission to quote from it. An earlier volume, covering the years 1943–44, was published as *Reporting from Palestine*, Nottingham: Five Leaves, 2008. For her experiences in Palestine during the 1930s, see Barbara Board, *Newsgirl in Palestine*, London: Michael Joseph, 1937.

35. For a remarkably detailed and vivid reconstruction of the bombing, see Thurston Clarke, *By Blood and Fire: The Attack on the King David Hotel*, London: Hutchinson, 1981.

36. Dehn, letter of 25 July 1946. (The exact date is unclear, but the letter was clearly written shortly after the bombing.)

37. Dehn, letters of 8 August 1946 and 8 March 1947. When Barker left Palestine, he expressed his feelings for it by urinating on its soil; Wm. Roger Louis (ed.), *The End of the Palestine Mandate*, London: I.B. Tauris, 1986, p. 14.

38. Louis (ed.), *The End of the Palestine Mandate*, pp. 19–20.

39. Dehn, letter of 29 November 1947.

40. Dehn, letter of 2 February 1948.

41. Larry Collins and Dominique Lapierre, *O Jerusalem!* New York: Simon & Schuster, 1972, pp. 176–179; Uri Milstein, *History of the War of Independence, Vol. III*, Lanham: University Press of America, 1996, p. 110.

42. Dehn, letter of 3 April 1948.

43. Dan Kurzman, *Genesis 1948: The First Arab-Israeli War*, London: Valentine Mitchell, 1970, pp. 133ff.

44. Kurzman, *Genesis 1948*, p. 141. The Haganah had not expected—and had certainly not approved—a massacre, but, as Kurzman makes clear, its

commander in Jerusalem, David Shaltiel, had given his guarded approval for the attack on the village.

45. Khalidi, *Memoirs of an Early Arab Feminist*, pp. 160–161.
46. Stubbs, *Palestine Story*, pp. 168–169.
47. Abu-Lughod, *Resistance, Exile and Return*.
48. John Marlowe, *The Seat of Pilate: An Account of the Palestine Mandate*, London: Cresset Press, 1959, p. 1.

5. ABDULLAH'S LITTLE KINGDOM

1. Mary C. Wilson, *King Abdullah, Britain and the Making of Jordan*, Cambridge: Cambridge University Press, 1987.
2. *Memoirs of King Abdullah of Jordan*, ed. Philip P. Graves, London: Cape, 1950, p. 37.
3. *Memoirs*, pp. 38–39.
4. Ilan Pappé, 'Kirkbride, Sir Alec Seath', *Oxford Dictionary of National Biography*, Oxford: Oxford University Press, 2004; accessed online.
5. Alec Seath Kirkbride, *A Crackle of Thorns: Experiences in the Middle East*, London: John Murray, 1956, p. 20.
6. Kirkbride, *A Crackle of Thorns*, pp. 25–27.
7. Quoted in Wilson, *King Abdullah*, p. 67.
8. Kirkbride, *A Crackle of Thorns*, p. 29.
9. 'A falcon trapped in a canary's cage': the phrase, from an unnamed contemporary, is quoted in Larry Collins and Dominique Lapierre, *O Jerusalem!* New York: Simon & Schuster, 1972, p. 92.
10. Ann Dearden, *Jordan*, London: Robert Hale, 1958, p. 51.
11. Wilson, *King Abdullah*, p. 115. Abdullah's long and largely secret relationship with the Zionists is the subject of Avi Shlaim's book, *Collusion across the Jordan: King Abdullah, the Zionist Movement and the Partition of Palestine*, Oxford: Oxford University Press, 1988.
12. Philip Robins, *A History of Jordan*, Cambridge: Cambridge University Press, 2004, p. 42. For a sympathetic, but not entirely uncritical, account of Glubb's life and work, see James Lunt, *Glubb Pasha: A Biography*, London: Harvill Press, 1984.
13. Barbara Board, *Newsgirl in Palestine*, London: Michael Joseph, 1937, pp. 72, 76–81.
14. Lunt, *Glubb Pasha*, pp. 78ff.
15. Dearden, *Jordan*, p. 105.
16. Shlaim, *Collusion*, pp. 113–119.
17. Ibid., pp. 136–137.
18. Quoted in ibid., p. 193.
19. Ibid., pp. 206–208.

20. Sir Alec Kirkbride, *From the Wings: Amman Memoirs, 1947–1951*, London: Cass, 1976, p. 28.

21. Quoted in Benny Morris, *The Birth of the Palestinian Refugee Problem, 1947–1949*, Cambridge: Cambridge University Press, 1987, p. 210.

22. Kirkbride, *From the Wings*, p. 48.

23. Wilson, *King Abdullah*, pp. 179, 190, 191.

24. Dearden, *Jordan*, p. 73.

25. Dearden, p. 85. As a journalist working for the *Guardian*, Dearden had witnessed the events she describes.

26. Wilson, *King Abdullah*, p. 198.

6. OIL AND EMPIRE

1. Ervand Abrahamian, *The Coup: 1953, the CIA, and the Roots of Modern US-Iranian Relations*, New York: New Press, 2013, p. 37.

 2. Quoted in Gordon Waterfield, *Professional Diplomat: Sir Percy Loraine of Kirkharle*, London: John Murray, 1973, p. 63.

 3. Manucher and Roxane Farmanfarmaian, *Blood and Oil: Memoirs of a Persian Prince*, London: Prion, 1991, pp. 32–40.

 4. Ibid., pp. 59–60.

 5. The apt phrase is Farmanfarmaian's; *Blood and Oil*, p. 122. For a critical account of the AIOC's record by someone who worked for the company in the 1930s, see L. P. Elwell-Sutton, *Persian Oil: A Study in Power Politics*, London: Lawrence & Wishart, 1955.

 6. Sir Reader Bullard, *Letters from Tehran*, ed. E. C. Hodgkin, London: I.B. Tauris, 1991, p. 168.

 7. Farmanfarmaian, *Blood and Oil*, p. 334.

 8. Bullard, *Letters from Tehran*, p. 27.

 9. Ibid., pp. 80–81. See also Annabelle Sreberny and Massoumeh Torfeh, *Persian Service: The BBC and British Interests in Iran*, London: I.B. Tauris, 2014.

10. Bullard, *Letters from Tehran*, p. 73.

11. Ibid., pp. 93 and 163.

12. Ibid., p. 221.

13. Richard Burton, *A Strong Song Tows Us: The Life of Basil Bunting*, Oxford: Infinite Ideas, 2013, p. 183.

14. Don Share (ed.), *Bunting's Persia: Translations by Basil Bunting*, Chicago: Flood Editions, 2012, p. 45. The extract is from the tenth-century poet Manuchehri.

15. Keith Alldritt, *The Poet as Spy: The Life and Wild Times of Basil Bunting*, London: Aurum Press, 1998.

16. Gerald Butt, *The Lion in the Sand: The British in the Middle East*, London: Bloomsbury, 1995, pp. 66–80.

17. Farmanfarmaian, *Blood and Oil*, pp. 87–88.

18. Daniel Yergin, *The Prize: The Epic Quest for Oil, Money, and Power*, London: Simon & Schuster, 1991, p. 451.

19. Abrahamian, *The Coup*, pp. 19, 64–65.

20. Farmanfarmaian, *Blood and Oil*, p. 218.

21. Interview with the author for the BBC World Service radio programme 'Oil and Empire', 1990, in the series 'The Making of the Middle East'. For McGhee's own account, see *Envoy to the Middle World: Adventures in Diplomacy*, New York: Harper & Row, 1983.

22. Farmanfarmaian, *Blood and Oil*, pp. 260–264.

23. Norman Kemp, *Abadan: A First-Hand Account of the Persian Oil Crisis*, London: Allan Wingate, 1953, pp. 244–246.

24. Yergin, *The Prize*, p. 464.

25. Dean Acheson, *Present at the Creation: My Years in the State Department*, London: Hamish Hamilton, 1970, p. 503.

26. Abrahamian, *The Coup*, pp. 126–127.

27. C. M. Woodhouse, *Something Ventured*, London: Granada, 1982; Kermit Roosevelt, *Countercoup*, New York: McGraw-Hill, 1979.

28. Farmanfarmaian, *Blood and Oil*, p. 156.

29. Burton, *A Strong Song*, pp. 327–328.

30. Ibid., pp. 330–332; Aldritt, *The Poet as Spy*, pp. 134–137.

31. Woodhouse, *Something Ventured*, p. 117.

32. Fitzroy Maclean, *Eastern Approaches*, London: Jonathan Cape, 1949.

33. Abrahamian, *The Coup*, pp. 190–192.

34. BBC World Service, 'Oil and Empire'.

35. Ibid.

36. Yergin, *The Prize*, p. 470.

37. Abrahamian, *The Coup*, p. 2.

7. THE PIGEONS OF DENSHAWAI

1. Roger Owen, *Lord Cromer: Victorian Imperialist, Edwardian Proconsul*, Oxford: Oxford University Press, 2004, pp. 335–336.

2. *The Times*, 29 June 1906.

3. Katherine Frank, *A Passage to Egypt: The Life of Lucie Duff Gordon*, Boston and New York: Houghton Mifflin, 1994, pp. 303–313.

4. J. G. Darwin, 'Baring, Evelyn, first earl of Cromer', *Oxford Dictionary of National Biography*, Oxford: Oxford University Press, 2004, accessed online; and Owen, *Lord Cromer*, p. 282. Baring did not become Lord Cromer until 1892, but for convenience I have referred to him as Cromer throughout.

5. Max Rodenbeck, *Cairo: The City Victorious*, London: Picador, 1998, pp. 174–176.

6. Owen, *Lord Cromer*, pp. 332, 337, 349–351.

7. Laurence Grafftey-Smith, *Bright Levant*, London: John Murray, 1970, pp. 17–18, 55–56.

8. Quoted in Elizabeth Monroe, *Britain's Moment in the Middle East*, London: Chatto & Windus, 2nd edn, 1981, p. 56.

9. Thomas Crowe (ed.), *Gathering Moss: A Memoir of Owen Tweedy*, London: Sidgwick & Jackson, 1967, p. 86.

10. Grafftey-Smith, *Bright Levant*, pp. 46–47.

11. Afaf Lutfi al-Sayyid Marsot, *A Short History of Modern Egypt*, Cambridge: Cambridge University Press, 1985, pp. 84–85.

12. Gudrun Krämer, *The Jews in Modern Egypt, 1914–1952*, London: I.B. Tauris, 1989.

13. Gilles Perrault, *A Man Apart: The Life of Henri Curiel*, London: Zed Books, 1987.

14. Robert Stephens, *Nasser: A Political Biography*, London: Allen Lane, 1971, pp. 36–37.

15. See Artemis Cooper, *Cairo in the War*, London: Hamish Hamilton, 1989.

16. Trefor E. Evans (ed.), *The Killearn Diaries, 1934–1946*, London: Sidgwick & Jackson, 1972, p. 215.

17. Mohammed Neguib, *Egypt's Destiny*, London: Gollancz, 1955, p. 14.

18. Butt, *The Lion in the Sand*, p. 137.

19. Extracts from an interview with Dave Wallis carried out by Julian Putkowski in 1983: http://www.marxists.org/history/etol/revhist/backiss/vol8/no2/wallis

20. Putkowski, 1983; and Dave Wallis, *Tram-Stop by the Nile*, London: Heinemann, 1958. For more on communism in the British army in wartime Egypt, see Richard Kisch, *The Days of the Good Soldier*, London: Journeyman Press, 1985. Wallis later achieved fame with another novel, *Only Lovers Left Alive* (1964).

21. One Egyptian recruit, the writer and diplomat Ibrahim Shukrallah, told the author how he would be summoned to a party meeting. Curiel's Rolls-Royce would arrive at the door of his modest home in Cairo and the chauffeur would ask him to accompany him to see Monsieur Henri.

22. William Stadiem, *Too Rich: The High Life and Tragic Death of King Farouk*, London: Robson Books, 1992.

23. Perrault, *A Man Apart*, pp. 155ff.

24. Afaf Lutfi al-Sayyid Marsot, *A Short History of Egypt*, p. 105.

25. Stephens, *Nasser*, pp. 109–110.

26. Keith Kyle, *Suez*, London: Weidenfeld & Nicolson, 1991; the best of the many books on the subject.

27. Even in exile, Curiel tried to help the Egyptian nationalists. He somehow got hold of the Anglo-French invasion plan and sent it, via one of the

Free Officers, to Nasser. But Nasser and his general staff would not take it seriously. Perrault, *A Man Apart*, p. 197.

28. Stephens, *Nasser*, p. 246.

8. REVOLUTION ON THE TIGRIS

1. The author's interview with Lamia Gailani, London, 1990.

2. For a graphic account of the siege of Kut and its aftermath, see Charles Townshend, *When God Made Hell: The British Invasion of Mesopotamia and the Creation of Iraq, 1914–1921*, London: Faber, 2010.

3. Letter dated 27 April 1917; Lady Bell (ed.), *The Letters of Gertrude Bell*, Vol. II, London: Ernest Benn, 1927. This was an early selection edited by Bell's step-mother. The full texts are now available at www.gerty.ncl.ac.uk

4. *Letters of Gertrude Bell*, 14 June 1920.

5. Ibid., 10 October 1920. For the rebellion of 1920, see Townshend, *When God Made Hell*.

6. Ali A. Allawi, *King Faisal I of Iraq*, New Haven & London: Yale University Press, 2014.

7. This was Sayid Talib of Basra, who was arrested and deported to Ceylon (modern-day Sri Lanka).

8. *Letters of Gertrude Bell*, 8 July 1921.

9. D. K. Fieldhouse (ed.), *Kurds, Arabs and Britons: The Memoir of Wallace Lyon in Iraq, 1918–1944*, London: I.B. Tauris, 2002, p. 95.

10. Fieldhouse, *Kurds, Arabs and Britons*, p. 96.

11. William Facey and Najdat Fathi Safwat (eds.), *A Soldier's Story: The Memoirs of Jafar Pasha al-Askari (1885–1936)*, London: Arabian Publishing, 2003, p. 19.

12. 'A prodigious manipulator of men': Larry Collins and Dominique Lapierre, *O Jerusalem!* New York: Simon & Schuster, 1972, p. 85.

13. Ida Donges Staudt, *Living in Romantic Baghdad: An American Memoir of Teaching and Travel in Iraq, 1924–1947*, Syracuse, NY: Syracuse University Press, 2012. Additional information on the American School is from Frank Walker, 'The Mission to Iraq', *Leben*, Vol. 2, Issue 1, 2006; accessed online. Catholics as well as Protestants helped educate the Iraqi élite; for the work of the American Jesuits who founded Baghdad College in the 1930s, see Anthony Shadid, 'The American Age, Iraq', *Granta*, 116, Summer 2011.

14. *Letters of Gertrude Bell*, 28 January 1925.

15. Ibid., 2 July 1926.

16. Phoebe Marr, *The Modern History of Iraq*, Boulder, Colorado: Westview Press, 1985, p. 49.

17. Quoted in Ali A. Allawi, *The Occupation of Iraq*, New Haven & London: Yale University Press, 2007, p. 17.
18. Fieldhouse (ed.), *Kurds, Arabs and Britons*, p. 205.
19. Fieldhouse, p. 209.
20. The official was Stewart Perowne; quoted in Wm. Roger Louis, *The British Empire in the Middle East, 1945–1951*, Oxford: Oxford University Press, 1984, p. 315.
21. Staudt, *Living in Romantic Baghdad*, pp. 218–219.
22. Freya Stark, *Dust in the Lion's Paw*, London: Murray, 1961; paperback edn, London: Arrow, 1990, p. 89.
23. Stark, p. 119; Tamara Chalabi, *Late for Tea at the Deer Palace*, London: Harper Press, 2010, p. 209.
24. Jane Fletcher Geniesse, *Passionate Nomad: The Life of Freya Stark*, New York: Random House, 1999, pp. 298–299.
25. Alaric Jacob, *A Traveller's War*, London: Collins, 1944, p. 155.
26. Hanna Batatu, *The Old Social Classes and the Revolutionary Movements of Iraq*, Princeton: Princeton University Press, 1978, pp. 487–522.
27. Batatu, *The Old Social Classes*, pp. 537–571.
28. David D. Newsom, *Witness to a Changing World*, Washington, DC: New Academia Publishing, 2008, pp. 125–126.
29. The diplomat was Harold Beeley; quoted in Donald Maitland, *Diverse Times, Sundry Places*, Brighton: The Alpha Press, 1996.
30. The author's interview with Lamia Gailani, London, 1990.
31. Sam Falle, *My Lucky Life*, Brighton: The Book Guild, 1996, p. 119.

9. THE BATTLE OF ALGIERS

1. Alistair Horne, *A Savage War of Peace: Algeria, 1954–1962*, Basingstoke: Macmillan, 1977, pp. 185–186.
2. John Ruedy, *Modern Algeria: The Origins and Development of a Nation*, Bloomington: Indiana University Press, 1992, p. 64.
3. Quoted in Nevill Barbour (ed.), *A Survey of North West Africa*, Oxford: Oxford University Press, 1959, p. 44.
4. Benjamin Stora, *Algeria 1830–2000: A Short History*, tr. Jane Marie Todd, Ithaca: Cornell University Press, 2001, p. 5.
5. Quoted in Charles-Robert Ageron, *Modern Algeria: A History from 1830 to the Present*, tr. Michael Brett, London: Hurst, 1991, p. 35.
6. The poem is quoted in Ruedy, *Modern Algeria*, p. 79. On the events of 1871–72, see Ageron, *Modern Algeria*, pp. 49–53.
7. Stora, *Algeria*, p. 7.
8. Edward Behr, *The Algerian Problem*, London: Hodder & Stoughton, 1961, p. 30.
9. Stora, *Algeria*, pp. 7–13.

10. Stora, *Algeria*, pp. 9–11. Stora, born in Constantine in 1950, is himself an Algerian Jew.

11. Stora, *Algeria*, p. 12.

12. Stora, *Algeria*, p. 24.

13. Martin Evans, *Algeria: France's Undeclared War*, Oxford: Oxford University Press, 2012, p. 55.

14. Quoted in Behr, *The Algerian Problem*, p. 48.

15. Albert Camus, *Algerian Chronicles*, tr. Arthur Goldhammer, Cambridge, Mass.: Harvard University Press, 2013; paperback edn, 2014, p. 43.

16. Olivier Todd, *Albert Camus: A Life*, tr. Benjamin Ivry, London: Chatto & Windus, 1997.

17. Ageron, *Modern Algeria*, p. 102; Stora, *Algeria*, p. 22. Estimates of the dead vary widely.

18. Ageron, *Modern Algeria*, p. 106.

19. Robert Merle, *Ben Bella*, tr. Camilla Sykes, London: Michael Joseph, 1967, p. 44. Merle, a French writer born in Algeria, taped a series of interviews with Ben Bella which form the basis of the book.

20. Merle, *Ben Bella*, pp. 67, 71, 82–90.

21. Mouloud Mammeri, *The Sleep of the Just*, tr. Len Ortzen, London: Cresset Press, 1956, pp. 67–69. Ortzen's *North African Writing*, London: Heinemann, 1970, provides translated extracts from several of the Algerian writers, and biographical information about them.

22. Evans, *Algeria*, p. 42.

23. Stora, *Algeria*, p. 59.

24. Todd, *Albert Camus*, p. 378.

25. Ted Morgan, *My Battle of Algiers: A Memoir*, New York: HarperCollins, 2005; paperback edition, 2007, pp. 91–92.

26. Morgan, *My Battle*, p. 106. Ramdane was later killed by rivals in the FLN.

27. Quoted in William Quandt, *Revolution and Political Leadership: Algeria, 1954–1968*, Cambridge, Mass.: MIT Press, 1969, p. 118.

28. Morgan, *My Battle*, pp. 124–125.

29. Ibid., p. 145.

30. Behr, *The Algerian Problem*, pp. 137ff.

31. Stora, *Algeria*, p. 84.

32. Horne, *A Savage War of Peace*, p. 517.

33. The estimate is Stora's, *Algeria*, p. 111.

10. ARABIAN ENDGAME

1. The author's interview with Doreen Ingrams, May 1993, for the BBC World Service radio series 'The Making of the Middle East'; for more details, see her memoir, *A Time in Arabia*, London: John Murray, 1970.

2. Tom Little, *South Arabia: Arena of Conflict*, London: Pall Mall Press, 1968, pp. 9–10.

3. Ingrams, BBC interview.

4. June Knox-Mawer, *The Sultans Came to Tea*, London: John Murray, 1961, p. 13.

5. Knox-Mawer, *The Sultans*, pp. 49ff.

6. Brian Lapping, *End of Empire*, London: Granada, 1985, p. 286.

7. Sir Kennedy Trevaskis, *Shades of Amber: A South Arabian Episode*, London: Hutchinson, 1968, p. 8.

8. Knox-Mawer, *The Sultans*, p. 211.

9. Spencer Mawby, *British Policy in Aden and the Protectorates*, London: Routledge, 2005, pp. 39–40.

10. Mawby, *British Policy*, p. 45.

11. Godfrey Meynell, unpublished manuscript, 2005. I am grateful to the author for letting me read the manuscript, a few extracts from which can be found in Peter Hinchcliffe, John T. Ducker, and Maria Holt (eds.), *Without Honour in Arabia: The British Retreat from Aden*, London: I.B. Tauris, 2006.

12. Mawby, *British Policy*, p. 48.

13. Ibid., pp. 52–57. Mawby records that some of the documents about the campaign were later destroyed by the British authorities in Aden.

14. Mawby, *British Policy*, pp. 77, 90.

15. Godfrey Meynell, unpublished manuscript, 2005.

16. Mawby, p. 97.

17. Mawby, p. 99.

18. Doreen Ingrams, BBC interview, May 1993.

19. V. V. Naumkin, *Red Wolves of Yemen: The Struggle for Independence*, Cambridge: Oleander Press, 2004, p. 92. Naumkin lived in Aden at the time and had good contacts with the NLF leadership.

20. Fred Halliday, *Arabia without Sultans*, London: Penguin Books, 1974, p. 190.

21. Quoted in Lapping, *End of Empire*, p. 295.

22. Naumkin, *Red Wolves*, pp. 104–105.

23. Mawby, *British Policy*, p. 105.

24. Hinchcliffe et al., *Without Honour in Arabia*, pp. 158ff.

25. Stephen Harper, *Last Sunset*, London: Collins, 1978, p. 71.

26. Mawby, *British Policy*, p. 145.

27. Godfrey Meynell, unpublished manuscript, 2005.

28. Mawby, *British Policy*, p. 167.

29. Godfrey Meynell, interview with the author, 2012.

30. Mawby, *British Policy*, p. 188.

EPILOGUE: THE POISONED WELL

1. Glen Balfour-Paul, *The End of Empire in the Middle East*, Cambridge: Cambridge University Press, 1991, p. 224, footnote 73.
2. Mahmoud Darwish, *Selected Poems*, tr. Ian Wedde and Fawwaz Tuqan, Cheadle: Carcanet Press, 1973, p. 74. Other examples include the stories of Ghassan Kanafani.
3. Balfour-Paul, *The End of Empire*, p. 103.
4. L. Carl Brown, *International Politics and the Middle East: Old Rules, Dangerous Game*, Princeton: Princeton University Press, 1984, p. 4.
5. Brown, *International Politics*, p. 18.
6. Roger Owen, 'North Africa and the Middle East', in Michael Howard and Wm. Roger Louis (eds.), *The Oxford History of the Twentieth Century*, Oxford: Oxford University Press, 1998, p. 262. See also his *State, Power and Politics in the Making of the Modern Middle East*, London: Routledge, 1992.
7. Maxime Rodinson, 'Islam Resurgent?' in his *Marxism and the Muslim World*, New York and London: Monthly Review Press, 1981, p. 298. (The essay was originally written as a series of articles for *Le Monde*, 6–8 December 1978.) On the issue of legitimacy, see Michael Hudson, *Arab Politics: The Search for Legitimacy*, Yale and London: Yale University Press, 1977.

ACKNOWLEDGEMENTS

I have incurred many debts in writing this book. My work as a Middle East analyst with the BBC World Service, from 1985 to 2010, produced the original idea for the book, and led to the radio series which was its precursor.

I am also indebted to those I've interviewed, over many years, who reminisced about their lives—and their family's lives—in different parts of the Middle East during the age of empire. I've learned much from listening to them and reading their letters, diaries, or memoirs, and on occasion debating with them the rights and wrongs of colonial rule.

Several universities have hosted me as a visiting researcher—the London School of Economics, King's College, London, and, most recently, Oxford. I have benefited from the advice of colleagues in all three places, and from the use of these institutions' libraries. In finishing and revising the book, I have relied heavily on the library of the Middle East Centre at St Antony's College, Oxford. Other libraries—at the School of Oriental and African Studies, the Arab-British Centre, and, in my new home, the South Oxfordshire public libraries—have been consistently helpful.

In March 2015 the Centre for International Studies in Oxford organised a workshop to discuss the book as a work-in-progress, and the participants came up with valuable suggestions and criticisms. In addition, I have had good advice on particular chapters from Michael Brett, Michael Provence, Naomi Shepherd, and Sami Zubaida. Among those who read the whole book in manuscript are Peter Clark, Peter Mangold, and Gerald Butt, who made numerous suggestions that have saved me from error or prompted me to rethink my ideas. I hope they will forgive me if I have not always heeded their advice. If mistakes remain, the fault is of course mine, not theirs.

My publisher, Michael Dwyer, has been a constant source of advice and encouragement. Finally, the book is dedicated to my wife, a life-long opponent of imperialism, and to my children, who belong to a genera-tion for whom Europe's empires are a distant shadow. My hope is that they, like other readers, can learn from the colonial past and its legacy, in order to gain a better understanding of the world they live in.

BIBLIOGRAPHY

(*An asterisk indicates recommended reading*)

Abdullah of Jordan, King, *My Memoirs Completed*, Harlow: Longman, 1978.

Abrahamian, Ervand, *The Coup: 1953, the CIA, and the Roots of Modern US-Iranian Relations*, New York: The New Press, 2013.

*Abrahamian, Ervand, *A History of Modern Iran*, Cambridge: Cambridge University Press, 2008.

Ageron, Charles-Robert, *Modern Algeria: A History from 1830 to the Present*, tr. Michael Brett, London: Hurst, 1991.

Allawi, Ali A., *King Faisal I of Iraq*, Yale University Press, New Haven & London: Yale University Press, 2014.

Almana, Mohammed, *Arabia Unified: A Portrait of Ibn Saud*, London: Hutchinson Benham, 1980.

Balfour-Paul, Glen, *The End of Empire in the Middle East*, Cambridge: Cambridge University Press, 1991.

Barr, James, *A Line in the Sand: Britain, France and the Struggle that Shaped the Middle East*, London: Simon & Schuster, 2011.

Batatu, Hanna, *The Old Social Classes and the Revolutionary Movements of Iraq*, Princeton: Princeton University Press, 1978.

Behr, Edward, *The Algerian Problem*, London: Hodder & Stoughton, 1961.

Behr, Edward, *'Anyone Here Been Raped and Speaks English?' A Foreign Correspondent's Life behind the Lines*, New York: Viking Press, 1978.

Bell, Sir Gawain, *Shadows on the Sand*, London: Hurst, 1983.

Birdwood, Lord, *Nuri as-Said: A Study in Arab Leadership*, London: Cassell, 1959.

Board, Barbara, *Newsgirl in Palestine*, London: Michael Joseph, 1937.

Board, Barbara, *Newsgirl in Egypt*, London: Michael Joseph, 1938.

Board, Barbara, *Reporting from Palestine, 1943–1944*, Nottingham: Five Leaves Publications, 2008.

BIBLIOGRAPHY

*Brendon, Piers, *The Decline and Fall of the British Empire, 1781–1997*, London: Jonathan Cape, 2007.

Brown, L. Carl, *International Politics and the Middle East: Old Rules, Dangerous Game*, Princeton: Princeton University Press, 1984.

Bullard, Reader, *The Camels Must Go: An Autobiography*, London: Faber, 1961.

Bullard, Reader, *Two Kings in Arabia: Letters from Jeddah, 1923–5 and 1936–9*, ed. E. C. Hodgkin, Reading: Ithaca Press, 1993.

Bullard, Reader, *Letters from Tehran: A British Ambassador in World War II Persia*, ed. E. C. Hodgkin, London: I.B. Tauris, 1991.

Butt, Gerald, *The Lion in the Sand: The British in the Middle East*, London: Bloomsbury, 1995.

Camus, Albert, *The First Man*, tr. David Hapgood, London: Hamish Hamilton, 1995.

Camus, Albert, *Algerian Chronicles*, tr. Arthur Goldhammer, Cambridge, Mass.: Harvard University Press, 2013.

Cesarani, David, *Major Farran's Hat: Murder, Scandal and Britain's War against Jewish Terrorism, 1945–1948*, London: Heinemann, 2009.

Chalabi, Tamara, *Late for Tea at the Deer Palace: The Lost Dreams of My Iraqi Family*, London: HarperCollins, 2010.

Clarke, Thurston, *By Blood and Fire: The Attack on the King David Hotel*, London: Hutchinson, 1981.

Collins, Larry, and Dominic Lapierre, *O Jerusalem!* New York: Simon & Schuster, 1972.

Connell, John, *The House by Herod's Gate*, London: Sampson Low, Marston, 1947.

Darwin, John, *The Empire Project: The Rise and Fall of the British World-System, 1830–1970*, Cambridge: Cambridge University Press, 2009.

Dearden, Ann, *Jordan*, London: Robert Hale, 1958.

de Bellaigue, Christopher, *Patriot of Persia: Muhammad Mossadegh and a Very British Coup*, London: Bodley Head, 2012.

Deighton, Len, *City of Gold*, London: Century, 1992.

Determan, Jörg Mathias, *Historiography in Saudi Arabia: Globalisation and the State in the Middle East*, London: I.B. Tauris, 2014.

Doty, Bennett J., *The Legion of the Damned*, London: Jonathan Cape, 1928.

Dueck, Jennifer M., *The Claims of Culture at Empire's End: Syria and Lebanon under French Rule*, Oxford: Oxford University Press, 2010.

Edib, Halidé, *The Memoirs of Halidé Edib*, New York: Century Company, 1926.

Edib, Halidé, *The Turkish Ordeal*, New York: Century Company, 1928.

Eliot, Sir Charles, *Turkey in Europe*, London: Edward Arnold, 1900; 2nd edition, 1908.

Elwell-Sutton, L. P., *Persian Oil: A Study in Power Politics*, London: Lawrence & Wishart, 1955.

BIBLIOGRAPHY

Evans, Martin, *Algeria: France's Undeclared War*, Oxford: Oxford University Press, 2012.

Evans, Trefor E. (ed.), *The Killearn Diaries, 1934–1946*, London: Sidgwick & Jackson, 1972.

Falle, Sam, *My Lucky Life: In War, Revolution, Peace and Diplomacy*, Brighton: The Book Guild, 1996.

Farmanfarmaian, Manucher and Roxane, *Blood and Oil: Memoirs of a Persian Prince*, London: Prion, 1997.

Field, Michael, *The Merchants: The Big Business Families of Arabia*, London: Murray, 1984; paperback edition, Woodstock, NY: Overlook Press, 1985.

Fieldhouse, D. K., *Western Imperialism in the Middle East, 1914–1958*, Oxford: Oxford University Press, 2006.

Fieldhouse, D. K. (ed.), *Kurds, Arabs and Britons: The Memoir of Wallace Lyon in Iraq, 1918–1944*, London: I.B. Tauris, 2002.

*Finkel, Caroline, *Osman's Dream: The Story of the Ottoman Empire, 1300–1923*, London: Murray, 2005.

Gallman, Waldemar J., *Iraq under General Nuri: My Recollections of Nuri al-Said, 1954–1958*, Baltimore: Johns Hopkins Press, 1964.

Gasiorowski, Mark J., and Malcolm Byrne (eds.), *Mohammad Mosaddeq and the 1953 Coup in Iran*, Syracuse, NY: Syracuse University Press, 2004.

Geniesse, Jane Fletcher, *Passionate Nomad: The Life of Freya Stark*, New York: Random House, 1999.

Gilmour, David, *Curzon*, London: Murray, 1994.

Golani, Motti, *The End of the British Mandate for Palestine, 1948: The Diary of Sir Henry Gurney*, Basingstoke: Palgrave Macmillan, 2009.

Golani, Motti, *Palestine between Politics and Terror, 1945–1947*, Waltham, Massachusetts: Brandeis University Press, 2013.

Grafftey-Smith, Laurence, *Bright Levant*, London: Murray, 1970.

Grondahl, Mia, *The Dream of Jerusalem: Lewis Larsson and the American Colony Photographers*, Stockholm: Journal, 2005.

Hinchcliffe, Peter, John T. Ducker, and Maria Holt (eds.), *Without Glory in Arabia: The British Retreat from Aden*, London: I.B. Tauris, 2006.

Hodgkin, Thomas, *Letters from Palestine, 1932–1936*, ed. E. C. Hodgkin, London: Quartet, 1986.

Holden, David, *Farewell to Arabia*, London: Faber, 1966.

Hopwood, Derek, *Tales of Empire: The British in the Middle East, 1880–1952*, London: I.B. Tauris, 1989.

Horne, Alistair, *A Savage War of Peace: Algeria, 1954–1962*, Basingstoke: Macmillan, 1977.

*Hourani, Albert, *A History of the Arab Peoples*, London: Faber, 1991.

Hourani, Albert, *The Emergence of the Modern Middle East*, London: Macmillan, 1981.

Howard, Michael, and Wm. Roger Louis (eds.), *The Oxford History of the Twentieth Century*, Oxford: Oxford University Press, 1998.

Idilbi, Ulfat, *Sabriya: Damascus Bitter Sweet*, tr. Peter Clark, London: Quartet, 1995.

Ingrams, Doreen, *A Time in Arabia*, London: Murray, 1970.

Jabra, Jabra Ibrahim, *The First Well: A Bethlehem Boyhood*, tr. Issa J. Boullata, Arkansas: University of Arkansas Press, 1995; London: Hesperus Press, 2012.

Jacob, Alaric, *A Traveller's War*, London: Collins, 1944.

Keith-Roach, Edward, *Pasha of Jerusalem: Memoirs of a District Commissioner under the British Mandate*, London: Radcliffe Press, 1994.

Kelly, Saul, 'A Succession of Crises: SOE in the Middle East, 1940–45', *Intelligence and National Security*, Vol. 20, No. 1, March 2005.

Khalidi, Anbara Salam, *Memoirs of an Early Arab Feminist*, tr. Tarif Khalidi, London: Pluto Press, 2013.

*Khoury, Philip S., *Syria and the French Mandate*, Princeton: Princeton University Press, 1987.

Kinross, Lord, *Atatürk: The Rebirth of a Nation*, London: Weidenfeld & Nicolson, 1964.

Kirkbride, Alec, *A Crackle of Thorns*, London: Murray, 1956.

Kirkbride, Alec, *From the Wings: Amman Memoirs, 1947–1951*, London: Cass, 1976.

Knox-Mawer, June, *The Sultans Came to Tea*, London: Murray, 1961.

Krämer, Gudrun, *The Jews in Modern Egypt, 1914–1952*, London: I.B. Tauris, 1989.

Kurzman, Dan, *Genesis 1948: The First Arab-Israeli War*, London: Vallentine, Mitchell, 1970.

*Kyle, Keith, *Suez*, London: I.B. Tauris, 1991.

Lacey, Robert, *The Kingdom*, London: Hutchinson, 1981.

Lapping, Brian, *End of Empire*, London: Granada, 1985.

Lazar, Hadara, *Out of Palestine: The Making of Modern Israel*, New York: Atlas, 2011.

Lesch, Ann Mosely, *Arab Politics in Palestine, 1917–1939*, Ithaca: Cornell University Press, 1979.

Lewis, Bernard, *The Emergence of Modern Turkey*, Oxford: Oxford University Press, 1961.

Lippman, Thomas W., *Inside the Mirage: America's Fragile Partnership with Saudi Arabia*, Boulder, Colorado: Westview Press, 2004.

Louis, Wm. Roger, *The British Empire in the Middle East, 1945–1951*, Oxford: Oxford University Press, 1984.

Louis, Wm. Roger, and Robert W. Stookey (eds.), *The End of the Palestine Mandate*, London: I.B. Tauris, 1985.

BIBLIOGRAPHY

Louis, Wm. Roger, and Roger Owen (eds.), *Suez 1956*, Oxford: Oxford University Press, 1989.

Louis, Wm. Roger, 'Sir Alan Cunningham and the End of British Rule in Palestine', *Journal of Imperial and Commonwealth History*, Vol. 16, Issue 3, 1988.

Lukitz, Liora, *A Quest in the Middle East: Gertrude Bell and the Making of Modern Iraq*, London: I.B. Tauris, 2006.

Mackworth, Cecily, *The Mouth of the Sword*, London: Routledge & Kegan Paul, 1949.

Maitland, Donald, *Divers Times, Sundry Places*, Brighton: Alpha Press, 1996.

Makdisi Cortas, Wadad, *A World I Loved: The Story of an Arab Woman*, New York: Nation Books, 2009.

Mammeri, Mouloud, *The Sleep of the Just*, tr. Len Ortzen, London: Cresset Press, 1956.

Mango, Andrew, *Atatürk*, London: Murray, 1999.

Mansfield, Peter, *Nasser's Egypt*, London: Penguin, 1969.

Marlowe, John, *Rebellion in Palestine*, London: Cresset Press, 1946.

Marlowe, John, *The Seat of Pilate: An Account of the Palestine Mandate*, London: Cresset Press, 1959.

Marlowe, John, *Late Victorian: The Life of Sir Arnold Talbot Wilson*, London: Cresset Press, 1967.

Marlowe, John, *Spoiling the Egyptians*, London: André Deutsch, 1974.

Mawby, Spencer, *British Policy in Aden and the Protectorates, 1955–67*, London: Routledge, 2005.

Mazower, Mark, *Salonica: City of Ghosts*, London: HarperCollins, 2004.

McDougall, James, *History and the Culture of Nationalism in Algeria*, Cambridge: Cambridge University Press, 2006.

McGhee, George, *Envoy to the Middle World: Adventures in Diplomacy*, New York: Harper & Row, 1983.

Milstein, Uri, *History of Israel's War of Independence, Vol. III*, tr. Alan Sacks, Lanham, Maryland: University Press of America, 1998.

*Monroe, Elizabeth, *Britain's Moment in the Middle East*, London: Chatto & Windus, 1963; 2nd edition, 1981.

Monroe, Elizabeth, *Philby of Arabia*, London: Faber, 1973.

Morgan, Ted, *My Battle of Algiers: A Memoir*, New York: HarperCollins, 2005.

Morris, James, *Farewell the Trumpets: An Imperial Retreat*, London: Faber, 1978.

Morris, James, *The Hashemite Kings*, London: Faber, 1959.

Moubayed, Sami, *The George Washington of Syria: The Rise and Fall of Shukri al-Quwatli*, Beirut: Dar al-Zakira, n.d. [c. 2005].

Moubayed, Sami, *Steel and Silk: Men and Women Who Shaped Syria, 1900–2000*, Seattle: Cune Press, 2006.

Neep, Daniel, *Occupying Syria under the French Mandate: Insurgency, Space and State Formation*, Cambridge: Cambridge University Press, 2012.

BIBLIOGRAPHY

Neguib, Mohammed, *Egypt's Destiny*, London: Gollancz, 1955.

Newsom, David D., *Witness to a Changing World*, Washington, DC: New Academia Publishing, 2008.

Ortzen, Len (ed.), *North African Writing*, London: Heinemann, 1970.

Owen, Roger, *Lord Cromer: Victorian Imperialist, Edwardian Proconsul*, Oxford: Oxford University Press, 2004.

Oz, Amos, *A Tale of Love and Darkness*, tr. Nicholas de Lange, London: Chatto & Windus, 2004.

Pappé, Ilan, *The Rise and Fall of a Palestinian Dynasty: The Husaynis 1700–1948*, London: Saqi Books, 2010.

Perrault, Gilles, *A Man Apart: The Life of Henri Curiel*, tr. Bob Cumming, London: Zed Books, 1987.

Perowne, Stewart, *The One Remains*, London: Hodder & Stoughton, 1954.

Provence, Michael, *The Great Syrian Revolt and the Rise of Arab Nationalism*, Austin: University of Texas Press, 2005.

Ranfurly, Countess of, *To War with Whitaker: The Wartime Diaries of the Countess of Ranfurly, 1939–45*, London: Heinemann, 1994.

al-Rasheed, Madawi, *Politics in an Arabian Oasis: The Rashidi Tribal Dynasty*, London: I.B. Tauris, 1991.

al-Rasheed, Madawi, *A History of Saudi Arabia*, Cambridge: Cambridge University Press, 2002.

Robins, Philip, *A History of Jordan*, Cambridge: Cambridge University Press, 2004.

*Rogan, Eugene, *The Arabs: A History*, London: Allen Lane, 2009.

Rogan, Eugene, *The Fall of the Ottomans: The Great War in the Middle East, 1914–1920*, London: Allen Lane, 2015.

Rogan, Eugene, and Avi Shlaim (eds.), *The War for Palestine: Rewriting the History of 1948*, Cambridge: Cambridge University Press, 2001.

Rodenbeck, Max, *Cairo: The City Victorious*, London: Picador, 1998.

Roosevelt, Kermit, *Countercoup: The Struggle for the Control of Iran*, New York: McGraw-Hill, 1979.

Rose, Norman, *'A Senseless Squalid War': Voices from Palestine 1890s-1948*, London: Bodley Head, 2009.

Ryan, Sir Andrew, *The Last of the Dragomans*, London: Geoffrey Bles, 1951.

Schami, Rafik, *The Dark Side of Love*, London: Arabia Books, 2009.

Seale, Patrick, *The Struggle for Arab Independence: Riad al-Solh and the Makers of the Modern Middle East*, Cambridge: Cambridge University Press: 2010.

*Segev, Tom, *One Palestine, Complete: Jews and Arabs under the British Mandate*, tr. Haim Watzman, New York: Henry Holt, 2000.

Shepherd, Naomi, *Ploughing Sand: British Rule in Palestine, 1917–1948*, London: Murray, 1999.

Shlaim, Avi, *Collusion across the Jordan: King Abdullah, the Zionist Movement and the Partition of Palestine*, Oxford: Oxford University Press, 1988.

BIBLIOGRAPHY

Sinderson, Sir Harry C., *Ten Thousand and One Nights: Memories of Iraq's Sherifian Dynasty*, London: Hodder & Stoughton, 1973.

Sluglett, Peter, *Britain in Iraq, 1914–1932*, London: Ithaca Press, 1976.

Sreberny, Annabelle, and Massoumeh Torfeh, *Persian Service: The BBC and British Interests in Iran*, London: I.B. Tauris, 2014.

Stadiem, William, *Too Rich: The High Life and Tragic Death of King Farouk*, London: Robson Books, 1992.

Stark, Freya, *East is West*, London: Murray, 1945.

Stark, Freya, *Dust in the Lion's Paw*, London: Murray, 1961.

Staudt, Ida Donges, *Living in Romantic Baghdad: An American Memoir of Teaching and Travel in Iraq, 1924–1947*, Syracuse, NY: Syracuse University Press, 2012.

Stein, Kenneth W., *The Land Question in Palestine, 1917–1939*, Chapel Hill: University of North Carolina Press, 1984.

Stephens, Robert, *Nasser: A Political Biography*, London: Allen Lane, 1971.

Stora, Benjamin, *Algeria 1830–2000: A Short History*, tr. Jane Marie Todd, Ithaca: Cornell University Press, 2001.

Stubbs, Richard, *Palestine Story: A Personal Account of the Last Three Years of British Rule in Palestine*, Brettenham, Suffolk: privately printed, 1995.

Thesiger, Wilfred, *Desert, Marsh and Mountain*, London: Collins, 1979.

Todd, Olivier, *Albert Camus: A Life*, tr. Benjamin Ivry, London: Chatto & Windus, 1997.

Townshend, Charles, *When God Made Hell: The British Invasion of Mesopotamia and the Creation of Iraq, 1914–1921*, London: Faber, 2010.

Trevaskis, Kennedy, *Shades of Amber: A South Arabian Episode*, London: Hutchinson, 1968.

Trevelyan, Humphrey, *The Middle East in Revolution*, London: Macmillan, 1970.

Tuqan, Fadwa, *A Mountainous Journey: A Poet's Autobiography*, tr. Olive Kenny, London: Women's Press, 1990.

Unwin, Peter, *1956: Power Defied*, Wilby, Norwich: Michael Russell, 2006.

Vaughan, James R., *The Failure of American and British Propaganda in the Arab Middle East, 1945–1957*, London: Palgrave Macmillan, 2005.

Wahba, Hafiz, *Arabian Days*, London: Arthur Barker, 1964.

Wahba, Magdi, 'Cairo Memories', in Derek Hopwood (ed.), *Studies in Arab History: The Antonius Lectures, 1978–87*, Basingstoke: Macmillan, 1990.

Wallis, Dave, *Tram-Stop by the Nile*, London: Heinemann, 1958.

Ward Price, G., *Extra Special Correspondent*, London: Harrap, 1947.

Wasserstein, Bernard, *The British in Palestine: The Mandatory Government and the Arab-Jewish Conflict, 1917–1929*, London: Royal Historical Society, 1978.

Wavell, Viscount, *Allenby in Egypt*, London: Harrap, 1943.

Wilson, Mary C., *King Abdullah, Britain and the Making of Modern Jordan*, Cambridge: Cambridge University Press, 1987.

BIBLIOGRAPHY

*Yergin, Daniel, *The Prize: The Epic Quest for Oil, Money, and Power*, New York & London: Simon & Schuster, 1991.

Zuhur, Sherifa, *Asmahan's Secrets: Woman, War, and Song*, Austin, Texas: Center for Middle Eastern Studies, University of Texas at Austin, 2000.

Zürcher, Eric, *Turkey: A Modern History*, London: I.B. Tauris, 1993.

DRAMATIS PERSONAE

Abbas, Ferhat (1899–1985)—Algerian political leader who led the Jeune Algérien movement in the 1930s which was committed to the union of Algeria and France; later, despairing of such a solution, he joined the FLN.

Abdullah I, King (1882–1951)—Arabian prince and founder of modern Jordan; born in Mecca, he spent his formative years at the Ottoman court, joined his father Hussein in leading the Arab Revolt of 1916–18 against the Turks, and was appointed emir of Transjordan by Churchill in 1921; he was assassinated in Jerusalem in 1951.

Abdul-Hamid, Sultan (1842–1918)—Ottoman ruler who tried and failed to halt the empire's decline; autocratic and secretive, he was overthrown by the Young Turk nationalists in a coup in 1909.

Abdul-Qader, Emir (1807–1883)—Algerian warrior and Sufi scholar who led one of the earliest and most sustained rebellions against the French; after his defeat, he lived in exile in France and Syria, and died in Damascus at the age of seventy-five.

Abu-Lughod, Ibrahim (1929–2001)—Palestinian academic, born in Jaffa, who became a university professor in the United States, before returning to his homeland to teach at Birzeit University in the West Bank, where he remained until his death.

Agronsky, Gershon (1894–1959)—Russian-born, American-educated editor of the *Palestine Post* who was close to Chaim Weizmann; after the birth of Israel in 1948, he became the mayor of Jerusalem.

Allenby, General Edmund (1861–1936)—British army officer, nicknamed 'the Bull', who captured Jerusalem from the Turks in WWI; he was High Commissioner in Egypt, 1919–25, during a crucial period in the emergence of Egyptian nationalism.

DRAMATIS PERSONAE

Askari, Jaafar al- (1885–1936)—Iraqi soldier and politician, brother-in-law of Nuri al-Said (see below); assassinated during a coup in 1936; his early career is described in his memoir, *A Soldier's Story* (English translation, 2003).

Asnag, Abdullah al- (1934–2014)—Yemeni politician who led the Aden Trades Union Congress and whose movement, Flosy, was defeated by its rival, the NLF, in the south Arabian struggle for independence; he later served as a government minister in Sanaa.

Atatürk, Mustafa Kemal (1881–1938)—Turkish soldier-statesman, born in Salonica, who led Turkey's war of independence and in 1923 founded the modern Turkish republic; a forceful secular reformer.

al-Atrash, Amal (1912–1944)—Syrian Druze princess, and one of the most popular singers of her day, who co-operated with the British during the invasion of Syria and Lebanon in WWII, and died in Egypt in a mysterious car crash.

al-Atrash, Sultan (1885–1982)—Syrian Druze warrior and Arab nationalist (great-uncle of the above), who led the Great Syrian Revolt of 1925–27.

Behr, Edward (1926–2007)—British journalist who, from 1957, covered the Algerian war for *Time;* he played a role in exposing the French use of torture, and was the author of *The Algerian Problem* (1961).

Bell, Sir Gawain (1909–1995)—British soldier and colonial official who served in Sudan, Transjordan, and Palestine; author of two volumes of memoirs, *Shadows on the Sand* (1983) and *An Imperial Twilight* (1989).

Bell, Gertrude (1868–1926)—British writer, traveller, and colonial official who helped install Faisal as king of Iraq in 1921, and whose experiences are vividly recorded in her letters to her parents in England.

Ben Bella, Ahmed (1918–2012)—Algerian nationalist leader who fought in the French army in WWII and became one of the founders of the FLN; after becoming the first president of independent Algeria in 1963, he was ousted two years later by Colonel Houari Boumedienne and placed under house arrest.

Ben-Gurion, David (1886–1973)—son of a notary in Plonsk, in Tsarist-ruled Poland, who emigrated to Palestine in 1906, becoming the head of the labour movement (Histadrut), a leading pioneer of Zionism, and Israel's first prime minister.

Bevin, Ernest (1881–1951)—British Foreign Secretary, with a trade-union background, who played a crucial role in the post-war Middle East, and especially in the closing years of the British mandate in Palestine, 1945–48.

Board, Barbara (1916–1986)—British journalist who reported from Palestine between 1936 and 1946 for the *Daily Sketch* and the *Daily Mirror*;

author of *Newsgirl in Palestine* (1937), *Newsgirl in Egypt* (1938), and *Reporting from Palestine, 1943–1944* (published posthumously, 2008).

Boullata, Issa J. (b. 1929)—Palestinian writer and translator, born in Jerusalem to a Christian family during the first decade of the British mandate.

Bullard, Sir Reader (1885–1976)—British diplomat who served in Ottoman Turkey, in Iraq (1914–20), and twice in Arabia between 1923 and 1939, before becoming British minister in Tehran (1939–46); author of a memoir, *The Camels Must Go* (1961), and two volumes of posthumously published letters, *Two Kings in Arabia* (1993) and *Letters from Tehran* (1991), both edited by his nephew Edward Hodgkin (see below).

Bunting, Basil (1900–1985)—British poet, born in Northumberland, who worked for MI6 in Iran during and after WWII, and married a young Iranian; in 1952, as *The Times*' correspondent in Tehran, he was expelled by Mossadeq; he admired Persian poetry, fragments of which he translated.

Cadman, Sir John (1877–1941)—British oil executive who ran the Anglo-Persian (later Anglo-Iranian) Oil Company from 1927 until his death; in 1933 he negotiated a new oil concession with Iran's ruler, Reza Shah; he was much admired for his diplomatic skills, unlike his blunt and inflexible successor, Sir William Fraser (see below).

Cafferata, Raymond (1897–1966)—British police chief who played a heroic role in Hebron during the Arab massacre of Jews in August 1929; he later survived an assassination attempt by the Irgun; he resigned, embittered, and left Palestine.

Camus, Albert (1913–1960)—Algerian-born French novelist whose posthumously published work, *The First Man*, provides a semi-fictional account of his impoverished early life in a *colon* family in Algiers.

Catroux, General Georges (1877–1969)—French soldier and colonial administrator who was General de Gaulle's representative in the Middle East in WWII.

Churchill, Winston (1874–1965)—British statesman who played a central role in the emergence of the modern Middle East after WWI, and in the conduct of the fighting there during WWII; in 1953, with Eisenhower, he sponsored the overthrow of the Iranian prime minister Muhammad Mossadeq.

Cornwallis, Sir Kinahan (1883–1959)—British official who was director of the Arab Bureau during WWI and accompanied Faisal to Baghdad in 1921, becoming his adviser; in 1941 he returned to Baghdad as ambassador, remaining until 1945.

Cromer, Lord (Sir Evelyn Baring) (1841–1917)—British official who ruled Egypt in the early years of the British occupation, from 1883 to 1907, and sought to reform its government and economy; he was nicknamed 'over-Baring'.

Curiel, Henri (1914–1978)—Egyptian-born political activist who grew up in a wealthy Jewish family in Cairo; one of the founders of the Egyptian communist movement and an active supporter of Algeria's struggle for independence; he was assassinated in Paris in mysterious circumstances.

Curzon, Lord (George Nathaniel Curzon) (1859–1925)—British statesman who played a significant role in policy towards Persia and the Gulf; he was viceroy of India and, after WWI, Foreign Secretary.

de Gaulle, General Charles (1890–1970)—French soldier-statesman who formed the Free French movement after the defeat of France in 1940; he was closely involved in the struggle for Syria and Lebanon in WWII, and in the French withdrawal from Algeria in 1962.

Dehn, Monica (1920–2017)—British journalist who worked in Palestine from 1944 to 1948, first for a clandestine radio station broadcasting to occupied southern Europe, then for the SOE-run Arabic radio station Sharq al-Adna, and finally for Richard Stubbs (see below) at the Public Information Office; she stayed on after the end of the mandate, married David Roy Elston (see below) in 1952, and worked as Jerusalem correspondent for *Time-Life*.

Doty, Bennett J. (b. 1900)—an American adventurer, born in Alabama, who joined the French Foreign Legion in 1925 and fought in Syria during the Great Revolt, an experience vividly recounted in his memoir, *The Legion of the Damned* (1928); after a year he deserted, was captured and spent eight months in French prisons before his eventual pardon and release. He reportedly went to Spain in the 1930s to fight Franco, after which his family never heard from him again.

Drake, Sir Eric (1910–1996)—British official of the Anglo-Iranian Oil Company who was involved in the crisis sparked by the Mossadeq government's nationalisation of the company in 1951.

Drif, Zohra (b. 1934)—Algerian politician who, as a young FLN militant, carried out the Milk Bar bombing in Algiers on 30 September 1956; after independence she became a member of the Algerian Senate.

Eddy, Colonel William (1896–1962)—American soldier, diplomat, and spy, born in Lebanon, who arrived as 'minister plenipotentiary' in Jeddah in 1944 and organised the war-time meeting between Ibn Saud and President Roosevelt; the architect of the US-Saudi special relationship.

Eden, Anthony (1897–1977)—British statesman who, as Conservative prime minister, was responsible for the Suez débâcle of 1956.

Edib, Halidé (1884–1964)—Turkish writer, nationalist, and feminist; the only woman in Atatürk's inner circle; author of two volumes of memoirs which vividly describe the struggle for national independence and the transition from empire to republic.

Eliot, Sir Charles (1862–1931)—British diplomat based in Istanbul during the 1890s; author of *Turkey in Europe* (1900).

Elston, David Roy (1900–1971)—British journalist; an ardent Zionist who, under the pen-name David Courtney, wrote a widely-read column for the *Palestine Post*; he was later *The Times*' correspondent in Israel, 1948–58; in 1952 married Monica Dehn (see above); author of *No Alternative: Israel Observed* (1960) and *Israel: The Making of a Nation* (1963).

Enver, Ismail (1881–1922)—Turkish army officer, known as Enver Pasha, who was a leading figure in the Young Turk revolution of 1908 and implicated in the Armenian genocide during WWI.

Faisal I, King (1883–1933)—Arabian prince, of the Hashemite family of the Hijaz, who was briefly king of Syria, then the first king of British-ruled Iraq.

Falle, Sam (1919–2014)—British diplomat who served in Iran and Iraq in the 1950s; he was sent on a mission to make contact with the NLF in Aden, prior to Britain's withdrawal in 1967; author of a memoir, *My Lucky Life* (1996).

Farmanfarmaian, Manucher (1917–2003)—Iranian oilman and politician, born a prince of the ruling Qajar dynasty, who became a senior official in the National Iranian Oil Company and later the Shah's ambassador to Venezuela; he spent his exile there after the Islamic revolution; author of a vivid memoir, *Blood and Oil* (1997).

Farouq, King (1920–1965)—ruler of Egypt from 1936 until the overthrow of the monarchy in 1952, well known for his corrupt and dissolute lifestyle.

Fraser, Sir William (1888–1970)—British oil executive, born in Glasgow, who ran the Anglo-Iranian Oil Company from 1941 until his retirement in 1956; he played a significant and much-criticised role in the crisis that followed Iran's nationalisation of the company in 1951; British and American officials, regarding him as stubbornly inflexible, tried without success to have him removed.

Ghazi, King (1912–1939)—ruler of Iraq from 1933 to 1939, following the death of his father, King Faisal; a nationalist critical of the British and sympathetic to the Germans; died in a car crash at the age of only twenty-seven.

Glubb, Sir John (1897–1986)—British soldier who spent thirty-six years in the Middle East, from 1920 to 1956, first in Iraq, in the early years of the monarchy, and then in Transjordan, where he became commander of the Arab Legion; he was finally expelled by the young King Hussein during a period of nationalist turmoil.

DRAMATIS PERSONAE

Gouraud, General Henri (1867–1946)—French general and colonial administrator in Africa and the Middle East; after serving in WWI, during which he lost his right arm at Gallipoli, in 1920 he became the first High Commissioner for Syria and Lebanon; he was a staunch Catholic.

Grafftey-Smith, Laurence (1892–1989)—British diplomat who served in Egypt, Iraq, and Saudi Arabia; author of *Bright Levant* (1970) and *Hands to Play* (1975).

Hodgkin, Edward Christian (1913–2006)—British official who during WWII worked for SOE in Egypt and Iraq, and after the war in Palestine as director of the Arabic radio station Sharq al-Adna, 1945–47; subsequently foreign editor of *The Times*.

Hourani, Albert (1915–1993)—British historian of Lebanese descent; as a young man he advised British officials on Middle East policy and testified before the Anglo-American Committee of Inquiry, which was investigating the Palestine problem; author of, among other books, *Arabic Thought in the Liberal Age* (1962) and *A History of the Arab Peoples* (1991).

al–Husseini, Abdul-Qader (1908–1948)—Palestinian commander, a cousin of Hajj Amin (see below); a natural leader, he fought as a commander in the Arab revolt of 1936–39 and in the first Arab-Israeli war of 1947–48, during which he was killed.

al–Husseini, Hajj Amin (1897–1974)—Palestinian from a leading family in Jerusalem, who became the leading Arab politician during British rule in Palestine; forced into exile during the Arab revolt of 1936–39, he spent WWII in Baghdad and Berlin supporting the Nazi cause.

Ingrams, Doreen (1906–1997)—British traveller and writer; wife of the colonial administrator Harold Ingrams (see below); author of *A Time in Arabia* (1970), which describes her ten years in south Arabia from 1934 to 1944.

Ingrams, Harold (1897–1973)—British colonial official who worked in Africa before being posted to south Arabia, where he established a tribal truce known as the Pax Ingrams.

Jabra Ibrahim Jabra (1920–1994)—Palestinian writer who described his early life in British-ruled Palestine in *The First Well: A Bethlehem Boyhood* (English translation, 1995).

Jemal Pasha, Ahmet (1872–1922)—Turkish politician, one of the Young Turk triumvirate; he was governor of Syria in WWI, and later assassinated by an Armenian.

Keith-Roach, Edward (1885–1954)—British official who served in Palestine from 1919 to 1943; an extrovert, larger-than-life character whose vivid and often trenchant memoir, *Pasha of Jerusalem*, was published posthumously in 1994.

DRAMATIS PERSONAE

al-Khalidi, Ahmad Samih (1896–1951)—Palestinian scholar and educationalist who ran the Arab College in Jerusalem from 1925 until the end of the British mandate; he left Palestine in 1948 and died in Beirut three years later.

Khalidi, Anbara Salam (1897–1986)—Lebanese-born wife of the above; a scholar and feminist who translated Homer into Arabic; author of *Memoirs of an Early Arab Feminist* (English translation, 2013).

Kirkbride, Sir Alec (1897–1978)—British soldier and colonial official who worked in Transjordan and Palestine between WWI and 1951; author of three volumes of memoirs, including *A Crackle of Thorns* (1956) and *From the Wings* (1976).

Knox-Mawer, June (1930–2006)—British writer and broadcaster who lived in Aden in the 1950s as the wife of the chief magistrate, an experience recorded in a memoir, *The Sultans Came to Tea* (1961), and a novel, *Sandstorm* (1991).

Lambton, Ann (1912–2008)—British scholar and authority on Iran; she was press attaché at the Tehran embassy in WWII and in the early 1950s advised the British government on how to undermine Mossadeq.

Lampson, Sir Miles (1880–1964)—British diplomat who was ambassador in Egypt in the 1930s and 1940s; an old-style imperialist, he later became Lord Killearn; his diaries provide a detailed record of his time in Egypt.

Luce, Sir William (1907–1977)—British diplomat closely involved in the end of empire in Sudan, south Arabia, and the Gulf.

Lyon, Wallace (1892–1977)—British political officer who spent twenty-six years in Iraqi Kurdistan, from 1918 to 1944; author of a posthumously published memoir, *Kurds, Arabs and Britons* (2002).

Makdisi Cortas, Wadad (1909–1979)—Lebanese educationalist and feminist whose memoir, *A World I Loved* (2009), describes her life under Ottoman and French rule and in independent Lebanon; the Palestinian writer Edward Said was her son-in-law.

Mammeri, Mouloud (1917–1989)—Algerian novelist, born in Kabylia and educated in Algiers and Paris; served in the French army in WWII; author of much-acclaimed novels, written in French, including *The Sleep of the Just* (1955).

Manning, Olivia (1908–1980)—British novelist, author of *School for Love* (1951), set in war-time Jerusalem, and the *Levant Trilogy*, which describes life in Egypt in WWII.

Mardam, Jamil (1894–1960)—a leading Syrian nationalist politician during the French mandate; he was prime minister in the 1930s, and took part in ill-fated efforts to secure a treaty with France.

Messali Hadj, Ahmed (1898–1974)—Algerian leader who in 1926 helped found his country's first nationalist movement, Étoile Nord-Africain, in Paris; after coming into conflict with the FLN, he was marginalised in the independence struggle and went into exile in France.

Meynell, Godfrey (b. 1934)—British colonial administrator who spent eight years as a political officer in southern Arabia, 1959–66; when it became clear Britain was to withdraw, he resigned in protest at this 'monstrous betrayal' of its Arab allies.

Middleton, George (1910–1998)—Britain's chargé d'affaires in Tehran in the run-up to the overthrow of Mossadeq in 1953.

Monroe, Elizabeth (1905–1986)—British historian of the Middle East who worked for the ministry of information during WWII, later joining Chatham House and becoming a journalist with the *Economist*; in the 1950s, with Albert Hourani, she established the Middle East Centre in Oxford; author of *Britain's Moment in the Middle East* (1963) and *Philby of Arabia* (1973).

Morgan, Ted (b. 1932, Sanche de Gramont)—French-born writer who settled in New York; his experiences as a young (and unwilling) soldier in Algeria in the 1950s are described in his vivid and bawdy memoir, *My Battle of Algiers* (2005).

Nasser, Gamal Abdul- (1918–1970)—Egyptian army officer, born in Alexandria, the son of a post office clerk, who seized power in 1952, becoming the pre-eminent Arab leader of the 1950s and 1960s.

Newsom, David (1918–2008)—American diplomat who served in various parts of the Middle East, including Iraq in the 1950s; author of a memoir, *Witness to a Changing World* (2008).

Perowne, Stewart (1901–1989)—British writer and colonial official; as a young man he was a schoolteacher in Palestine in the 1920s; during WWII he produced anti-German propaganda in Aden and Baghdad with Freya Stark, whom he later, briefly, married; author of a Palestine memoir, *The One Remains* (1954).

Philby, Harry St John (1885–1960)—British traveller, writer, and colonial official who first visited Arabia in 1917; he settled in Jeddah in the 1920s, converted to Islam in 1930, and became a friend and adviser to Ibn Saud.

Quwatli, Shukri al- (1891–1967)—Syrian nationalist; born in Damascus to a family of wealthy landowners, he derived his wealth from his family's extensive orchards; a prominent member of the National Bloc in the 1930s who went on to become the first president of independent Syria.

Qawuqji, Fawzi al- (1890–1977)—soldier of fortune, born in Tripoli, Lebanon, who fought in Syria against the French and in Palestine and Iraq against the British; a braggart whose defeats he proclaimed as victories.

DRAMATIS PERSONAE

Reza Shah Pahlavi (1878–1944)—Iranian army officer who seized power in 1921, ending the rule of the Qajar dynasty, and in 1925 became the new Shah; in 1941, after the Anglo-Soviet occupation of the country, he was forced to abdicate in favour of his son Muhammad Reza Shah, a much weaker figure who ruled the country until the Islamic revolution of 1979.

Roosevelt, Kermit (Kim) (1916–2000)—American CIA official, grandson of President Theodore Roosevelt, who led the coup against Mossadeq in 1953; he wrote a not-altogether-reliable account of the episode, *Countercoup* (1979).

Rutenberg, Pinhas (1879–1942)—Zionist entrepreneur, and former Russian revolutionary, who in the 1920s founded the Palestine Electric Corporation, a hydroelectric project harnessing the waters of the Jordan and Yarmuk rivers.

Said, Nuri al- (1888–1958)—Iraqi politician and loyal ally of Britain; fought for Faisal in the Arab Revolt, 1916–18, and subsequently joined him in Baghdad; known as a shrewd manipulator, he served as prime minister fourteen times, and was killed in the revolution of 1958.

Samuel, Sir Herbert Louis (1870–1963)—British politician and Zionist, who was the first High Commissioner in Palestine between 1920 and 1925.

Saud, Ibn (1876–1953)—Arabian tribal leader who, in the first three decades of the twentieth century, united most of the Arabian peninsula under his rule, a process completed in 1932, when the new state of Saudi Arabia was born.

al-Solh, Riad (1894–1951)—Lebanese politician and Arab nationalist, considered the father of independent Lebanon; he is the subject of Patrick Seale's study, *The Struggle for Arab Independence: Riad al-Solh and the Makers of the Modern Middle East* (2010); he was assassinated on a visit to Jordan in 1951.

Soustelle, Jacques (1912–1990)—French academic and colonial official, a liberal Gaullist who was the governor-general of Algiers, 1955–56.

Spears, Sir Edward Louis (1886–1974)—British soldier and diplomat closely involved in the struggle for Syria between 1941 and 1945, an episode he described in *Fulfilment of a Mission* (published posthumously in 1977).

Stark, Freya (1893–1993)—writer, traveller, and war-time propagandist in Egypt, Palestine, and Iraq; in 1947 married Stewart Perowne (see above).

Staudt, Ida (1875–1952)—American Protestant missionary who, with her husband Calvin, settled in Baghdad in 1924 and founded the American School for Boys; they remained in Iraq until 1947; her memoir *Living in Romantic Baghdad* was published posthumously in 2012.

Stubbs, Richard (1909–1996)—British spokesman in Palestine from 1946 to 1948, whose experiences are recounted in a memoir, *Palestine Story* (1995).

Thesiger, Wilfred (1910–2003)—British soldier, explorer, and writer who, as a young man, fought alongside the Druze in Syria in 1941.

Trevelyan, Humphrey (1905–1985)—British diplomat who served as ambassador in Egypt during the Suez crisis, in Iraq after the revolution of 1958, and as High Commissioner in Aden in the run-up to the British withdrawal in 1967; all three experiences are described in his book, *The Middle East in Revolution* (1970).

Trevaskis, Sir Kennedy (1915–1990)—British colonial official who in 1951 became a political officer in south Arabia and was the architect of the Federation of South Arabia created in 1959; he became High Commissioner in 1963 but was sacked the following year by the incoming Labour government in Britain; author of *Shades of Amber: A South Arabian Episode* (1968).

Tuqan, Fadwa (1917–2003)—Palestinian poet and feminist who lived throughout her life in Nablus, in the West Bank; author of an autobiography, *A Mountainous Journey* (English translation, 1990).

Urabi, Ahmad (1841–1911)—Egyptian army officer, born in a village in the Nile delta, who led the country's first national revolt; its suppression led to the start of the British occupation in 1882.

van der Meulen, Daniel (1894–1989)—Dutch consul in Jeddah in the 1920s; author of a number of books on Arabia, including *The Wells of Ibn Sa'ud* (1957).

Wahba, Hafiz (1889–1969)—Egyptian who worked as foreign-policy adviser to Ibn Saud and later as his ambassador in London; author of *Arabian Days* (1964).

Wallis, Dave (1917–1990)—British novelist and teacher who, as a young communist, served as a soldier in Egypt during WWII, an experience described in his novel, *Tram-Stop by the Nile* (1958).

Ward Price, George (1886–1961)—British correspondent for the *Daily Mail* during WWII, controversial because of his pre-war relations with Hitler and Mussolini; interviewed the young Atatürk and witnessed the fire at Smyrna in 1922.

Weizmann, Chaim (1874–1952)—Russian-born scientist who became one of the leading advocates of Zionism, helped bring about the Balfour Declaration of 1917, and in 1948 became Israel's first president.

Woodhouse, Christopher Montague (1917–2001)—British army officer, politician, and spy who worked in Greece for SOE during WWII; he masterminded the joint MI6-CIA operation to overthrow Mossadeq in 1953, an episode recounted in his memoir, *Something Ventured* (1982).

Yacef, Saadi (b. 1928)—Algerian nationalist, born in the Casbah of Algiers, where he worked in his father's bakery; he joined the FLN in 1955 and played a central role in the 'battle of Algiers', 1956–57.

Zaghlul, Saad (1859–1927)—Leading Egyptian nationalist of his day; of *fellah* origin, he trained as a lawyer and became the immensely popular leader of the Wafd Party.

INDEX

245

INDEX

INDEX

INDEX

257

INDEX

INDEX

INDEX

INDEX